D1175114

Victorian Novelists and Publishers

J. A. SUTHERLAND

Victorian Novelists and Publishers

THE UNIVERSITY OF CHICAGO PRESS

The University of Chicago Press, Chicago 60637
The Athlone Press of the University of London, London WC1

Published 1976

Library of Congress Cataloging in Publication Data

Sutherland, John, 1938–
Victorian novelists and publishers.

Includes bibliographical references and index.
1. English fiction—19th century—History and criticism.
2. Publishers and publishing—Great Britain. I. Title.
PR878.P78S9 823′.03 76–8216
ISBN 0–226–78061–9

Printed in Great Britain by
Western Printing Services Ltd, Bristol

Acknowledgements

I am grateful to Mrs E. M. Gordon and Colonel Murray-Smith for permission to use material relevant to the firm of Smith, Elder and Co. I should also like to record my gratitude to the late Sir Tresham Lever who helped me greatly with information about George Smith. Wing Commander G. D. Blackwood and Lady Hermione Cobbold have kindly allowed me to use correspondence of John Blackwood and Bulwer Lytton, now held in the National Library of Scotland. My thanks are also expressed to the manuscript departments and officials of the National Library of Scotland, the British Library, the Victoria and Albert Museum Library, the Bodleian Library and the Library of the University of Illinois at Urbana. The Henry E. Huntington Library generously gave me a grant to study there which was of great assistance to my research. I am also grateful to the British Academy for a fellowship which enabled me to work over the summer of 1973 in the Pierpont Morgan Library. I would like to thank Alan Bell, Scott Bennett, Professor Kenneth Fielding, Patrick Scott and Richard Taylor for their assistance. Professor R. L. Patten, who is preparing a book on Dickens and his publishers, read this study in proof and made a number of corrections for which I am grateful.

Contents

Introduction

The concentration which we bring to the study of literary texts tends to focus out the surrounding detail of how manuscript becomes print. For most modern critics nineteenth-century fiction has thus come to mean the great Victorian novelists and their rather shadowy accomplices, the Victorian reading public. Comparatively scant attention is paid to the figures whom the publishing world threw up in the 1840s to match the new generation of writers. Yet commonly in this era we find a business genius like John Blackwood's, George Smith's or Alexander Macmillan's partnering or fostering a creative genius like George Eliot's, Thackeray's or Charles Kingsley's. Some of fiction's triumphs were actually begotten by publishers rather than authors. (*Pickwick* is the most brilliant example, but the whole career of Charlotte Brontë could be cited as the outcome of one publisher's discrimination and protectiveness.) Even where they did not directly interfere in the novelist's life, the composition of his fiction or the form of his literary vehicle, the publisher's skills were often as instrumental to success as anything the author might contribute. A good house could take material as unpromising as an unknown novelist's 'Manchester Love Story' and turn it into the bestseller we know as *Mary Barton*;[1] a bad one could bring a novel as great as *Wuthering Heights* to still birth.

In this respect fiction is itself an untrustworthy witness. The better publishers are nothing like Thackeray's philistine couple, Bacon and Bungay, or the commercial vampires who destroy Edwin Reardon in New Grub Street. These figures had their counterparts (and sometimes their originals)[2] in the trade but on the whole Dickens, Thackeray, Trollope and other novelists of their standing were blessed in the publishers they found. There were imaginative patrons as well as commodity merchandisers in Victorian publishing houses. Granted patronage sometimes took unorthodox forms and did not always feel bound to confine itself to the traditional measures of praise, encouragement, money and the warrant of a famous name. Since they paid the piper even the most enlightened publishers felt justified in calling the tune at times—more so since no firm of name regarded fiction as its most respectable line of goods. Richard Bentley, for example, had discrimination enough to bring out Herman Melville's *Mardi*, *Redburn*, *Whitejacket* and *The Whale* (i.e. *Moby Dick*) which argues a literary sensibility far ahead of that of contemporary criticism. But when in March 1852 he totalled up his losses on these projects (£453 4s. 6d.—Melville by contrast had made some $3,000 on their sales to date)[3] and Melville offered him yet another novel Bentley countered with a condition which makes one's blood run cold. He would take *Pierre, or the Ambiguities* only on half profits and if the author would allow it to be altered by a 'judicious literary friend' (of Bentley's) so as to 'restrain' Melville's imagination and cast the work 'in a style to be understood by the great mass of readers'. *Pierre* should be disambiguated.

One may not generalise too easily from such instances. Against Bentley's crass interference one can set such examples as John Blackwood's in forgoing his prerogative and withholding any breath of criticism on George Eliot's early fiction at a time when she was still a chancy proposition.[4] By so doing he helped keep intact the 'mental greenhouse'[5] which the timid authoress needed to bring her novels to fruition.

George Eliot was, in fact, particularly fortunate in the publisher she did business with. Each of the major houses had a distinct personality which materially affected an author, especially one who had still to make a name. Blackwood's retained the spirit of their early *Magazine* days. 'Blackwood's authors' no longer foregathered in the Princes Street saloon to air their smart conservative views but there was still much of the coterie about them. Although the house did not give 'fancy prices'[6] and was careful about what it took, the publishers were good at forming life-long friendly relationships with writers.

Bentley, on the other hand, was much more opportunistic. But characteristically this same opportunism which often gave him the edge over competitors regularly lost him authors; Richard Bentley could pick winners but unlike John Blackwood never managed to hold a major writer throughout his career. Ainsworth, Dickens, Wilkie Collins, Trollope, G. P. R. James, Charles Reade all left with the suspicion that Bentley had somehow done them down and an atmosphere thick with accusation and sometimes even law suits. The publisher was forced to make his living largely from hacks paid less than £300 a novel. It was a far from thriving living and any one or two of the major novelists whose career he helped launch, indentured to the house by bonds of friendship, would have relieved Bentley from the financial crises which bedevilled him during the 1840s and 50s.

If Blackwood's looked back to the author-publisher clubs of the eighteenth century, Bentley's looked forward to the commercialism of the twentieth. So, in a rather more dignified way, did Smith, Elder and Co. In George Smith's day this was the most freely spending of the houses. They did pay 'fancy prices' and specialised in outbidding rivals for any novelist who had caught the public. (They poached George Eliot from Blackwood's, for example.) Enriched by years of connection with the East India Company they could afford to cut something of a dash among their fellows who got by solely on what profits they made from publishing. And although he was nick-named the 'prince of publishers' there was always a savour of trade about Smith. Mrs Gaskell once discovered that he could get her 22½ per cent off her furniture which, with feminine logic, she was prepared to take advantage of since he was paying Wilkie Collins two-and-a-half times as much for *Armadale* as she was getting for *Wives and Daughters*.[7]

Macmillan's came into the business rather later than some others and were very careful about money. Their books were 'chosen to last'.[8] From their bookselling days in Cambridge they maintained a strong University connection which gave an intellectual cast to their list. They were founded, it was said, 'on Broad-Church theology and Cambridge mathematics'.[9] For this reason, perhaps, they were unusually conscientious in their dealings with novelists, especially inexperienced novelists. There were few better nurseries for the beginner than Macmillan's. As their books lasted so the house prospered. Macmillan's, despite their late arrival, expanded inexorably to command a major place in the national and international market by the end of the century and were, under Frederick Macmillan, leading organisers in the trade counter-attack against discount selling, a campaign that led to the net book agreement of 1899 and the relative stability of bookselling in the twentieth century.

Chapman and Hall were the easiest going, and in many ways, the kindest of firms to old friends, with whom they 'never refused a book and never haggled at a price'.[10] It was their amenability that kept Dickens with them during the heady days of his rise to literary stardom—that and the fact that they were always willing to entrust their affairs to plenipotentiaries like John Forster and George Meredith. Edward Chapman, in particular, seems to have been too full of the milk of publishing kindness and not to have minded having Mrs Gaskell, Trollope, Thackeray and Kingsley suborned or drift away from him at one time or another. As a firm Chapman and Hall were noticeably innovative when it came to finding new ways to market fiction. During their most innovative phase (1836–50) they pioneered the monthly shilling number (1836), the Christmas book (1843) and the cheap collective reissue of the work of living novelists (1847). They also made some brave but futile attempts in the same period to bring down the price of new fiction.

Their great rivals, Bradbury and Evans, were by contrast the least imaginative of the houses. They were not, like Chapman and Hall, 'Booksellers and Publishers' but 'Printers and Publishers'. But what they lacked in the pioneer's bright ideas they made up in technical expertise in production and distribution. They were also lucky. They happened to be *Pickwick*'s printers; they happened to be *Punch*'s printers in 1842 when it was going for a song;[11] they happened to be nearest when Dickens flounced away from Chapman and Hall in 1844 annoyed at having his whims crossed and resolved that 'a printer is better than a bookseller'.[12] Even so this was a gift horse they were unwilling to accept at first. Another stroke of luck was the runaway success of *Punch* in the early forties. Bradbury had the wisdom to leave the running of the magazine to a convivial group of brilliant young men and the venture did amazingly well; eventually it earned the house £5,000 a year profit.[13] Moreover from its ranks emerged another best-selling novelist, Thackeray. It was not all luck. Where Bradbury and Evans excelled was in marketing on an industrial scale and the times were propitious for manufacturing publishers. Consequently this rather featureless house, which had published no book before 1844, came to occupy a dominant position by 1847 and held it for ten years, bringing out the bulk of Thackeray's and Dickens's best fiction and giving it a circulation no English novelist of first rank had previously enjoyed.

Bradbury and Evans were among the most tradesmanlike firms in 'the trade'. Longman's, with their distinguished pedigree (Longman, Rees, Orme, Brown, Green and Longman) felt themselves somewhat above fiction. Trollope once heard a member of the firm declare that an author 'had spawned upon them (the publishers) three novels a year'.[14] Such language Trollope thought more appropriate to the fecundity of the herring than the novelist's muse. Yet for all their dynastic hauteur Longman's name was on the title page of *Waverley*, Victorian fiction's great progenitor. And it was Longman's who offered the novel its highest reward of the century—£10,000 for Disraeli's *Endymion*; partly, one feels, because it was written by no mere scribbling novelist but a recent Prime Minister of England.[15]

These are the main firms we shall be dealing with. There were, of course, others: Tinsley Brothers, Hurst and Blackett, T. C. Newby, Sampson Low and Marston, Saunders and Otley, Routledge and many more. But on the basis of the seven selected here one can generalise fairly confidently about the production of the 'literary novel'. One uses the epithet advisedly since there was another kind of novel produced in much greater numbers throughout the century. Louis James in his *Fiction for the Working Man* lists ninety publishers of penny-installment fiction between 1830 and 1850, which at a conservative estimate means that for every producer above the literary threshold there were ten beneath it. In this as much as anything else Victorian England was two nations. However much the literary novelist's mouth might water at the prospect of the 'unknown public' of three million readers it was, as Wilkie Collins regretted, 'impenetrable'.[16] Our business here has to do with the relatively few great novelists, major houses and respectable readers. Similarly, I deal only with new novels or with those that have at least a bloom of freshness on them.

The following chapters fall into two sections. The first (Chapters 1–3) deals generally with the Victorian publishing world. The second (Chapters 4–10) examines particular novelists, novels and careers in connection with the circumstances in which fiction was published. There is, I hope, some originality in both sections but the first may usefully be read in conjunction with such standard works as R. D. Altick's *The English Common Reader* and Kathleen Tillotson's *Novels of the Eighteen-Forties*. Publishing history is almost unique in literary studies in having an embarrassing richness of manuscript materials. I have drawn freely on the wealth of material in publishers' archives and unpublished business correspondence. At times this has led me to cross the lines of such specialist studies as R. A. Gettmann's on Richard Bentley and Guinevere Griest on Mudie's Circulating Library. But my aims are essentially different from theirs. I have not sought to trace the history of any one institution (or novelist) but rather to investigate some various interactions of artists and publishing institutions. Many of the great novels of the period which appear to be the unaided product of creative genius were often, as I set out to show, the outcome of collaboration, compromise or commission. Works like *Henry Esmond*, *Middlemarch* or *Framley Parsonage* cannot be fully appreciated unless we see them as partnership productions. Similarly much of the fiction, good and bad, of the period was written not in response to what the public or critics demanded, but what the publisher would take. There is, I would maintain, no Victorian novel (and I would include even literary eccentricities like *Wuthering Heights*) which was not materially influenced by the publishing system, for good or ill. It is this influence which I have tried to isolate and evaluate in the following pages.

PART ONE

The Novel Publishing World
1830–1870

1

Novel Publishing 1830–1870

Various as they were, most of the great Victorian publishing houses may be gathered under some generalisations. All had grown out of the retail selling, printing, or wholesale trade and were mostly family concerns with the memory of some near ancestor who had served in the shop with its window display in front and press or warehouse at the back, or had come to London with the traditional half-a-crown in his breeches pocket. A significant number of founders were Scottish and largely self-improved. The guiding principle of such men is summed up by the prayers for 'right conduct' at the head of Smith, Elder's first daybook,[1] above the cash transactions that began a huge financial empire. They saw no contradiction in their service to God and commerce:

> We booksellers [wrote Daniel Macmillan], if we are faithful to our task, are trying to destroy, and are helping to destroy, all kinds of confusion, and are aiding our great Taskmaster to reduce the world into order, and beauty, and harmony...At the same time, it is our duty to manage our affairs wisely, keep our minds easy, and not trade beyond our means.[2]

A portion of this mingled high-mindedness and hard-headedness was transmitted to later, more polished generations (although aesthetic idealism tended to replace religious). After he had taken his grand tour, *en prince* with tutor in attendance, like any rich gentleman's son, John Blackwood, like any tradesman's son, went to work as apprentice in a London publishing firm and found himself lugging a commission-collecting bag all over London.[3] This was a superintended phase of the family's training for him as future head of the house. When at thirty-two he assumed command he brought to it a sensibility capable of advising George Eliot on points of narrative and a toughness in trade bargaining which got for her books a higher price in the cut-throat library market than any other author's.

Blackwood was one of the 'new men' who had, as an American admirer noted, completely ousted the 'old fogies'.[4] There was in the forties a whole infusion of such young men. Smith was only twenty-two when he took over the family firm, Blackwood thirty-two, the Macmillans twenty-five and thirty when they started, Mudie only twenty-two when he started his own library; Chapman, Hall and Dickens had barely seventy years among them when *Pickwick* had its fabulous success catapulting them into the forefront of their professions.

There was much dead wood for the new men to clear. Traditionally publishing had proved itself to be a notoriously conservative profession. Most early nineteenth-century publishers were utterly incurious about the growth of markets and slow to keep up with a rapidly changing world. The attitude of the fathers of the trade is aptly illustrated by John Murray's declining Disraeli's *The Young Duke* because of 'his fears for the future of the country owing to the passing of the Reform Bill'.[5] Caution with regard to fiction in particular was encouraged by the fate of Constable and Ballantyne in 1826. Constable had dreamed of a 'total revolution' in bookselling, by which was meant, among other things, offering fiction to the 'millions' at a price that could be generally afforded. The dream was forestalled by bankruptcy. A firm which had held the copyrights of Scott, the *Encyclopaedia Britannica* and the *Edinburgh Review*, all three of them goldmines, collapsed with upward of a quarter of a million pounds worth of debt. It was a terrible precedent. For a while afterwards the banks would not change the bills of any bookseller and the whole publishing industry quaked. Even Longman's with a hundred years of prosperous trading behind them were rumoured to be at risk.[6]

This calamity together with the deaths of Byron and Scott, who had inaugurated the new era of huge readership and correspondingly huge payments, stifled publishing ambitions and inventiveness for years afterwards. A letter of Bentley and Colburn's written in December 1831 to the author of a manuscript in which they were clearly interested conveys the time's spirit of smothered enterprise and toe-dipping caution:

the publication of novels has lately become an affair of greater risk than usual, and our prospective arrangements will not admit of our engaging to bring out any new work of fiction for several months. If however it would suit you to wait till the next year now about to commence shall be somewhat advanced, we would undertake on our own responsibility, to introduce your volumes to the world; but as we should only feel justified in printing in the first instance a very small number in order to ascertain the public feeling towards the work we could propose no other remuneration to you than a certain number of copies.[7]

And this, one reminds oneself, was the leading producer of fiction in England.

In this damped-down world of publishing, competition between the major houses was kept to an acceptable minimum by a comfortable degree of co-operation, especially on remaindering and price maintenance. Booksellers and book publishers were more involved in each other's spheres than was later to be the case. Much of the trade sale of new and surplus books was conducted at dinners, with lots being auctioned over the walnuts and wine. Unlike the German trade fairs and the American book auctions, these dinners did not indicate the future course of British publishing and, although they survived almost throughout the century (the very last was held by Bentley's at the Hôtel Metropole on 3 December 1897), the post-prandial auction came to be regarded by most as a pleasant, antiquated ritual.[8]

Prices were high, exorbitantly so. In the 1790s, the cost of novels, which had been falling throughout the century, steadied at around 3s. a volume.[9] With the universal price and tax rises brought about by the Napoleonic wars it rose sharply again until by the 1820s it had attained the half-guinea per volume mark, where it stuck. The post-war supply of fiction, like corn, was thus stabilised by expense, taxation and shortage—but books provoked no repeal lobby to agitate for the cheapening of an inessential to life. Similarly, while the 'taxes on knowledge' were obnoxious, a tax on fiction might seem quite proper. As a result, the average purchaser was pushed out of the market at a time when the appetite for fiction generally was quickening and growing and the novel taking over from the stage and poetry as the dominantly attractive form for young talents.

Not surprisingly editions of the 1830s were kept small. ('Second editions' might well be the fag ends of first editions with reprinted title pages, a practice which gives a spurious glow of good health to the publishers' lists of the period.) And to prop prices up it was common for dealers who specialised in remainders to burn a large part of their stock. New fiction, like other new books, was a luxury and in the same class as the records of leisured foreign travel, field sports and memoirs by 'persons of rank' so popular in the period. When it began in 1828 the critical weekly, the *Athenaeum*, founded its reviewing on the assumption that 'no Englishman in the middle class of life *buys* a book'.[10] If author or publisher thought about their public it was probably as Carlyle's 'reader on a sofa', certainly not the man in the street. It is estimated that the accessible reading public in this period amounted to some 50,000.[11]

The general constraint had a morbid effect on the novel which is consumed more greedily than other literary forms and thrives, naturally enough, on its novelty. It can be no accident that in the stagnant years between Constable's collapse and Chapman and Hall's innovation of the monthly serial with *Pickwick* there emerged little that we recognise as worth reading today; certainly no masterpiece. Many who know their George Eliot, Dickens and Trollope would be stumped to name one major novel of the early 1830s, or to say whether Lady Bury, Captain Marryat and Catherine Gore were the authors or the principal characters of best-selling fiction of the period. Yet this was a time of steady output and, if nothing else, established the library edition, three-volume, guinea-and-a-half novel as fiction's standard form, with the 6s. reprint following up after a few years.[12] Arguably this was the most important single development in the history of the nineteenth-century novel.

Overlong, overpriced and almost from the first overdue for extinction the three-decker at 31s. 6d. which began with Scott saw out Thomas Hardy's novel-writing career. It is likely that the new novel, that most speculative of commercial ventures, was the most stably priced and sized commodity in the whole nineteenth-century market place. There is something wonderful about its longevity (seventy-three years from *Kenilworth* to the circulating libraries' ban on it as 'unacceptable' at any price in

1894).[13] Much exaggerated reports of its death were recurrent throughout the period: 'it is the remnant of a past age', snarled Charles Reade in 1853, 'and can no more stand before the increasing intelligence of this age than an old six horse coach can compete with a train whirled past by a single engine'.[14] He gave it ten more years of life;[15] by a pleasing symmetry it survived ten years after Reade's own death in 1884. In fact the three-decker would seem to have been less a pre-industrial anachronism than the very embodiment of the present age. As Lytton Strachey said of the heroic couplet and the Augustans, the three-volume novel was the Victorians' 'criticism of life', massive, expensive, moral and enduring. As the century progressed it was common to compare it not with old fashioned stage coaches but the other grand durables of the British Empire—the Queen, the Constitution and the Navy.

Like these other imperial pillars the three-volume novel was not only stable in itself but a source of general stability. This may be better understood if we briefly examine the chain of supply which established itself, around the three-volume form, during the century. Retailing at a notional 31s. 6d. the novel would be sold to booksellers with a normal trade allowance of 25 per cent, a reduction of some 8s. on the sale price fixed by the publisher. The order for the book would go into a running account on which settlement was made half-yearly, in June and December. If the account were settled by cash within a month a further discount of 2½ per cent of the gross sum was allowed, bringing the price down another 9½d., roughly. As a further bonus to entice his customer the publisher would often offer his book to be 'subscribed' among the trade. They would have an early copy to sample and would be given the day, even the hour of publication. In addition they might subscribe at a pre-publication rate of 13 for the price of 12 or, more usually, 25 for 24. This brings the minimum price of our hypothetical novel down another 11d.[16] If the house were one of those which held trade sales yet another deduction might be made.

So far this gives the publisher a lowest return of about a guinea on his three-decker. But this price would only obtain for his London outlets, whom he could supply direct. For his country and export sales (as much as 30 per cent of his trade at midcentury) there would be the interposition of commission agents in the principal towns who would subdistribute the books. Their cut of the profits would be negotiated but would hardly be less than 10 per cent—which to round off we might calculate as 5 per cent of the total. This brings the minimum cost below the £1 mark. Special, and often thumping, discounts were expected by the large circulating libraries, Smith's, metropolitan bookshops, wholesalers and others making bulk orders. These would carve still further into the profit margin. A novel that was no longer the latest thing might be cut in price so as to clear it from the publisher's shelves. A usefully representative picture of how things might finally stand is given by a marked-up Bentley trade-dinner sales catalogue of September 1852. Three-decker novels are printed there with three prices: 'sells: £1 11s. 6d.' 'Subs. [i.e. subscription price]: £1 4s. 3d.' 'Sale [i.e. price to those attending the trade sale]: £1 3s. 0d.' Entered in ink beside each title are the prices of last resort or maximum discount; these range from 9s. to 14s. (Dinner sales were particularly used for disposing of remainders—'books with broken prices'.)

In all, then, our publisher is left with something under £1 average income from his novel once it has left his warehouse. To continue at a more specific level we may now look at a particular example, Trollope's *The Three Clerks*, brought out by Bentley in 1857. The first edition of 1,000 was all but sold out, a happy outcome for both parties. This is the breakdown we find in the publication ledger (note, particularly, Mudie's price):

	£	s.	d.		£	s.	d.
Printing 1000	130	5	6	38 presented			
Paper	91	0	6	500 Mudie	288	0	0
Binding 750	47	10	3	210 sold	227	8	9
A. Trollope (payment in full)	250	0	0	119 sold	115	12	6
Advertising	63	7	8	23 sold	24	19	0

Profit on first year, £74 9s. 7d. Of the 123 left on hand 97 were sold off at cut price in the next year, yielding £32 16s. 7d. profit for the publisher.[17]

This may be taken as a fairly representative example and if one considers all the unaccounted items, office expenses, overheads and the fact that not every edition sold out, it can be seen that the three-volume novel, in the usual smallish edition, did not make a fortune for the publisher (some £100 in this case). Why then was the three-volume, 31s. 6d. novel persisted with? The simple answer is that it was demanded by the circulating libraries, famously Mudie's. But this is too simple an explanation. For one thing the three-decker had been riding high for thirty years before Mudie ever became a major buyer. For another, although Mudie would help explain the retention of the three-volume form (since he worked on a volume-subscriber system this paid him), price maintenance at an exact 31s. 6d. is not to be explained by the libraries—for their buying was largely unaffected by it. The price Mudie paid for a novel was related not to its market price but the size and terms (i.e. cash or credit) of his order. Thus from Bentley in this period, 1857–8, Mudie took 100 of one title for £72, 250 of another for £180, 500 of *The Three Clerks* for £288, 150 of another novel for £108. The prices to him in this year were either 11s. 6d. or 14s. 5d. per copy according to the terms he could make with Bentley. For the small retail supplier, however, the standard price on all these titles was 22s. 6d.[18] And the shop price was the advertised guinea-and-a-half. Any underselling was vigorously discouraged by the publishers (although after 1852 there was no legal way of preventing it).

The three-decker seems to have been kept going all those years for the dullest of literary reasons—because it was commercially safe. The English publisher, as the *Westminster* noted (disapprovingly) in 1852, 'finds it easier and more profitable to sell 500 copies of a work at a guinea and a half per copy, than 5,000 at half a crown, or 50,000 at a shilling'.[19] As well as being easier and profitable the system was also surer. Much of an edition's sale was cut and dried even before publication day. Charles Lever, for example, wrote to his wife recording disappointment about the sale of a novel in April 1857 because

> Glencore was 'subscribed' today in the slang of 'the Trade'—and I grieve to say—not very successfully—with 300 copies taken by

Mudie the Gt. Library man, we can only make *600 in all* but this Chapman seems content with—the book costing one guinea and [a] half—a fearful price. On my own part I expected to have seen the whole edition of 1000 taken—but I am not so clever a fellow as I think myself.[20]

To have sold out three-fifths of an edition before the book even came onto the open market might, today, seem cause for rejoicing rather than otherwise.

In other ways it might well be argued that a safe, stable commercial framework was no bad thing for literature. The generous margins of the three-volume system sustained the long, expensive lines which brought a constant supply of fiction to the public. In today's publishing world an edition of a thousand copies would hardly be thought worth embarking on for a full-length novel. The point of return which would make it a reasonable source of income to author and publisher would not be reached. (In America in the nineteenth century there was commonly nothing paid to the author until *after* the first thousand had been sold, then royalties on a sliding scale.) But with *The Three Clerks* Bentley could afford to give Trollope £250 and still make a profit of some £100 with the prospect of a reprint harvest to come (and since Trollope had sold the entire copyright *all* those profits would be Bentley's). With a bit of scrimping £250 was a tolerable annual salary. When he started for Chapman and Hall as reader in 1860 Meredith received something under that and even though the stipend was later raised (probably to £300)[21] it remained his staple source of income for thirty years.

Trollope had a payment equivalent to a 17 per cent royalty, Bentley had a return on investment of 18 per cent, the manufacturers had £268, the advertisers £63 and the trade some £500 to divide among themselves after the first year's sales. Not least of all the reading public had a fine novel which in other countries might never have seen the light of print. Publishers were encouraged to take risks because the three-volume system had a kind of built-in insurance against loss. Take an obscure and unsuccessful novel of the period, *Zaidee* by Mrs Oliphant, which Blackwood's brought out in 1856. They had 1578 copies of this work printed at a cost of £358. A paltry 496 were sold,

25 as 24, for 22s. 6d.; this yielded £535 10s.[22] So with just two-thirds of the stock still on hand (1031 copies) Blackwood had covered his costs. The novel was by any standard—except the commercial—a failure: half the edition was still on the publisher's shelves six years later. In a crueller world than the three-decker permitted it would probably never have been gambled on.

This ability to make ends meet on small editions created what is a very benign state of affairs for the production of fiction. Nowhere more than with novels is the trade adage true that of five books three lose money, one covers costs and the fifth makes a profit. The golden age of the English novel, as we like to think of the Victorian period, probably owes its distinction to more causes than can be reasonably discovered. But one main cause was the sheer superabundance of the novel in the period—the fact that publishers could offer so large an invitation to ambitious literary talents.

Thinking, as the casual observer is bound to do, of the daunting cost of the three-decker and the general incapacity of most Victorians to pay it outright one can cite some startling anomalies. In 1850, for example, Bohn contrived to put in hand a 1s. edition of *The Scarlet Letter* only a month after its first publication in America.[23] He paid Hawthorne nothing. It is likely that Bohn made money on his book (notoriously shrewd, he rarely lost money on anything). Meanwhile Bentley was bringing out Melville's novels in three volumes, paying the author as honourably as he would any Englishman, and losing as he reckoned up to £170 on each title. Could not something have been achieved, satisfactory to all parties, at some intermediate point on the thirty-shilling range that separated *The Scarlet Letter* from *Moby Dick*? Probably not. As it expanded the English market had stabilised on a high-price equilibrium which was unexpectedly clement to the writing and sale of fiction. The American market which had stabilised on a low-price equilibrium (and whose methods Bohn was imitating) was clement to producers and retailers but less so to writers. Copy for copy American publishers vastly outproduced English; title for title English novelists vastly outproduced American. In America the nineteenth century may have been a 'gilded age' of publishing but it was certainly not a golden age of fiction.

Looking at 'American tales, wordy past all belief, trashy beyond all description, one would say unreadable were it not that there exist such signs of their being read' Trollope concluded, in 1855, that 'a good article cannot in literature be supplied at a low price.'[24]

The trade's concurrence on this subject was reinforced by the failure of the occasional attempts which were made to introduce cheap, new, good fiction. In 1833 Smith, Elder's 'Library of Romance' bravely attempted to market new fiction at 6s. a volume and collapsed after a short life. In November 1838 Bentley took up a great deal of advertising space to announce to 'the Booksellers and Proprietors of Circulating Libraries in the United Kingdom' his intention henceforth to publish new fiction at 8s. instead of 10s. 6d. the volume, not to dispose of remainders for three years from publication day and to cut back production of new novels so as to allow purchasers to take largely of those he did issue. Although Bentley prophesied new novels by big names (Lytton, Trollope, James, Ainsworth, Gore) and courageously threw his current bestseller in as the first novel (*Oliver Twist*, 25s. for three volumes—the extra shilling for the Cruikshank illustrations) the scheme failed and Bentley fell back into line with his competitors after a few months. In February 1845 Chapman and Hall, in their turn, announced the inception of a 'Monthly Series' by which a purchaser could have a full length novel at less than half-price by buying it in four 3s. installments. In 1847 the same firm launched their 'Original Works' which offered full-length fiction in two volumes for 18s. as opposed to 31s. 6d. and three volumes. Although one occasionally in the subsequent years comes across Chapman and Hall advertisements still pushing the cheap 'original' novel, neither series made any significant impact on the pattern of production and purchase. Neither did the most ambitious and carefully mounted of the cheapening experiments, Bentley's in 1853. In the autumn of this year Bentley again proposed to reduce the price of fiction; this time, however, by a slashing two-thirds, issuing it at 3s. 6d. a volume, the three-decker to cost a mere 10s. 6d. After a couple of months and a couple of novels on the new plan Bentley was back to the guinea-and-a-half standard.[25]

All these projects foundered on the ingrained conservatism of the English reading public and, more significantly, because it was not economic to buy copyrights from the best authors for sale in cut-price series. The numerous 'Libraries' with their reassuring epithets (Colonial and Home, Empire, English, Family, Standard, Parlour)[26] which might provide a novel for between 1s. and 6s. could normally do so only by dealing in fiction which was undersize, underquality, where the copyright was aged, dead, pirated or no longer the property of the author. Bentley could bring out *Uncle Tom's Cabin* for 3s. 6d. as a new book but it would have cost nine times as much had Mrs Stowe been one of his authors and not some American powerless to protect her copyright. (As it was Bentley had to compete with pirated 1s. editions and even, it was rumoured, a serialised 6d. version costing 1d. the part.) Bentley informed one of his English authors, Captain Marryat, that it was 'out of the question' for him to offer more than £50 for publication in the Standard Novels, selling at 6s. No self-respecting author was going to write new novels for such a payment.

Nonetheless the price of non-fiction books fell consistently after the midcentury and the novel's resistance to this lateral pressure on its high cost is remarkable. The facts may be shown by breaking down Bentley's publishing list, either side of the 1850s. In 1835 Bentley put out 58 titles of which 41 sold at over £1; 20 novels were published costing 31s. 6d. and two costing 21s. In 1865 Bentley put out 57 titles of which only 26 cost over £1; 15 of these were 31s. 6d. and three 21s. novels. The total output and the output of expensive fiction had thus remained perfectly constant over the thirty years in which other kinds of books were plummeting in price. Meanwhile, too, reprints were creeping down from 6s. to 3s. 6d. or less and books were running through their career from first printing to reprint form much more quickly.[27] Among all this change the three-volume, 31s. 6d. novel remained rocklike, immutable. Britain in 1865 may not have been what it was in the 1840s, 'the dearest country in the world for books'—but it was still the dearest country for new novels. And yet the novel and novelist prospered there as nowhere else in the world.

II

For these reasons publishers and authors generally were complacent about the high cost of fiction. No one involved in the making of novels was over-concerned to drop prices prematurely. As George Bentley once put it with artless candour: 'it is questionable whether any persons benefit by cheap literature but the public'.[28] A rogue novelist attempting to break the mutual benefit between writer and publisher on this point would be smartly disciplined as was Alison Carmichael when she suggested compressing her novel into a cheaper, two-volume form:

> [Mr Bentley] would much prefer the work being extended to three volumes as he has invariably found that nothing can be expected in the way of profit either to author or publisher from the publication of works of fiction in two volumes. This arises from the expenses in the latter case being almost as great as those in the former while the price of the work in two volumes [i.e. 21s.] is a third less. He has therefore ordered me to make out the agreement which is annexed for three volumes.[29]

Assuming that one had to buy fiction, and buy it in volume form, Bentley's logic was unassailable. For seventy years, therefore, English fiction was subject to the inflationary pressure of the three-volume format.

It is a paradox of the Victorian publishing world, however, that while it retained the three-volume novel as the foundation stone of its production, it was constantly trying to find ways around the barrier which the high price erected. The desired effect was not to undermine the three-decker, but to underpin it, creating an interdependence of expensive and cheaper forms serving an ever expanding and fiction-hungry market. One could go only so far with the 6s. reprint; if this followed too hard on the three-volume issue it competed and upset the publishing apple cart. Something new was needed to supplement the traditional multi-volume novel. In the period from the forties to the sixties four major breaches were made in the established system which opened an enlarged supply of fresh, quality fiction to literate, but not necessarily wealthy classes of the population. These were: part publication, the 'Leviathan' circulating library, the prompt collective reissue and magazine serialisation.

The first of these innovations occurred in 1836 when Dickens, together with Chapman and Hall, revived the serial publication of fiction in shilling monthly numbers, with immense success. The part issue of fiction had a venerable history, going back at least 200 years but the better novelists, following Scott, had tended to avoid it in the 1820s and 30s. For some time before *Pickwick*, however, there had been experimental stirrings with new, or nearly new novels in numbers, such as the 1836 issue of Lytton's *Pilgrims of the Rhine* from Saunders and Otley in 2s. 6d. parts. (The work was a travel book whose interest lies in a number of digressive tales; this was one of the original conceptions of *Pickwick*, as declared in the advertisement of 26 March 1836.) And for a year or so before that Colburn had been running his 'Colburn's Modern Novelists' series which offered novels in weekly 1s. parts. (Numbers 1–6, for example, made up Lytton's *Pelham*.)

Dickens's serial differed from its predecessors in one simple and all important feature. Whereas Colburn took a novel published originally in volumes and broke it down into 1s. parts Chapman and Hall had *Pickwick* designed from the first as 1s. parts with a view to subsequent consolidation in volumes. The reader had the fiction, as the phrase went, 'warm from the brain' and usually before any critical judgement could be imposed on it, giving the work a singular freshness. The process by which this mode of serialisation was arrived at seems to have been largely accidental but, once it caught on, *Pickwick* established 1s. monthly numbers as a pre-eminent form of Victorian publishing. By it as many as 40,000 subscribers were provided with a 300,000-word, well printed, large paged, illustrated, original novel at £1, in easy payments. Dickens brought out all but two of his full length works in this way, Thackeray four of his six, Ainsworth, Lever, Trollope and (in modified form) George Eliot a number of theirs. All in all serialisation in monthly parts accounts for a rich slice of our canonised Victorian fiction.

Rich in every sense. Monthly serials, one should emphasise, were a way of producing novels as sumptuous as the three-decker, but at a more affordable price. Illustration, which was a luxury the multi-volume novel did not normally offer, was of an expensively high standard. Dickens illustrated by Phiz, Trollope by Millais or Thackeray by Thackeray were at least equivalent to Smollett illustrated by Rowlandson or Sterne by Hogarth. And in the forties and fifties reproductive processes were costly—roughly £120 of the £400 total monthly expense of a 30,000 issue (but in the sixties illustration costs were cut by one-third with new technology—interestingly this coincides with decline of the monthly number novel).[30] Nor is it true to say that the novel in numbers catered for 'a new naive public... the shopkeeper and the working man'.[31] The semi-literate public had its own presses, churning out penny serials before, during and after *Pickwick*'s success. Admittedly Chapman and Hall and Bradbury and Evans borrowed some of the techniques of the slum publishers but they refined them for an essentially middle-class readership. (The same line was pursued, even more profitably, by Cassell's.) In itself the novel in monthly numbers remained an article for the discriminating, literate and fairly affluent for whom it was that beloved Victorian thing, 'a cheap luxury'.

The value of the monthly serial was not just that it lowered the price of expensive novels. It also raised the reward for authors. 'No novel would be worth £10,000 to a publisher by any author,' declared Trollope magisterially to a correspondent who had mentioned that magic number, 'no house could afford to give such a sum.'[32] In the normal course of publishing this economic commonsense held true enough. But serialisation broke the rules. It was certainly worth Chapman and Hall's while to give Dickens £10,000 for *Our Mutual Friend* and for Smith to offer the same amount for *Romola*.[33] Serialisation rendered the old ceiling payments irrelevant. Not all novelists got higher wages but the fact that any novelist might attain to fabulously high rewards changed the whole notion of the profession. Writing of Dickens in 1858 Cordy Jeaffreson made the point that his huge individual earnings had raised the art of writing novels generally: 'With us every calling, however mean in itself, becomes honourable by custom, if it can be shown to be lucrative by experience, for the simple reason that the enterprizing of the best ranks of society join it.'[34] By dying a rich man (unlike

Scott) and leaving an estate of £93,000 Dickens had helped make fiction writing as professionally respectable as the law, medicine or the civil service. No longer was authorship a 'beggarly profession', nor did the aspiring writer have to console himself with the famously incommensurate rewards of literary history; £10 for *Paradise Lost*, £60 for *The Vicar of Wakefield*. It is probable that Dickens's gross fortune, which was made largely from monthly serials, did more to raise the profession than any number of Thackerayan or Carlylean lectures on 'The Dignity of Literature', or 'The Hero as Man of Letters'.

Although Dickens himself continued to make money from the monthly serial up to the time of his death in 1870, it declined as a form in the late fifties and sixties. The probable reason was that it had been overtaken by the increasing efficiency and cheapness of reproduction which made feasible even better bargains for the consumer. Comparing some costs for *Dombey and Son* (1846) and *Our Mutual Friend* (1865) one can see how the industry had advanced in a purely technical sense:[35]

	Dombey (3rd Number)				*Our Mutual Friend* (3rd Number)		
printed	32,000				30,000		
composing	£5	15s.	6d.		£4	10s.	0d.
Corrections	5	5	0		3	4	0
Stereotyping	4	0	0		2	8	0
Working							
64 rms. at 7s. 9d.	24	0	0	60 rms. at 6s. 6d.	19	10	0
Pressing at 2s.	6	8	0	(at 1s. 6d.)	4	10	0
Paper,				(60 rms. at			
64 rms. at 32s.	102	8	0	25s. 6d.)	76	10	0
Illustration work	118	0	0		79	9	9
Advertiser	67	5	0		64	10	0
Stitching: 23s. 6d. per 1,000				16s. 0d. per 1,000			
(*Total Costs*	£416	18s.	2d.		£217	15s.	9d.)

In the sixties there were richer pickings to be had from the magazine which capitalised on the cheaper machine processes (especially for illustration); the *Cornhill* for 1s. could offer *two* fiction serials by big names, illustrations and a wealth of supplementary material. This and the heavy production costs of monthly numbers (even a modest serial could cost £5,000) account for their being used only by a relatively few best-selling authors over a relatively short period. Nonetheless the monthly serial in shilling numbers probably did more than anything else to open up a mass market for fiction.

III

Serialisation by no means threatened the three-decker in which the majority of lesser novelists continued to appear. The *Publishers' Circular* listed six times as many in 1887 (184) as in 1837 (31). A prime factor in its survival, and increased prosperity, in the mid-century period was the dramatic growth in the circulating library business. In the 1840s and 50s Mudie's library in particular expanded to control a major section of the metropolitan market and a sizeable portion of that in the country and overseas.[36] At his zenith, in the 1860s, he earned up to £40,000 a year in subscriptions.[37] His biggest selling point was cheapness: for an annual fee of only a guinea (a fraction of what early rivals charged) the customer was entitled to the loan of a volume which could be exchanged as often as he cared. Proportionately more lavish subscriptions were available and it was calculated that using Mudie's facilities a year's reading for half-a-dozen members of a family could be had for two to three guineas, equivalent to £200 worth of new books bought in the shops. But it was the talismanic one guinea, one volume, one year offer which remained Mudie's trademark throughout his century of trading.

As he grew from Southampton Row to New Oxford Street and across the country Mudie rationalised not just the library system but many aspects of production as well. Before his Select Library established itself novels were delivered in quires and sold in an undignified scramble by the dealers who could bind them first in the ugly, grey boards which one still finds on some old copies.[38] Mudie bound books himself and soon encouraged publishers to follow his example. At the same time the order and supply of novels was regularised. Mudie entered into treaty with the major houses for subscription rates and pre-publication orders. (Of the 3,864 novels Bentley sold by subscription in 1864, 1,962 were bought by Mudie). This helped set up orderly sequences of manufacture and delivery. There were no price wars in new fiction while Mudie's dominated the scene. In this process of centralising, cheapening and expanding service Mudie may be seen as literature's Rowland Hill.

Other forms of rationalisation followed. It was no accident that the two greatest entrepreneurs of fiction in mid-Victorian England, Mudie and W. H. Smith, set themselves to impose middle-class decencies on the English novel, 'purifying the sources of amusement and information' as Smith's biographer puts it in an image that links railway reading and contemporary sanitary reform.[39] Mudie read likely novels himself and, as his brochure discriminated with subtle accentuation, his library contained 'the best New Works' but 'the *best* Works of Fiction are also freely admitted'.

Mudie, another Scottish founder, had fundamentalist religious views. He had begun providing books for the new population of London University students and intellectuals around Bloomsbury and it is conceivable that he might just as well have gone on to become a great bookseller like Blackwell or James Thin. Arguably he might have been happier than he was satisfying the age's insatiable demand for novels; but on the other hand his natural censoriousness was good business in his chosen line. Mudie prospered partly because the West-Central area of London was becoming more bourgeois. There had been circulating libraries plying there when Mudie 'could scarcely have reached the dignity of long clothes'.[40] But the aristocracy and gentry moved further westward and the old genteel libraries did not adapt to the new clientele. Mudie did adapt. It was the new middle classes who must have taken out most of his subscriptions and they were principally reading groups of mixed ability and mixed age; the family circle had replaced the 'reader on a sofa'. Mudie had a 'Juvenile Department' larger than many of his predecessors' total stocks. If he truckled to Mrs Grundy he was repaid by the little Grundys' custom.

It is undeniable, however, that Mudie's influence was frequently a trespass on artistic freedom. The severe moral tone of his judgement is evident in a crusty little note he sent Bentley in 1876:

dear Mr Bentley

Readers and Critics differ in opinion as to the 'New Godiva'—My own personal opinion is that the too suggestive title is the worst thing about it.

I do not intend to withdraw the book entirely from circulation, but I must ask you to be so good as to take back 50 of the 75 copies I have still uncut.[41]

Publishers doubtless needed few such touches of the whip to know who was in the driving seat and what were his ways. 'Mr Mudie', *The Saturday Review* observed in 1860, 'is in a position to make himself the dictator of literature.'[42] He was not entirely disinclined to assume that power. In ten years his annual acquisition of volumes rose, as his advertisements tell us, from 5,000 to 120,000; this must have made him the largest single purchaser of novels in the world. And as his business grew he would occasionally interfere directly with the novelist (by a ban as on Reade's *Cream* or by withholding a work from general circulation as with Meredith's *Ordeal of Richard Feverel*). 'Novels of objectionable character or inferior ability are almost invariably excluded' his advertisements declared—'almost' is an interesting concession. Occasionally he was accused outright of refusing a book on moral or religious grounds but the indirect pressure of his 'petticoated mind'[43] on publishers and thereby on authors was both more pervasive and in its way more irresistible than a clear exclusion. The source of his power may be estimated from the sales figures of Trollope's *Barchester Towers* in its first three-volume edition, 1857:

750 printed and advertised at a cost of £266 15s. 1d.
6 author's free copies
26 presented
200 sold to Mudie, 25 as 24, at 13s. 6d. Receipts £129 12s. 0d.
126 sold to trade, 25 as 24, at 21s. Receipts £127 1s. 0d.
Amount short of expenses £10 2s. 1d.[44]

On the basis of these figures Longman's felt justified in going on with a highly remunerative cheap, one-volume edition in Spring 1858, another in June 1859 and yet another in June 1860, making some 4,000 cheap copies in all. More importantly for Trollope this success with *Barchester Towers* got his career as a novelist off the ground. Yet it is obvious that the Mudie sale was the pivot of commercial success. Without these 200 cleared off (even at the near giveaway price of 13s. 6d., giving only half-a-crown's profit at most) the project would have been a dead loss. At June 1860 123 copies of the first edition remained on hand; without Mudie's purchase there would have been half the impression still in the warehouse after three years. No publisher could have gone forward on those figures.

The notoriously straight-laced, hymn-writing Mudie could not, therefore, be offended and his crotchets were elevated to precautionary rules of the trade. When he read the manuscript of *Barchester Towers* Longman's adviser insisted on its being extensively purged of its 'vulgarity' and 'exaggeration.'[45] (It would be nice, Michael Sadleir muses, to read the 'uncensored' *Barchester Towers*.) One example of the kind of alteration required is on record; 'fat stomach' had to be changed to 'deep chest'. It is a prime instance of what came to be called 'Mudie-itis'.[46]

Like most of the great breakthroughs in the nineteenth-century fiction market Mudie's triumph was the outcome not of cautious whittling down of costs but of slashing them dramatically, so short circuiting the gap that existed between high book prices and low income. Yet unlike, for example, Bentley's stab at reducing the three-decker's price to 24s. in the late 1830s,[47] it was achieved not by cheapening the product but by exploiting the expendability of fiction once it is read. One reason that fiction tends to gravitate towards the cheapest form of publishing is that in most cases it is read once only, and then quickly. In America this economic logic led to books of incredible cheapness, designed to be thrown away after use. In Britain it was not the book which was cheapened but the reading of it.

To the public Mudie was a benefactor. For less than the price of a new novel one had English fiction at one's disposal. For publishers, on the other hand, Mudie was a harsh opponent, beating them down on bulk orders and sometimes withholding payment until dunned. He was also capable of sharp practice; in October 1852 he bought 430 copies of Thackeray's *Esmond* at the library discount price (probably around 18s.). In February he was selling off surplus copies of the novel—after they had had the run of his shelves—for 15s., in direct competition with Smith's second edition of the novel at 31s. 6d. If he had a publisher in his hand Mudie squeezed relentlessly. Shilling by shilling he pushed down what the book producer could expect for his product. In September 1850 Bentley's wrote proposing a standing order arrangement by which Mudie would have any three-volume novel for £1 (25 for 24). Eight years later the publisher was glad to get 13s. 6d. for the same kind of novels.[48] In this way Mudie undoubtedly helped create the uncomfortably Hobbesian world of bookselling between the introduction of 'free trade in books' in 1852 and its regulation in 1899 with the net book system.

It was not mere cussedness or ruthlessness that made Mudie deal so competitively with the publishers. Although he made his money from novels every new three-decker he took posed a financial problem. Hence we find him negotiating and renegotiating, often on single titles. The nature of his problem is clear if we look at his advertised list. It was made up of established favourites and classics (mostly in one-volume editions) and new multi-volume novels. Assuming that an average subscriber took out the three-guinea, eight-volume option and changed his books every fortnight this would mean that a volume in Mudie's stock earned less than 6d. on every loan (before deductions for carriage, warehousing and overhead costs). Bearing this in mind, consider a typical novel, *The Ladies of Bever Hollow*, by Miss Manning, brought out by Bentley in two volumes at 12s. in June 1858. On July 16 Mudie took 1,000 copies of this novel at just over half price, 6s. 6d.[49] In November Bentley, having cleared his expensive edition, brought out a 5s. one-volume reprint. (Mudie would often try to enjoin publishers not to bring out cheap editions of novels he had taken in bulk, for a year; such requests were, as the trade was not slow to point out, unenforceable.)[50]

The cheap version of *The Ladies of Bever Hollow* would to a large extent syphon off the immediate popularity of the novel. Either subscribers would buy it at the cheap price or it would have lost the aura of being the latest thing. Now there was little chance that at 6d. a journey the two thousand volumes of *Bever*

Hollow could have earned what Mudie paid for them, plus service costs, in three months. Admittedly there was a substantial rebate in selling off surplus copies at a reduced price to lesser libraries and in his sales department. But in the main *Bever Hollow* and other new fiction of its kind, must have been regarded as loss leaders to attract and keep subscribers. His real money must have come from the one-volume veterans of his shelves or those few multi-volume copies he kept in stock after a novel lost its bloom.

Mudie's was particularly strong on fiction (although after 1860 he always put it at the end of his catalogue). Of the million-or-so volumes he bought between 1853 and 1862 half were novels.[51] In 1858 his stock stood thus:

History and Biography	56,472 volumes	slow turnover
Travel and Adventure	25,552	
Fiction	87,780	fast turnover[52]
Miscellaneous	46,450	

Since he worked on a subscriber-volume allowance it suited Mudie to build his sytem round the redundancy of the three-decker, which meant that his expensive, fast turnover fiction went that much further. Looking over his catalogues one perceives a distinct trend towards more multi-volume fiction between 1850 and 1870. Rather than restock with one-volume reprints Mudie tended rather to keep back a proportion of his original three- or double-deckers. Thus in 1857 Lytton had twenty titles listed in the Mudie catalogue of which five are multi-volume works; in 1871 he had twenty-one titles of which eighteen are multi-volume. It was, one imagines, partly by this means that Mudie contrived to show such an increase in his stock in the early 1860s.

It also suited Mudie to keep the price of novels sky-high for those who, unlike himself, did not enjoy a 60 per cent discount. This would include not only the private buyer but the small libraries whom he was driving to the wall. Thirty-one shillings and six pence on the open market gave a scarcity value to his stock and a glamorous overvaluation in the public eye. To acquire fiction cheaply whilst keeping intact its luxurious reputation was good business.

All this served to reinforce the expensive, multi-volume form long after one would have expected it to disappear. With the help of the libraries English fiction thus had the security which came from assured high prices and concurrent wide circulation. It was obviously an artificial situation. For one thing it meant that novelists had to write in what many of them felt was an unnaturally long format. But it is probable that the artificial maintenance of the thousand-page novel in this way made for greater as well as bigger fiction. In the weaker artist it encouraged diffuseness, bulking and padding (Miss Manning, for example, was prevailed on by Bentley to add two chapters to *Bever Hollow* to give each volume a respectable girth); but for the novelist trying to do something great in fiction it allowed that 'epische Breite'[53] which seems inextricably tied in with physical massiveness. A curtailed *Mill on the Floss* or *Esmond* is unthinkable. The three-decker was thus an ordeal and at the same time an opportunity for the novelist. Charles Reade, in a letter, expresses its possibilities and burdens eloquently: 'I am a writer. I *cannot scribble.* A 3 vol Novel is a great prose Epic. I hope never to write another...'[54]

IV

The third, and in some ways the most significant innovation, was the cheap reissue in 'collective editions' of the works of authors who had achieved classic status in their lifetimes; notably Dickens and Bulwer Lytton, though Lever, Eliot, Disraeli and Ainsworth were subjected to the same honorific treatment. These collectives were the nearest the Victorian publishing world came to issuing good fiction, at minimal prices, while it was still seasonably fresh.

Although they were not synonymous with novels for railway reading a main precondition of the collective reissues was the railway 'mania' of 1846. By their very nature Victorian rail-travellers were an up-market, literate class with money and leisure. The thousands of miles of rail-line laid in the mid 1840s meant that journeys were now long enough to take up the reading of a novel. And the franchise awarded to W. H. Smith, who insisted on certain standards in the fiction he purveyed, gave the better novelists a foothold in this new market. A selective chronology will give some idea of the suddenness with which price levels fell in the novel-publishing boom that swept along with the railway boom:

1831 Bentley and Colburn's 'Standard Novels' selling at 6s.
July 1844 Smith, Elder begin a collective of G. P. R. James at 8s. per volume.
1845 Saunders and Otley complete their collective of Lytton at 6s. per volume.
1846 Simms M'Intyre introduce the 'Parlour Novelist' at 2s. and 2s. 6d. per volume.
March 1846 Longman's bring out their collective of Mrs Bray's novels at 6s. per volume.
February 1847 Simms and M'Intyre announce that their 'Parlour Library' will bring out new works of fiction 'of the highest character' at 1s. and 1s. 6d. per volume.
March 1847 Chapman and Hall announce their 'Cheap' edition of the novels of Dickens selling at 1½d. a part and (on average) 3s. 6d. the entire novel.
Autumn 1847 Bentley issues a 'New Edition' of the 'Standard Novels' (109 titles) at 5s. per volume.
October 1847 Chapman and Hall announce their cheap edition of Lytton's novels on the same pattern as Dickens's, earlier in the year.
November 1848 Routledge's 'Railway Library' begins with a collective of Fenimore Cooper's novels at 1s. per volume.
1849 Bentley drops the 'Standard Novels' to 2s. 6d. and 3s. 6d.
November 1849 Chapman and Hall begin a collective of Ainsworth's novels at 1s. and 1s. 6d.
1849 Simms M'Intyre purchase all G. P. R. James's copyrights for issue at 1s. and 1s. 6d.
1852–3 Bentley's 'Standard Novels' are supplemented by his 'Shilling Series' and Bentley's 'Railway Library' at 1s.
April 1853 Bryce brings out a collective of Disraeli's novels at 1s. 6d.
1854 Routledge purchases all Lytton's copyrights to be brought out in the 'Railway Library' at 1s. 6d. and upwards.

The most daring in conception and admirable in quality of these ventures were, probably, Chapman and Hall's cheap editions of Dickens and Lytton in 1847. The scheme worked by fixing rock bottom prices and going for the widest possible sales. The format for the issue of these novels was, in fact, taken from the world of popular journalism; specifically Sharpe's weekly *London Magazine* which was started up in October 1845, offered sixteen double columned pages and sold for a 1½d. a week or 7d. monthly. (It advertised itself, unironically, as 'the cheapest of cheap journals' a tag which gives one some notion of the respectability of the adjective 'cheap' at this time.) With Chapman and Hall's 'Cheap Edition' *Martin Chuzzlewit* (a book less than three years old in March 1847) would cost a subscriber 4s. in thirty-two weekly 1½d. parts. *Oliver Twist* on the same terms would cost 2s. 6d. The novels could also be had in monthly 7d. parts or bound up as volumes after issue was complete. These were tiny sums and great conveniences compared with fiction in the orthodox three-volume form.

Success with these collective editions required a shrewd knowledge of the market, a big name on the title page and a long haul for profits. Both prices and the books themselves were fractionalised to their smallest tolerance. Huge figures were involved. In 1847, for example, Chapman and Hall printed 2,290,000 'parts' of Dickens's novels.[55] The profit from this output produced around £1,000 a year for the interested parties, which was relatively small considering the capital investment on the one side and the literary investment on the other. Its overriding value, however, was its durability and what it was doing for the better class of the reading public. Charles Lever, who was dealing with Chapman and Hall at the time, rightly saw the 'Cheap Edition' as 'the greatest trial of cheapness ever made in bookselling'. But, as he pointed out, 'it has shown that the profits...cannot be reckoned on till after a considerable lapse of time. When an author's popularity has lasted long enough to be more than a passing taste and to stand the test of a new generation of readers—then, and only then can successive editions be regarded as profitable.'[56]

In other words it was necessary to have a public educated in the discriminating reading of novels. The general application of critical standards in the evaluation of fiction had become something more than a belletristic exercise. As part of the general uplift that occurred about this period one witnesses the emergence of reliable reviewers, publishers' readers and a public capable of judgement based on sound critical reasoning. This presented a new and stimulating challenge to the author. 'The public', Reade told his publisher in 1852, 'is more intelligent than it was...I am ready for them.'[57]

What the collective editions demonstrated most tellingly was the hitherto unplumbed depth of the fiction market. The cheap edition of *Oliver Twist* had to compete with the novel's original magazine publication (1837–9), Bentley's first book edition in 1838 together with several reprintings, Chapman and Hall's three-volume edition of 1841, Bradbury and Evans's issue in ten numbers (January–October 1846) and their one-volume edition of 1846. There was, in addition, a whole gallery of plagiarisms and pirated copies. Almost every publishing finger had been in this pie, and, unlike pies, books do not disappear once they are consumed. Yet it was still worthwhile to bring out the biggest ever issue in 1850.

Ostensibly the collective editions were democratic. Lytton's declaration in Chapman and Hall's advertisements of October 1847 indicates the general feeling that publisher and author were breaking upon a new, uncolonised territory:

> May these works, then, thus cheaply equipped for a wider and more popular mission than they have hitherto fulfilled, find favour in those hours when the shop is closed, when the flocks are penned, and the loom has released its prisoners;—may they be read by those who, like myself, are workmen.

But one suspects that the cheap collective edition found a richer market in professional people like the young Anthony Trollope. Trollope had been educated at Harrow, clearly had a literary bent yet was earning only about £100 a year in the early 1840s—about enough to buy a three-volume novel a week and a loaf of bread a day. However was someone in his position to get the best contemporary novels which were now the vehicle for the best contemporary writers? Book clubs tended to favour improving literature; Mudie's worked best for family groups;

new novels were for the rich and monthly serials only offered half an hour's ration of reading every month, poor fare for a diet trained on three-deckers.

Chapman and Hall went in for the cheap reissue methodically in the 1840s and after, doing it for Lytton, Dickens, Ainsworth and Lever—but especially Dickens and all while the authors were in their prime. At one point they were handling simultaneously the 'Library', the 'People's', the 'Cheap', and the 'Charles Dickens' editions for Dickens, as well as his new fiction (after 1859). In the 1850s the system was brought to its highest pitch of success by Routledge's with their 'Railway Library'. By backing the market's insatiability Routledge was to make a fortune through acquiring copyrights which more orthodox publishers thought worn out. His most famous coup was the ten-year purchase of nineteen of Lytton's copyrights for £20,000, which he started to exercise in 1854 with thirty-five separate volumes, including a twenty-volume 'complete' Lytton for £3 11s. 6d. The risk was considerable and three years later the traditional publishing world was gloating over the fact that he was still ten thousand pounds out of pocket.[58] But using fiction's new outlets, Smith's bookstands, Routledge saturated the market with his Railway Library editions of these 'FIRST CLASS WORKS' eventually proving, in Lytton's case at least, that it was impossible to exhaust a good book by a good author. At first not even Lytton himself (who was not a modest man) believed that Routledge could make money from the agreement: 'he pays high for a leading article in order to set up a periodical',[59] he told John Blackwood. But Lytton's copyrights were not, finally, the expensive gilt on the Railway Library; they returned the publisher's investment, and more. In 1857 W. H. Smith reported Lytton as 'heading the list' of popular reading fare, a position that novelist held for twenty years. Take one title, *Pelham*, which had been first published in 1828 and was in and out of print between then and Routledge's purchase in 1853. With its new owner this somewhat moth-eaten novel sold 46,000 in five years in its 1s. 6d. Railway Edition. The 2s. Railway Library Edition of 1859 sold 35,750 copies in 34 years.[60] In various more or less expensive forms the work continued to sell consistently for Lytton's lifetime. When he died in 1873

(Routledge commemorated the event with a 3s. 6d. edition) this still extremely popular 'Adventures of a Gentleman' of 1828 must have had the flavour of an antiquity.

Basically the collective reissue worked by turning a prime disadvantage of the writing profession in the practising author's favour. The disadvantage was that, as one writer complained, 'we suffer...from the competition of great writers who have passed beyond the necessity of earning their bread'.[61] In 1832, for example, Bentley bought five of Jane Austen's copyrights for the paltry sum of £210.[62] For forty years these novels ran in the Standard Novels at a few shillings. In a market which was dominated by limited money supply for fiction there is no doubt that Jane Austen was taking work from contemporary writers with whom she shared Bentley's list.

In the superheated conditions of the midcentury an author could achieve early in his lifetime the classic status previously accorded only after death. Dickens was keenly aware of this, and waxed fulsome on the prehumous nature of the venture in the launching advertisement for the first series:

> It had been intended that this CHEAP EDITION, now announced, should not be undertaken until the books were much older, or the Author was dead...To become, in his new guise, a permanent inmate of many English homes, where, in his old shape he was only known as a guest, or hardly known at all; to be well thumbed and soiled in a plain suit that will be read a great deal by children, and grown people, at the fireside and on the journey; to be hoarded on the humble shelf where there are few books, and to lie about in libraries like any familiar piece of household stuff that is easy of replacement: and to see and feel this—not to die first, or grow old and passionless, must obviously be among the hopes of a living author, venturing on such an enterprise.[63]

Certainly in their own day Lytton and Dickens's work was, all of it, continuously on display before the public. Some idea of the scale of production (and the relative popularity of the novels) may be gathered from the printing figures[64] for the 'Charles Dickens' edition, the last collective that the novelist saw through the press. (Royal 16mo, illustrated, it sold at 3s. and 3s. 6d., the eighteen-volume set costing £2 18s. plain, £3 10s. fancy.)

	HT	PP	MC	DS	NN	GE	DC	OT	OCS	CB	BH	LD	BR	UT	TTC	SB	AN	OMF
1867		50	30	30	25		25	25	25	25								
1868			5					5	5		22	22	25		22	25	20	
1868	18	13	5		5	22	5	5						15				20
1869				5	5		5		5	5	5			5				5
1869		5	5	5			5	5					5					
1870	5	8			5		5		5	5		5					5	5
Totals	23	76	45	40	40	22	45	40	40	35	27	27	30	20	22	25	25	30

Grand Total: 612,000

Legend: units are in thousands printed. *HT* = *Hard Times*, *PP* = *Pickwick Papers*, *MC* = *Martin Chuzzlewit*, *DS* = *Dombey and Son*, *NN* = *Nicholas Nickleby*, *GE* = *Great Expectations*, *DC* = *David Copperfield*, *OT* = *Oliver Twist*, *OCS* = *Old Curiosity Shop*, *CB* = *Christmas Books*, *BH* = *Bleak House*, *LD* = *Little Dorrit*, *BR* = *Barnaby Rudge*, *UT* = *Uncommercial Traveller*, *TTC* = *Tale of Two Cities*, *SB* = *Sketches by Boz*, *AN* = *American Notes*, *OMF* = *Our Mutual Friend*.

Printing figures for the 'Charles Dickens' edition

One effect of this kind of collective issue was to keep all of Dickens simultaneously before the public. Almost four-fifths of the volumes printed by Chapman and Hall in this edition were works written before 1850. In this way Dickens had a kind of total and continual existence for the readers of his age.

V

At first many novelists were inclined to be suspicious of 'cheap rascals'[65] like Routledge, or Chapman. It was Dickens who had the keenest business mind of all his colleagues who took up the collective edition and profited most from it. Dickens also made the most of the fourth of the innovations in the practice of fiction selling. This occurred in the late fifties and early sixties when he, Bradbury and Evans, Smith, Macmillan's, Bentley and others established magazines and weeklies with circulations of up to 100,000 copies and more as vehicles for top grade fiction. In essence this was a new lease of life for serialisation and did for it what monthly numbers had done in the forties and mid fifties. Thackeray's later novels came out in this form as did many of George Eliot's, Wilkie Collins's, Reade's, Trollope's, Mrs Gaskell's and Hardy's.

The development of these fiction-carrying journals was part of the logic of the increasing growth and power of a nucleus of very large firms. The peculiar organisation of English fiction publishing meant a necessarily heavy expenditure on advertising. Publishing is anomalous in this respect since it is the manufacturer rather than the retailer who bears the cost of enticing the purchaser. When firms became rich enough it was practicable to have their own house journal (according to some authorities it was essential) so as to give the house's products adequate exposure. These journals were ideal for selling fiction as well, and at costs even lower than monthly numbers could achieve. The *Cornhill*, for example, offered two serials by name novelists every month, and a wealth of other matter.

It is likely that the fiction-carrying journal did not merely offer an alternative mode of purchase, it actually enlarged the gross size of the reading public by taking in a whole new sector of customers. Charles Reade, a professionally thoughtful novelist, made this point in 1856 on the subject of serialising a story in the *London Journal*:

It is I am aware the general opinion that a story published in a penny journal is exhausted—I do not think so. I am a great believer in *rascally* bad type—I believe there is a public that only reads what comes in a readable form. I may be wrong—we shall see: if I am right the London journal will do little more than advertise my story to Public No. 2.[66]

Events would seem to bear out Reade's belief that magazine and journal serialisation created second markets rather than redeploying old ones. George Eliot at the same period was reluctant to run *Mill on the Floss* through *Blackwood's Magazine* for fear that it would 'sweep away perhaps 20,000—nay, 40,000—readers who would otherwise demand copies of the complete work from the libraries'.[67] In the same spirit she withdrew a promised serial from *Harper's* in 1861. The truth was that readers were swept up rather than away. After *Great Expectations* had run through *All the Year Round*, the biggest selling of the quality fiction carriers, Mudie was still prepared to take 1,400 three-volume copies and Chapman and Hall cleared their 3,750 three-decker version of *Great Expectations* with no trouble whatsoever, the work going through five editions in a year.[68]

In the period we are dealing with, every major house eventually acquired its own journal and used it as a vehicle for top quality fiction. These journals after the initial and considerable expense of founding them, earned revenue for the publisher, displayed his wares and enabled him to test the market to see how a novel 'pulled' with the public. The advantages even went so far as to outweigh the occasional unprofitability of the venture from a purely book-keeping point of view. Tinsley cheerfully sustained a loss on his *Tinsleys' Magazine* observing: 'what cheaper advertisement can I have for twenty five pounds a month? It advertises my name and publications and it keeps my authors together.'[69] There was, in fact, a fearful increase in the expense of advertising between the mid fifties and sixties. It cost Bradbury and Evans around £200 to advertise the early numbers of *Little Dorrit* in 1855. Chapman and Hall spent £1,000 in pre-publication advertisement of *Our Mutual Friend* ten years later (among their expenses were 1,000,000 bills).[70] Since the unit cost had been brought down by only about a penny on the production of a shilling number (from 3d. to 2d.) this meant that advertising was beginning to bite sharply into profits.

From every point of view, then, the magazine was a rational investment and fiction carrying journals prospered for thirty years or so. To some they seemed the securest of all literary institutions. In April 1861 the *Publishers' Circular* speculated about 1960 when the *Cornhill* premises would have expanded to take over Wimbledon Common. But in fact things were no more stable in the publishing world than they had ever been. Novels in volumes were given a new impetus by the price reductions of the 1890s and the journals became less clients of publishing houses and more independent bodies in their own right and then went on to a new phase of existence in which fiction was to play a less important part.

High prices, multiple outlets, wide sales and abundant creative genius combined to make 1850–80 one of the richest periods that fiction has known. The variety of channels by which the great novelist might reach his public can be seen from the following list of George Eliot's novels, together with the ways in which they first presented themselves:

1857 *Scenes of Clerical Life*. Magazine serial (*Blackwood's*, 2s. 6d.)
1859 *Adam Bede*. Three volumes (31s. 6d.)
1860 *Mill on the Floss*. Three volumes (31s. 6d.)
1862–3 *Romola*. Magazine serial (*Cornhill*, 1s.)
1866 *Felix Holt*. Three volumes (31s. 6d.)
1871–2 *Middlemarch*. Bimonthly numbers (8 × 5s.)
1876 *Daniel Deronda*. Monthly numbers (8 × 5s.)
1878–85 Cabinet Edition. 24 vols. Collective reissue.

Part-issue, Library editions (which is what the three-deckers were in essence), Bookstall editions (which is what the collective reissues were in essence) and magazine serialisation had one feature in common. They could each bypass the bookshop. This bypass was a valuable, perhaps even a necessary, facility after

1851. 'From what I hear', Blackwood's London manager wrote to his chief in October of that year, 'it seems not unlikely that we are on the eve of a revolution in trade prices.'[71] It had been a decade of revolutions and publishing did not escape. Free trade in books became the rule after 1852 when Lord Campbell's judgement abolished retail price maintenance by publishers' pact as 'indefensible and contrary to the freedom which ought to prevail in commercial transactions'. The unbridled competition which resulted led to the elimination or degradation of many bookselling retailers. Outside London, Alexander Macmillan claimed in 1868, 'the trade has become so profitless that it is generally the appendage to a toyshop, or a Berlin wool warehouse.'[72] The innovations we have examined created an arterial system by which new, or nearly new, fiction might still reach a mass, countrywide readership. They supported the novel until the 1890s brought in the net book, the reduction of the price of novels on first publication to 6s. and a market vastly expanded and enhanced by the literacy acts of the previous twenty years.

2

Mass Market and Big Business: Novel Publishing at Midcentury

None of the four innovations discussed in the first chapter was, strictly speaking, an invention. Serialisation of fiction, in numbers and magazines, dated back to the eighteenth century and survived unbroken in the slum publishing of G. W. M. Reynolds who is supposed to have sold 40,000 a week of his lurid *Mysteries of London.* The numerous journals Colburn and Bentley spawned in the thirties and forties (especially the *Miscellany*) were in many ways the pattern for the later quality periodicals like the *Cornhill.* The collective reissue during the novelist's lifetime was pioneered by R. J. Cadell's legendarily profitable 'Author's Edition' of the Waverley Novels in 1829.[1] There had been numberless experiments in setting up fiction libraries both of the cheap purchase and book lending variety before the 1840s. Mudie merely rationalised and systematised what had existed for at least a hundred years.

What was different about each of these four initiatives was, above all, the scale of their operation. The expansiveness of the novel-reading market and the eventual efficiency with which publishers exploited it can be seen from the printing figures of Dickens's *Our Mutual Friend*:

No. 1	40,000 (30,000 sold in first two days)
No. 2	35,000
Nos. 3–5	30,000
Nos. 6–12	28,000
Nos. 13–20	25,000[2]

Dickens usually had less of a fall-off than this, but we may assume that the wastage rate here was precisely responded to by Chapman and Hall. What the dwindling represents, in part at least, is the publisher's efficiency in extracting revenue from the desultory reader prepared to speculate a shilling or two on a work he might or might not like. (The same reader would be unlikely to plunge 31s. 6d. on the same experiment.)

Total sales of *Our Mutual Friend* in this first edition amounted to £27,000—assuming that all the 536,000 printed sold. And these were the equivalent of first-day sales. Expensive and cheap reprints could be thought about immediately. Dickens was £10,000 the richer (£6,000 advance, the balance receipts on sales) and his publishers £4,000 in pocket.

Figures are even more dramatic if one takes the magazine serialisation of a novel like *The Woman in White,* whose forty instalments in *All the Year Round* (2d. a weekly copy) represented on completion a sale of over 100,000 at 7s. the entire novel. And these bookstand sales, vast as they were, in no way impeded the runaway success of the novel in three volumes and cheaper book forms. After the journal serialisation Collins sold the first three-volume edition of 1,000 on the day of publication and 350 copies of the second edition within five days. Seven editions went in six months. This pace kept up until the end of the year. Six months later in April 1861 10,000 cheap copies at 6s. were in production with plans for 40,000 to follow.[3] Collins positively tired of sitting for photographs for new edition frontispiece portraits, so many were there. All this represented a quite different scale of operation from what had been achieved earlier. (*Bentley's Miscellany,* carrying *Oliver Twist,* sold 11,000 of its first numbers in 1837.)[4]

Viewed objectively successes like that of *The Woman in White* did no more occasionally than what the slum publishers did regularly and had been doing for several years. (Reynolds not only had his own press but his own paper mill, so vast was his output.) But the difference was that each of the four innovations was directed at, and found, a significantly larger *middle class* readership than conventional trading wisdom assumed to exist and one that was prepared to put its hand into its pocket to get the fiction it liked. The invariable surprise of the establishment in the face of these successes is well caught in the comment of the trade journal, the *Bookseller,* to the *Cornhill*'s triumph in 1860:

The Cornhill Magazine has opened our eyes to the great fact of there being a very large, and hitherto overlooked mass of readers for literature of high class. Whoever believed that a hundred thousand buyers could be found, month after month, for that serial?[5]

II

The simple answer to the *Bookseller*'s question was that George Smith believed in the 'hundred thousand buyers'. Smith, who entered his father's firm at fourteen and ran it before he was twenty, was first the 'boy wonder' and later the 'prince' of nineteenth-century publishers. His princeliness manifested itself in a legendary open-handedness with money. The willingness to put his cash out in literary ventures he judged good marks him off from his more cautious professional colleagues. In this respect his own account of the founding of the *Cornhill* is, as he intends it to be, impressive:

> I have said that our payments to contributors were lavish. As figures are generally interesting, I may mention that the largest amount expended on the literature of a single number was £1,183 3s. 8d. (August 1862), and the total expenditure under that head for the first four years was £32,280 11s. 0d., the illustrations costing in addition £4,376 11s. 0d. In the years between 1860 and 1879, the sum of £84,675 was paid for purely literary work in connexion with the magazine. Expenditure on this scale for literary work alone was, up to this time, unprecedented in magazine literature.[6]

The sums involved in running the *Cornhill* and buying Thackeray as its figurehead (Smith was paying him up to £600 a month)[7] indicate another important fact about the production of fiction at this period, namely that it had become very big business indeed. As a trade, publishing in England has always been long in expertise and short in capital. In the nineteenth century it was no longer necessary, as it had often been in the eighteenth, to raise money by purchaser subscription in advance of printing, or by sharing investment in a copyright but cash was always in fairly small supply. One reason Smith was so successful was that he had capital from his firm's activities in banking and the Indian agency and was prepared to plough it into the publishing operations. By injecting money in this way and by always putting it behind the best talents, even if they were the most expensive, he increased his firm's annual volume of trade from under £50,000 to £600,000 within twenty years.[8]

The prosperous diversity of Smith's firm was exceptional but by legitimate publishing profits a number of other houses had achieved by the late fifties what Victorians would have called 'leviathan' status. This relatively small constellation of rich firms dominated the publishing of quality fiction. One may state almost as an axiom that every work written between 1840 and 1870 which is now recognised as a classic was first published by Chapman and Hall, Bradbury and Evans, Macmillan's, Longman's, Smith, Elder, Bentley or Blackwood's. The only notable exceptions are some first efforts which gained wide readership on the strength of their author's subsequent fame and a very few mavericks like *Wuthering Heights*.

To put this in perspective: Hodson's *Directory* of publishers for 1855 lists 372 firms working in London.[9] Many, of course, like the 'Religious Tract Society', specialised exclusively in fields other than entertaining fiction, but a good proportion did trade in novels whether new or reissued. Yet, for the purposes of most students of the nineteenth-century novel, little would have been lost if 365 of Hodson's publishers had never issued a book; *Nineteenth Century Fiction* would be scarcely a learned article the shorter.

There were good economic and book-making reasons why the seven houses came to monopolise the best in fiction during and after the forties. Following Dickens, popular novels were increasingly well paid for and few firms had purses long enough to reward a bestselling author. But even if such a novelist gave his novel away (as Mrs Gaskell was prepared to do with her first effort)[10] it would not have done much good, unless it fell into the right publishing hands, for only the large houses had the flexibility or the directorial flair to recognise talent and promote it to its full potential. Without a capable publisher the novelist simply could not lift himself out of the rut of writers who lived from one small-edition novel to the next.

This state of affairs may be illustrated by the fate of Trollope's first novel, *The Macdermots of Ballycloran*. T. C. Newby on 15

September 1845 agreed to publish 'any number not exceeding 800'[11] copies of the hopeful young author's work. Newby was a hand-to-mouth purveyor of low quality fiction and a man of dubious honesty; Richard Bentley once refused to talk with him unless there were a witness in the room and 'good enough for Newby' was a clinching rejection by his publisher's reader. Newby in fact has achieved a kind of shabby immortality from Mrs Gaskell's oblique account of him in the *Life of Charlotte Brontë*. In describing his treatment of Emily and Anne, the intrepid biographer was fully prepared to sustain a libel suit in order to 'warn others off trusting to...Newby'.[12] Her account of his villainies seems just enough but unpublished novelists cannot be choosers and Trollope was probably grateful to have anyone, even Newby, take his work.

The agreement for *The Macdermots* was of the joint net-profits kind. Newby, who reserved all printing and publishing decisions, decided on an initial edition of 400; this would allow him a second edition, without renegotiation, if the book caught on. In the first instance Trollope would get nothing until the 200 or so copies needed to cover costs were sold, leaving about £150 to be divided equally between author and publisher when the edition was cleared. (This legally primitive variety of contract was common in the nineteenth century, especially with starting authors.) In the event the break-even point was not reached and the edition was judged a dead loss after a few months. It was published in the Spring; Newby ceased advertising it in June.

A vigorous tale which depicts the brutal realities of life in Ireland of the 1830s, *The Macdermots* was not an inherently unsaleable novel—just the opposite in fact. In 1860, after Trollope had risen in the literary world, it was worthwhile for Chapman and Hall, acting on the advice of John Forster, to buy up the writer's share in the novel, have the novelist trim the narrative down, and bring out several cheap editions in the sixties. So within fifteen years *The Macdermots* had passed from being a dead loss in one publisher's hands to a useful copyright in another's.

The cause lay not in the work but its handler. Even if *The Macdermots* had sold reasonably by Newby's standards when it first came out it would not have benefited Trollope much. Newby was terrified by the prospect of dead stock left with him, so he did not print more than the minimum required for profitability, a niggardly 400, giving at best overhead and a small margin of profit for him, nothing more than pocket money for Trollope. If he meant to live writing novels for employers like Newby he was caught in the exhausting cycle Gissing dramatises in *New Grub Street*; rapid production, low reward, disincentive for the artist to write at his best and the early extinction of whatever talent he had.

To have a chance of hitting the public it was necessary that a novel should have a certain staying power, even if this meant its taking up shelf or storage space for some months. Wilkie Collins put these facts persuasively to his publisher Tinsley (again a fairly dubious operator, though a notch or two above Newby) on hearing that Mudie's had only ordered a disappointing 500 copies of *The Moonstone*:

> Both you and I might have good reason to feel discouraged, if this list indicated anything more important than the timidity of the Libraries—and possibly the poverty of the Libraries—as well. As things are, we have only to wait a few weeks—until the book has time to get *talked about.* I don't attach much importance to the reviews—except as advertisements which are inserted for nothing. But the impression I produce on the general public of readers is the lever that will move anything—provided the impression is favourable. If this book does what my other books have done, in the way of *stimulating the first circle of readers among whom if falls*—that circle will widen to a certainty. It all depends on this.[13]

It is a nice little lecture on the mechanics of literary popularity; and Collins was right. Publishers who had the actual weight of unsold volumes on their hands were notoriously prone to despair and premature remaindering. This was especially the case with men like Tinsley who were somewhat out of their depth and whose bills were thought 'queer' by the more established members of the trade. It is likely that Tinsley was nervous about producing the large number of copies appropriate to a novelist of Collins's stature in the sixties. He could only afford to give the writer £300 of the £1,400 promised him in the contract in cash.[14] All the rest was bill of hand or postponed until sales receipts were in. Nor could Collins persuade him to go ahead and take the risk of printing a further 500 after the first 1,500 were sold.[15]

The novelist was vindicated and Tinsley rescued when, after a very hesitant start, *The Moonstone* went on to become a sales success. But with Trollope's *The Macdermots* it was not simply a question of nerve; there simply was insufficient bulk to make the initial splash, or exert the necessary leverage. Newby did not put enough life into the production for it to be anything but still-born. Printing amounts as small as 400 did not incline a publisher to advertise, moreso since he was to have only half of any profit. Advertisement was a surprisingly high item of production cost when done properly (between 25 and 50 per cent); but, as one author put it, 'to be effectual it must be done with something that looks like prodigality'.[16] Newby was hardly prodigal. Early advertisements of *The Macdermots* are almost as rare as that collector's dream, a first edition. To add insult to neglect, in the few advertisements for the novel that he put in the newspapers Newby dishonestly gave the author as 'Mrs Trollope', Anthony's famous mother. Trollope was doubly a loser in this since a novelist's first work was principally useful to its creator not as a source of income but an announcement of his existence to the public. So obscure was Trollope's debut that Cordy Jeaffreson, writing a history of the novel in 1858, assumed that he had written nothing before 1850.

The whole marketing of *The Macdermots* was marked by a deadening attitude of minimising the loss. With new fiction from an unknown the riskier strategy of maximising the gain was required (at least from the ambitious author's point of view). Almost all the great Victorian novelists burst upon the world. There was no hope of this happening with *The Macdermots*. Even if by some fluke it had caught on it is highly unlikely that Newby could have responded quickly and flexibly in bringing out a second edition to catch the market while it was still interested. At exactly the same period it took him six months to get out an execrable edition of *Wuthering Heights* and *Agnes Grey*,[17] for example, while Smith took the exactly comparable *Jane Eyre* from first reading of the manuscript to shopwindow in just over six weeks for the Autumn market. And Smith was similarly rapid in replenishing booksellers' stock, bringing out the first edition in October 1847, the second in January 1848 and the third in April. When it came, success had to be taken by the forelock and to do the best for an author it was necessary that publishing houses could move from standstill to mass production in a few days. But in such matters, as Charlotte Brontë noted tartly, 'Mr Newby...does not do business like Messrs Smith and Elder.'[18] The truth was that he *could* not do business like Smith, Elder and Co. and it was not until he moved to Longman's in 1854 that Trollope's career began to take shape.

We may compare Newby's methods with those of Longman's for *The Warden*. Trollope made a half-profits agreement for 1,000 copies of this one-volume story in October 1854. The publisher's sales figures and the remittances made over to Trollope are instructive. Trollope, unlike Dickens, Thackeray, Charlotte Brontë or Mrs Gaskell, crept rather than leapt into public favour. But it was clearly the patience and substantial investment that Longman's were prepared to make which made this gradual popularity possible:

	sales	*payments*		
		£	*s.*	*d.*
Dec. 1854–June 1855	388	9	8	8
June 1856	70	10	15	1
June 1857	21	3	10	6
June 1858	61	10	2	7
June 1859	90	15	0	3
June 1860	10	1	15	0
June 1861	4		14	0
June 1862	8	1	8	0

The cheap edition 1859: 1750 produced, by June 1860 1435 sold. Trollope received £24 8s. 8d. June '60 another 1,000 cheap copies printed. Trollope received £39 16s. 2d. Thereafter cheap editions dribbled out regularly until 1877, when Trollope received his last remittance for £5 12s. 6d.[19]

A firm as massive as Longman's could print a substantial edition and wait years for their return. It had taken Newby only a year to judge *The Macdermots* a failure. A year after its publication, with under a half sold, *The Warden* might well have seemed similarly unfortunate. In fact when Trollope got in touch with the firm a month or so after publication they were so discouraging that he stopped work on the sequel (*Barchester Towers*, then one third completed). With Newby the affair would have ended there. Trollope would have recoiled back into the unsuccessful author's limbo. But by waiting five years Longman's managed to clear enough to warrant a second, lucrative, cheap reprint and, looking back at the time of Trollope's death, Henry James could see *The Warden* as signposting the start of his popular career. One main difference between Longman's and Newby was, evidently, that the large and more famous firm had a certain loyalty to any book that came out under their name and were reluctant to let something of theirs be a failure. The remaining copies of the first edition of *The Warden*, now getting on for ten years old, they did not remainder, pulp or sell off cheaply.[20] Instead they bound them into a fresh edition so in the long run, and it was a very long run indeed, all the copies were cleared.

In his way Newby was an efficient book producer, but it was a wretchedly small and obscure way. Bentley, for example, reckoned that on a sold-out edition of 500 copies of a three-decker at this period there would be only £80 to share between novelist and publisher. Newby could squeeze twice this amount out of a similar venture. But Bentley's was a mechanised and sophisticated firm which could as easily bring out an edition of 5,000 as 500. And as Bentley would point out a successful 'small affair' with him would 'pave the way for a good book probably', since he would normally spend up to £80 or so advertising a small edition by a promising young author, laying the ground for a cheap edition.[21] It was not until Trollope left the second-rank publishers and moved up to Longman's that he had any such 'good book'. Even so his career was put back at least eight years by his false starts among the minor publishing houses.

III

Why, one may wonder, did not other small firms of the century emulate the career of Chapman and Hall with *Pickwick*? That novel's monthly circulation soared in a year from 500 to 40,000, shooting both publishers and novelist from obscurity to the forefront of their professions. The reasons for the uniqueness of the Chapman and Hall–Dickens triumph are complex. Partly Dickens was in this, as in most other things, 'inimitable'. Partly in 1837 the publishing world had not consolidated as it would ten years later. Chapman and Hall had, moreover, shown a courage verging on recklessness in launching *Pickwick*. (The early numbers were brought out at a loss which would have proved bankrupting if sustained.) Nor is it too much to say that by good luck they had introduced the monthly serial formula at precisely the right historical moment for it to succeed. And by another stroke of luck, they had as their printers Bradbury and Evans,[22] a progressive firm with modern equipment.

For these, and probably other reasons, shoe-string firms did not follow Chapman and Hall's lucrative experiments with serialisation, and would have been foolhardy to do so. The method offered the best way of sounding the market, since one month's sales figures could be fed back to control the succeeding month's production but it required physical resources that were beyond the small firm and a total commitment which was alien to the philosophy of the one-man business. To look at the manuscript of *Vanity Fair* which has a dozen or more printers' marks and almost as many different names on each monthly number is to realise that the major serials of the 1840s required less the printing shop than the printing factory. The pace and volume exceeded the capacity of a small firm—it also exceeded the capacity of some of the large firms as they had been ten years earlier.

The capital and machine intensity required for serialisation on the large scale probably accounts for the spectacular growth of Bradbury and Evans during the 1840s. Their name appears on *Pickwick* as contracted printers but by 1846 they had expanded to have the century's best-selling novelist all to themselves. They also had Thackeray on their list for the best part of his novel-writing career. Critics, Victorian and modern, naturally think of *Vanity Fair* and *Dombey*, *Pendennis* and *Copperfield*, *Little Dorrit* and *The Newcomes* as rival novels competing for the 'top of the tree'. It is salutary to remember that for their publisher the decade's two greatest novelists were making common cause and earning huge sums for Bradbury and Evans. In this way Bradbury and Evans grew to become the fifth largest printing business in the country, employing between eighty and ninety men (as many as *The Times*).[23]

Bradbury and Evans's domination of the serial publishing field was largely due to the fact that they combined the functions of printer and publisher. Historically these operations have tended to separate; the reason is suggested by Sir Stanley Unwin in his book, *The Truth about Publishing*:

> Many authors think it is a great advantage to a publisher to possess his own printing works. This is a delusion. It may even be a positive disadvantage. To be run economically, and therefore profitably, a printing plant needs an even supply of manuscripts to print. No one firm, however large, can ensure that the supply will arrive sufficiently regularly to keep all the machinery steadily employed. If there is a lull, either the machinery is idle, or, in order to make full use of his plant, the publisher is tempted to embark on some new publication which he would otherwise have declined. There is thus a perpetual conflict between the requirements of the printing and publishing sides of the business.[24]

Bradbury and Evans's exploitation of the monthly serial, did, in fact, keep their presses turning at full capacity with a regular supply of the best fiction (they also had *Punch*, their weekly journal, to help keep things moving at a controlled full speed). And as 'printers and publishers' they were able to take all the complicated decisions connected with stereotyping, illustration and production in the shop rather than the office. Just how delicately these matters had to be judged may be gathered from the printings of the first two numbers of *Dombey and Son*, in 1846:

	Number 1		*Number 2*
30 Sept.	25,000		
10 Oct.	5,000		
		30 Oct.	30,000
7 Nov.	2,000		
21 Nov.	2,000	21 Nov.	2,000
9 Jan.	2,000		
		6 Feb.	2,000
17 Apr.	2,000		

	Number 1		*Number 2*
		11 Sept.	1,000
8 Apr. (1848)	2,750	8 Apr.	2,750[25]

Add to this that much of the work had to be done at great speed ('night work' is a recurring item on cost schedules) and one can see that direct control of production was desirable in serial publication. And for as long as serialisation in monthly numbers was dominant this seems to have given the manufacturing publisher, like Bradbury and Evans, a distinct edge over 'bookseller' competitors.

It was, however, only an edge and the seven leading firms were, as a body, streets ahead of lesser producers of fiction. It is characteristic of the first half of the nineteenth century that large businesses formed, then consolidated remarkably quickly becoming, as it seemed, venerable institutions almost overnight. In 1811 William Blackwood was no more than 'a diligent antiquarian bookseller and the Scotch agent of the great London publisher, Murray'.[26] By 1850 'the House of Blackwood' exacted feudal devotion from its employees, Simpson, John Blackwood's Edinburgh manager being legendary for his 'perfect, almost whimsical, devotion to the house of Blackwood, of which and all the incidents of its history he used to speak with bated breath, as if it were at least a grand ducal family and he a hereditary Chamberlain'.[27] John Blackwood, whose father had been an apprentice, himself took on the manner and appurtenances of a laird, hobnobbing with the great men of the Conservative party and preferring, whenever he could, to retreat to golfing leisure at his country house at Strathtyrum.

Firms who missed the period of flux were to a large extent excluded after the period of consolidation in the 1840s and 50s. All the houses and businesses with whom we are concerned—Chapman and Hall, Macmillan's, Blackwood's, Bentley's, Bradbury and Evans, Mudie's, Smith's, Smith, Elder, Longman's, Routledge—either achieved their 'leviathan' status in this period or were one of the smaller band of firms who had survived from an earlier period. Between 1850 and 1880 there were few major producers of good fiction established. And it was the young, rather than the old firms who made the running.

More was involved, of course, than merely being in the right place at the right time. To achieve their pre-eminence each of those firms needed large amounts of disposable capital. If one looks over the history of the 'young leviathans' one can usually discern a critical moment when they suddenly, and often unexpectedly, found themselves in possession of large amounts of incoming money. With Blackwood's it happened with the success of their *Magazine*, early in the century; with Chapman and Hall the windfall was *Pickwick*; Bradbury and Evans, *Pickwick* again and the success of *Punch* in the early 1840s; Smith, Elder when George Smith took over, put the firm on its feet and began pumping in the firm's collateral resources; Bentley's capital bonus came from a number of sources in the early and mid-thirties—the success of his Standard Novels, and bestsellers like *The Last Days of Pompeii*, *Rookwood* and *Oliver Twist*. These profits enabled him to pay cash for printing and paper (gaining up to 10 per cent discount) and 'with the surplus remaining [he] put by a handsome sum: at least £6000—which was reserved for a considerable time, as a sort of nest-egg'.[28]

IV

It was in the 1840s that progressive innovation, expansion and professionalisation combined to shape the manufacture and distribution of fiction into forms which survived until the end of the century. The transitional point at the end of the 1830s may be located with nice accuracy by an invitation which Bentley made Ainsworth in 1840 to choose between hand printing or machine work for *The Tower of London*.[29] Ten years later the offer would have seemed ridiculous. The distance covered in the decade from manual to manufactory modes of production may be gauged from a comparison of two contracts entered into by the same author, Bulwer Lytton. The first is for *The Last Days of Pompeii* (1834), the second for a cheap collective edition of his works with Chapman and Hall in 1847. As is usual with contracts they are uniquely honest documents which record, better than any amount of discursive commentary, the exact state of play between author, publisher and public.

The Last Days of Pompeii would seem to have originated with a letter from Lytton to Bentley offering him a 'Novel yet unborn' which he 'could not...agree to sell for a less sum than £1200'.[30] As an established best-selling novelist Lytton could reconnoitre in this way, testing publishers with ideas rather than samples or complete manuscripts. Bentley was certainly interested. But with his usual sharpness he whittled down the price given for the novel by a hundred. Even so it remains surprisingly high. (In 1832, for example, a novel by Lytton rated only £400 from Bentley.[31])

Some haggling and a reciprocal give and take seem to have carried on through the agreement meeting of 2 April 1833. The memorandum contains a number of afterthought additions which were, presumably, made while final details were being thrashed out between principals. It was, however, a mark of his importance that Lytton had a tailor-made agreement; lesser authors were given a printed form to sign:

> ...it is further agreed (by consent of both parties) between the said parties, that the said Edward Lytton Bulwer Esq. will write a novel in three volumes post 8vo. of the usual number of pages to be published by the said Richard Bentley, who is to pay for the entire copyright of the same the sum of Eleven Hundred Pounds, in bills not exceeding the date of twelve months from the time in which the MS. is given to Mr. Bentley (viz. a bill for the one half at 6 months date and the other half of the same at nine). NB. Mr. Bulwer is to have the sole right (and profit) of sending proofs...to America and the Continent.[32]

This is a gentleman's agreement in layman's language. Legally it is only one step away from a purely verbal contract. (Indeed Lever commented in 1838 that it was only 'great publishing people' like Bentley who bothered with written contracts at all.)[33] One can see quite plainly what either party stands to gain and all the various moves and concessions. Lytton, still under thirty years old has an excellent price for his chattel. Bentley's going rate for the ordinary novel was between one and three hundred; £1,100 was double anything he had ever previously paid on his own account for a novel. His normal price is reflected by the £100 he gave a few days later to Mary Shelley for *Lodore*, a three-decker, with the bonus of £50 if the edition of 750 copies were sold out. In the first six months 3,250 copies of *The Last*

Days of Pompeii were printed which makes it by far the most numerous new novel Bentley had brought out to date. In spite of the fact that the gamble paid off handsomely (the novel was still selling for him, though not for Lytton, twenty years later)[34] there is no doubt that Bentley was taking a big risk with this one work. Moreover, putting all his eggs in one basket in this way was quite alien to Bentley's philosophy. His formative years had been spent in partnership with Colburn and despite an inveterate rivalry with his former ally he took away with him many of the older publisher's habits. Colburn was wonderfully indestructible and had survived the great Constable crash, had even prospered during it,[35] by not having his money tied up in large single projects. Consequently while all other firms were paralysed Colburn was still bringing up his myriad novels and romances of high life, each of which involved only a tiny outlay on the publisher's part. Putting his money in lots of small parcels had hitherto been Bentley's way of operating, and in general continued to be throughout his business life. So low were his usual prices that Mrs Gore, the most prolific novelist of the period, called him the Scylla and Colburn the Charybdis of the trade.[36] (Thackeray less politely, but with a similar sense of their equivalence, called them Bacon and Bungay in *Pendennis*.)

On the other hand, although the sum was large, Bentley had contrived to reduce his risk by making payment doubly conditional. First by waiting until the manuscript arrived and could be inspected at leisure, secondly by then handing over bills rather than ready money. Double postponement in this way allowed payment to be made from realised profit, or at least narrowed the gap between the income from moneys owed by booksellers and outgoings to the author. The arrangement meant, of course, that the novelist's money was at loan and used speculatively by the publisher to finance the operation.

Payment in this fashion had disadvantage to the novelists as great as any corresponding advantages to the publisher. Nominally the interval before a bill matured represented how long it was calculated to be before sales revenue was in. But the author was invariably tempted to cash the promissory note prematurely at a discount for whatever he could get in advance. This would yield ready money, but it encouraged him to live off a book that had yet to pay its way, with his income heavily taxed by the bill discounter. This in turn often induced a precipitate start on a new book, or a botched job on the work in hand. With serials, especially, there was a temptation to sign new contracts before the old one was served out (and occasionally prohibitions against such forwardness were included in the agreements of known offenders, like Charles Lever).[37]

In the case of Bentley versus Lytton the invitation was for the author to dash off his thousand pages of manuscript as soon as possible, take his money and leave the rest to the publisher who thereafter would be the sole guardian of the literary property. Having unconditionally signed over his interest in the copyright, Lytton was not encouraged to have any say in how the work was to be produced and marketed. A line of strict demarcation fenced him off from all such technical mysteries. This, of course, was standard practice in the 1830s. Charles Lever was conscious of his subordinate place in the book producing process when he wrote to his agent in 1838: 'Of course McGlashan [his publisher] will consider as his exclusive province all the details of getting up of the work...but I hope he intends presenting me in a good coat.'[38] Novelists were in no position to cut their own cloth in this matter. It was a point on which Richard Bentley could be quite peremptory. When, for example, G. P. R. James complained in the late thirties he was sharply told: 'The form in which I publish the work...is a matter upon which I alone have a right to exercise my judgement.'[39] And so it was.

The Last Days of Pompeii 'had the most spectacular success of any novel issued since *Waverley*'.[40] From the subscription sale five days before publication, where 729 copies were sold for £750 2s. 6d., until Bentley's closed at the end of the century the work sold powerfully and consistently. Its success made it an important novel in Lytton's career and an even more important one in Bentley's, adding substantially to his 'nest egg'. Yet it is hardly surprising that the novel's composition and production reflect the somewhat haphazard circumstances of its conception. Lytton's narrative tone is casual and dilettantish; he affects a Byronic *insouciance* of address, airily announcing at one point,

'Italy, Italy, while I write your skies are over me—your seas flow beneath my feet…'[41] The manuscript bears witness to the novel's having been written at speed, with plentiful reliance on improvisation. Scenes relating to the complicated Nydia subplot were inserted, somewhat clumsily, at a later date than their surrounding narrative.[42] Improvisation is also evident from Lytton's rather engaging habit of jotting down good ideas for future episodes in margins or at the heads of chapters. Proportion and structure suffered both from the writer's mode of composition and from the arbitrary demands of the three-volume form. Bentley undertook to print the first two volumes[43] but while setting up the third, which was being done by another printer 'for the sake of expedition', it was discovered that it made up only 260 pages, some fifty short. The finished text shows that the difficulty was solved first by the reduction of lines on the page from twenty-four to twenty-two (giving around twenty extra pages)[44] and one suspects that the remaining deficit was made up by the introduction of a redundant chapter at the beginning of the third volume ('A Classic Funeral', seventeen pages) together with a quantity of the songs and lyrics which Lytton could turn out by the yard when required to.

To make the obvious points about the incoherence of the narrative line in *The Last Days of Pompeii*, especially in its flabby middle sections, is not to damn the novel as somehow reprehensible. It is, simply, a novel of its time. Almost every aspect reveals it as belonging to the period when writing and production were operated by the rule of thumb. When *Last Days* was finally made up its outward appearance was so slovenly as to throw Lytton into apoplectic rage at 'the infamous and most neglectful manner in which my two first volumes are printed—many of my corrections wholly unheeded and many verbal errors pertinaciously restored after revision'.[45] Lytton was not, like Bentley's plebeian writers, the kind of man who would take this treatment lying down. But fulminate as he might, there was no redress other than fulmination. And for his pains he was regarded not as an aggrieved partner but a troublesome and eccentric author invading the publisher's domain.

For contrast turn now to a deal which Lytton made fifteen

years later with Chapman and Hall for a cheap collective issue of his works in 1847. This was a project which had long been dear to the novelist,[46] who conceived himself in middle age to have inherited the mantle of Scott (just as in youth he had assumed the more romantic airs of Byron). The venture was based, from the publisher's point of view, on the recent successful cheap edition of Dickens's works, which it followed by six months. The memorandum of agreement is not the most readable of documents, but its very density makes some useful points about what had happened in the intervening years:[47]

It is hereby agreed that the said Edward Chapman shall publish the works of Sir Edward E. G. L. Bulwer Lytton in the form and manner and upon the terms and conditions hereinafter mentioned—that is to say—the said (Chapman) doth hereby promise and agree with the said (Lytton) to print and publish such of the works of the said (Lytton) as the said (Lytton) shall from time to time direct in weekly numbers in the same form as the last edition of the work called 'Pickwick'—but in type a little larger—and that each such number shall sell for the price of three half-pence and no more or less and the expenses of publishing the said numbers shall not exceed in price to be charged to the said (Lytton) the estimate set forth in the first schedule hereinunder written and the account of the sales shall be made on the basis of one shilling per every dozen numbers as set forth in the second schedule, hereinunder written as the trade price thereof without any other deduction whatsoever save and except a commission of Ten percent as appears in the said second schedule and an additional Ten percent to such country agents as may be appointed subject to the approbation and consent of the said (Lytton) and shall bear and pay all and every expense charge or outgoing whatsoever—save and except the charges set against the proceeds of the work in the first schedule and the expenses of advertising and bear and suffer all bad debts defalcations and lapses of whatsoever nature or kind the same may be and from time to time and at all reasonable times produce and shew forth all and every account accounts memorandum and agreements relating in anywise to the said publication in order the better to evidence the number published being published and sold and the stock unsold and shall pay over to the said (Lytton) the profits of the said works half yearly upon accounts to be settled each and every half year such half yearly accounts to be made up to the Christmas and Midsummer of each year.

FIRST SCHEDULE

Estimate 10,000			
Composition per sheet of 16 pp.	2	4	
Stereotyping		17	
Working and coldpressing 10 reams dble. 5/-	2	10	
Paper 10 reams dble. crown 24/-	12		
Folding 10,000 1/8d.		16	8
	18	7	8

Per 1,000 extra			
Working and coldpressing 1 ream dble. paper		5	
Paper 1 ream dble.	1	4	
Folding		1	8
	1	10	8

SECOND SCHEDULE

Produce of 10,000 769 Dozen (9997) at 1/- £38 9s. Commission £3 17s.	34	12	
Produce of 1,000 77 Dozen (1001) at 1/- £3 17s. Commission 7/8d.	3	9	4

RESULT

NO.	PRODUCE	COSTS	ESTIMATED PROFIT
10,000	34 12	18 7 8	16 4 4
20,000	69 4	33 14 4	35 9 8
40,000	138 8	64 7 8	74 0 4
60,000	207 12	95 1	112 11

This is anything but layman's language and one needs something of a legal mind to perceive the hedges, blocked loopholes and points of vantage. Indeed in the 1840s Lytton seems to have employed a lawyer to scrutinise his contracts and there is no doubt that Dickens's spectacular dispute with Bentley in 1838 and the 1842 Copyright Amendment Act led to a general tightening up in this area. (Lytton, incidentally, was a founder member of the abortive 'Society of Authors' in 1843[48]—one of whose main aims was the education of authors in contract-making.) Immediately apparent in this agreement with Chapman and

Hall is the frigid terminology necessary for documentary precision. There is nothing of the bargain-striking, hand-shaking spirit which accompanied the agreement for *The Last Days of Pompeii*. But actuarial precision was required because these were no longer the days when a house could stake its prosperity on single winners, or on one good season, as Bentley had in 1833.

Some other features stand out. The predicted sales figures, scaled up to a possible 60,000 are impressive. (Dickens's schedule, however, went up to 100,000.)[49] Impressive too is the rock-bottom price of 1½d. Risk is not deferred but carefully calculated and engrossed at 10 per cent. (Mainly it would cover bad debts from retailers who failed, as many had in the crash of 1846.) The expected profits are not, on the face of it, vast; but they are qualitatively different from the cash bounty offered by Bentley. What Chapman and Hall's project held out was a steady and supportive income, a *cadeau de saison* every Christmas and midsummer for years to come. An author living on such income was more likely to work consistently than one who was given a lump sum on delivery.

It was also less likely to produce the festering disagreements which so often infected publisher-novelist relationships in the period. Bentley had a very lucrative sideline in selling novelists back the copyrights which they had signed over to him 'entirely'. In 1840 Lytton was asked to pay £750 for the partial recovery of *The Last Days of Pompeii*, together with two other of his novels. This clawed back a big lump of the £1,100 payment and must have been the more chagrining for the knowledge that Bentley had made thousands for himself from the novel while he owned it and as part of a very hard bargain had tried to exact more fiction from Lytton at a 'proportionately reduced price'.[50] Not surprisingly Lytton was aggrieved and made a bitter comment in his preface to *Ernest Maltravers*. There is, when one thinks of it, something absurd in Bentley selling, or offering to sell, Ainsworth, Wilkie Collins, Dickens and Reade—as well as Lytton—their work after having made a healthy publisher's profit from it. To others it seemed sharp practice. When Jerdan reflected sarcastically in his *Autobiography* on the Lytton resale, Bentley exploded with a self righteous barrage of letters for the papers about 'abuse of confidence', demanding, among other things, that Jerdan should make a public retraction.[51] Dickens and Forster were drawn in; statements were made and sides were taken. Whoever was right Bentley lost Lytton as a regular novelist, just as he lost every major artist who came his way, sooner or later.

Bentley's relationship with Lytton, a man whom he needed to run in harness with, was thus irredeemably poisoned. The depth of mutual suspiciousness which came to separate publisher and novelist is evident from a memorandum by Bentley's business manager on learning that his chief had made an offer of £2,000 for two works by Lytton in 1846:

> ...What I dislike in the negociation is that you have to combat with some sort of unfavourable prepossession existing towards you—embittered no doubt by his recollection of the 'sell' sought by himself in which he outwitted himself in the affair of the 3 novels. Now I think him capable of trying to revenge himself on you for this—by giving you perhaps a *paw-paw* novel—that might in a literary point of view be safe for him to write, but which would be proscribed and ergo a failure as a speculation. It is the dread of this makes me wish you to withdraw when a fair opportunity offers...I repeat if he took to the task in *good faith* there is nothing disastrous in this prospect. But his self exaggeration and inextinguishable conceit will very likely soon release you from the offer.[52]

With this kind of contempt and distrust in the way how could a profitable and co-operative partnership ever be formed?

Things were quite different with Chapman and Hall the following year. Since he expected income for some considerable time from the arrangement Lytton took a thorough interest in production, distribution and advertising. One of the singular differences between this and the previous contract was that Chapman and Hall defined, exactly, what their undertakings were in these departments. Lytton plagued his new publishers with enquiries and instructions about commission, binding, format, engravings, foreign editions. He carefully revised his novels for his new series (including *The Last Days of Pompeii*). He was anything but amateurish on technical matters; in January 1848 he reminded Chapman, who might be expected to know about such things already, that 'stereotyping is now much cheaper than it was'.[53] No longer was the publisher's ledger the publisher's business only. On receiving his Christmas 1848 accounts Lytton declared himself 'dismayed' at the way in which he found the works 'clubbed together pell mell'.[54] Instead of loose papers he proposed: 'let there be two Books, one for you—one for me—and separate books for the 6d. edition kept in the same manner'.

The two ledgers aptly sum up something of the strides which had been made in ten years towards a systematic, co-operative and modern author–publisher relationship. Half a century later the Society of Authors was to insist on open books and the right of audit as the pre-requisite for a secure partnership. Nor can it be entirely fortuitous that in the 1840s and 50s one perceives a new constructiveness in the English novel. Dickens labours to organise *Dombey and Son*, Bulwer Lytton apologises for the lack of care in the hasty books of his youth, Thackeray writes his first 'careful' book, the exquisitely shapely *Esmond*. Even Charles Lever, that most cavalier of craftsmen, proudly declares in 1846: 'No popularity I ever had—have—or shall have will make me trifle with the public—by fast writing—or careless composition.'[55] And in the late 1850s we have with George Meredith and George Eliot artists more interested in narrative control and order than any who had hitherto written in English.

V

One may not be artificially precise or put too much weight on two individual contract relationships. But as a generalisation it is safe to assert that something of a revolution had occurred between the first publication of *Pickwick* and *Dombey and Son*. And, as these chronological markers suggest, Dickens was at the centre of the revolution, inspiring change and benefiting from it. According to the best judgement we can make, the great Victorian reading public and the mass market that went with it were formed in the early 1850s.[56] Certain preconditions in the previous two decades are discernible. Looking back at the end of the century the veteran printer J. F. Wilson noted how when he began to work in the 1830s advertisements were taxed at 3s. 6d., paper at 3d. per pound.[57] These burdens had been alleviated (around the time of *Pickwick*, significantly) and finally removed; printing shops, which were once converted town houses, were now factories. The only thing that had not changed, Wilson noted, was the price of skilled labour: throughout the century one could get a twelve-hour day from a craftsman for about 10s.

The increased spending power of the middle and literacy of the lower classes contributed to the heyday of the fifties. In production sectors new machinery enabled publishers to extend operations on an ever larger scale. Power machinery which did the work of an army of edition binders made possible the binding of the huge library editions of Routledge and Chapman and Hall.[58] The scale of Routledge's operations alone may be gathered from the 10,000 copies of *Uncle Tom's Cabin* which he was sending out *every day* for a period in the early 1850s. Other technologies which created leisure to read and surplus value wherewith to buy played a reciprocal part. The railway system which expanded 6,000 miles in the forties, the improvement of roads, penny postage (introduced in 1839) and such conveniences as *Bradshaw's Timetable* (also 1839) assisted the trade in numberless ways. So, too, did improved standards of clerical and book-keeping methods throughout commerce generally. The publishing trade in particular had notably improved its internal communication with the setting up of the *Publishers' Circular* in 1836.

The effect of such advances was indirect but ultimately massive. Once interconnected they allowed the operations involved in the making and distribution of novels to become complex and efficient in new ways. Mudie's device, for example, was the Pegasus—it promised and performed speedy delivery. Mudie would send out his list by post, receive country and overseas order by return post, process them in his office, expedite boxes of books by rail or van (for city orders). This kind of operation would simply have been impossible in the 1830s. Similarly when Blackwood's set up their London branch in 1840;[59] if they had had to wait a week for a letter and send parcels of books down by sailing boat (as was the case twenty years before) this consolidation between capitals would have been impracticable. The Great Western steam-powered crossing in 1838 now made it almost as easy to communicate with New York as it had once been with Edinburgh.

As regards the sale of fiction, it was now feasible to circularise provincial booksellers and for the wholesale distributors to send out hordes of bagmen. It was in the forties and fifties that the 'commercial room' (immortalised in Trollope's *Orley Farm*) began to feature prominently in English business life. By the same token booksellers in the 1850s could come up to London and stay in one of the many boarding houses which advertised their cleanliness and low prices to the trade. Movement between country and capital was further rationalised by the growth of wholesale distributors who took over in the forties from the London booksellers as publishers' most reliable purchasers.

London pulsed out, in this way, a regular supply of reading matter. Joseph Shaylor describes working to midnight on every 'magazine day' at Simpkin and Marshall's in the mid-sixties and counting himself lucky because a few years earlier employees were expected to sleep under the counter on these hectic occasions when the monthly parcels of books were made up for despatch around the country.[60] When it began in 1859 *All the Year Round*'s business manager scheduled a tentative 22,000 for country and export sales, 20,000 for London sales and 6,500 for sales via Smith's for customers moving up and down the country.[61] These proportions are a fairly good guide to the relative equality of the two large market sections at midcentury. And both were expanding vastly during this period; between 1830 and 1890, Walter Besant calculated, the reading public for books published in England grew from 50,000 to 120,000,000.[62] Like other forms of trade 'Colonial editions' of the English novel followed the flag round the world.

Writing as a cultural historian, Q. D. Leavis has grimly described these advances as 'economic developments making for disintegration.'[63] But whatever they did for the sensibility of the age their commercial effect was quite opposite. They integrated the country as a national market with London at its centre, drawing all literary talent to it. Charles Lever, who lived out of England, wrote to his wife from London in May 1856:

It is sheer madness for any man who has to live by his brains to be removed from this great market. I can now see how recklessly I have played my cards this life—and that if I had settled down here I should have been a rich man today.[64]

One may disagree with Lever's estimate of his chances in London or anywhere else—but his perception of the centrality of the capital for any literary activity was sound. When Macmillan's moved back to London in the late fifties[65] they were unconsciously witnessing the economic truth that it was no longer possible, as it had been twenty years earlier, to run an ambitious publishing venture from the provinces. Macmillan's opening a a branch in New York in 1869 conveniently signposts another major enlargement of the market. Through agencies, treaties, the export of books and portable stereotype plates English publishing now had a world-wide sales territory. In 1860 the book exporting trade was worth half a million pounds. (It would probably have been much more had international copyright been quicker in coming.)

Of all literary forms none has a greater immediate impact than the novel, and none loses it quicker. It is not merely riddling to suggest that novels and novelty are intimately linked. New fiction also enjoys a metropolitan *chic* which is short-lived but, while it lasts, an effective selling agent. Hence in the 1850s one finds Alexander Macmillan, the head of a large firm, writing personally to Glasgow and Devon, wheedling local booksellers into taking a few more copies of *Westward Ho!* at the special pre-publication price. Macmillan judged that every advance copy 'planted' in this way would call for a dozen more when sold which could be supplied by rail the next day.[66] The London headquarters could, in this way, feed sales in the furthest corners of the kingdom. In some respects the effectiveness of the nineteenth century probably surpasses our own. Lever, for example, assured his London publishers that within twenty-four hours any of his books could be got to any part of Ireland. No one need wait for their fiction any more.

Railways were not important merely as agents of delivery. Their increasing comfort, at least in the first two classes of carriage, released leisure time for reading. In 1859 one leading railway publisher was supposed to have sold 750,000 books, varying in price between a shilling and half a crown.[67] These volumes are beneath our notice here, concentrating as we are on work of some literary quality. But better fiction also benefited from the railway boom. A railway bookseller would take up to 5,000 copies of a popular 'literary' novel and by the late forties the outlet had been made safe for respectable fiction with the Smith monopoly. On a horse-drawn coach the only feasible recreation, as on Mr Pickwick's journey to Birmingham, was strong drink or sleep to annul the discomfort of jostling along on unmade roads. Very few books, one imagines, were sold at staging posts, whereas railway stations were taken into account by every wide-awake wholesaler. George Routledge complacently noted seeing six first-class passengers in one compartment of the Brighton train all reading his edition of *Uncle Tom's Cabin*—'first-class' is a nice touch. 'A man's seat in a railway carriage is now, or may be, his study', Trollope observed in 1855.[68] It was not, therefore, peevishness or *amour propre*, though he was amply supplied with both, that made Lytton write to Chapman in complaint that he did not find his cheap collective being sold 'in *any* station along the Birmingham line …not even the London one Euston Square were there any of my works in the cheap editions—and I heard one passenger ask if they had any—and the reply was no we don't have them.'[69] (W. H. Smith's launched their railway bookstall network at Euston Station on 1 November 1848.)

'Novels for railway reading' were often regarded somewhat contemptuously by the cultivated, but they testify to the growth of the fiction-reading habit and its respectability (it could clearly be done in public), and its convenience. In this last respect even improved domestic lighting must have helped increase the sale of fiction; 'gas and steam', as the *Bookseller* commented in 1859, 'have enlightened and quickened everything'.[70]

By 1852 the English novel was as much a triumph of industrial progress as anything in the Great Exhibition, and inspired much the same kind of pride as Sheffield steel or Wedgwood china: 'those were the days' an old publisher lamented nostalgically, 'when new English fiction was the strongest and best in the world'.[71] But with the novel this strength was not simply the outcome of steam presses and machine-made paper. It was at the centre of a confluence of factors transforming English life in what *The Times* called 'our marvellous Railway era'. It is not far-fetched to conceive, for example, that Trollope was serving the novel by helping speed postal services in the forties and improving clerical efficiency in the fifties as much as by lecturing on fiction as a 'rational amusement' in the 1870s.

The 1840s were thus a period of consolidation and establishment in which were formed the big organisations that were to control smaller organisations of retailing (and often writing) fiction. All this happened with a suddenness that surprised some observers. Carlyle, for example, went through life scornfully referring to publishers as 'booksellers'. The appellation may have been appropriate to William Blackwood and Archibald Constable whom he remembered in his youth as dealing with the stocking and disposition of gentlemen's libraries. It was not appropriate to Chapman and Hall in the 1850s or John Blackwood's firm. These were publishing businesses in a modern sense.

During the 1850s the framework for the production of fiction was set and remained fairly fixed until the demise of the three-volume novel in 1894. In the 1860s one can see the auguries of further drastic change, but in the event little came of them. There seems to have been a lot of money floating around the publishing world at this period. Payments for the best novels were often many thousands of pounds; magazines proliferated (the topographical theme was a tribute to *Cornhill*'s enviable success)—*Once a Week*, *Belgravia*, *Macmillan's*, *Cornhill*, *Temple Bar*, *Tinsley's*, *Argosy*, *All the Year Round*, *St James's*, *St Paul's*, were all set up in or just preceding this decade. Mudie expanded into his vast New Ionic Hall; Simpkin and Marshall took over new premises; Smith's subscription library got under way. With the boom in joint stock companies in the early sixties there was money enough for a rival to Mudie to be floated, the Library Company Ltd of Pall Mall which, disastrously, offered a half-guinea subscription, undercutting Mudie by a full 50 per cent. For a while this meant that publishers could expect to double their London library sales, which with the magazine boom and Smith's orders (mainly for cheaper, one-volume editions) meant golden days for fiction.

Most interesting of all the trade movements in the 1860s were the hesitant steps towards mutual incorporation which brought together parties previously opposed. In July 1864 Mudie's went public under the pressure of financial difficulty[72] and half of the £100,000 worth of shares were taken up by people other than Mudie. Publishers took out stock in their main customer: Bentley had £400 worth of shares, as part payment for £434 owed him. Bradbury and Evans were meanwhile represented on the board of Inspectors who had to ratify all Bentley's publishing decisions. (He too had had his financial difficulties.) A proposed merger between Mudie and W. H. Smith fell through but in another area of co-operation Smith's and Chapman and Hall collaborated on the production of cheap one-volume novels ('yellow backs'), combining their manufacturing and distributive skills. Chapman and Hall would also rent out their book-keeping facilities to free-lance magazine proprietors.[73] Dickens turned himself into a publisher with *All the Year Round*. These were exciting developments; if, for example, the publishers had turned themselves into limited liability companies and novelists had taken out stock (as Chapman and Hall did, and as Trollope did in 1880), a new era of co-operative publishing might have been inaugurated, but it was not. Possibly the financial crashes of 1866 had something of an inhibiting effect. Whatever the reasons the family-business nature of nineteenth-century publishing which had resisted, in large part, even partnerships outside the kinship group remained intact.

VI

Although *laissez-faire* economists might, and probably did, argue that the conditions in which novels were published in the 1850s and after was the pure result of free-market forces they were, in fact, idiosyncratically English. If one compares them with the German model at the same period one finds a quite different situation. In England everything came to be centralised in London (and to a lesser extent Edinburgh); paper-makers, printers, publishers, commission houses, the major booksellers and generally authors and a large proportion of readers were all concentrated in the metropolis forming a kind of literary-commercial ganglion. In London in 1860 there were, as a result of this concentration, 211 booksellers and publishers, 566 booksellers, 23 foreign booksellers and 12 law booksellers (Edinburgh's figures for the first two categories were 30 and 90).[74] In the German confederation at the same period, the production of literature was decentralised. Books were printed all over the state, then despatched to Leipsig to the commission houses who would then either display the work at one of the famous fairs or circularise it on a sale or return basis to booksellers throughout the land.

As a result of this efficient network German publishing differed from the English in some important particulars. The sale-or-return circulation of books through commission agents meant that there was no need for the punitively heavy expenditure on advertising and salesmen to make works known which oppressed the English producer. Competition was reduced by a system in which a central control encouraged some kind of equity between supply and demand. Nor was there the claustrophobic literary 'world' of London where critics, authors, publishers and readers were thrown promiscuously together.

Theorists in England pointed enviously to Leipsig in the 1860s: a town of 66,000 inhabitants and no less than 120 publishers and booksellers, a commercial centre dominated by the *Börsen-Gebäude*, a kind of stock exchange for books. In Germany, it was said, a publisher took precedence over a prince. But the cool, rational agency houses of Leipsig do not seem to have encouraged the growth of fiction in the same way as the hot-house atmosphere of London's Paternoster Row. Book production in general was roughly twice what it was in London (10,000 titles as opposed to 5,000 in 1862). Of these 10,000, however, by far the greatest single variety were theological works; novels came well down the list. In England novels came equally at the top of the list with theology. In fact Germany's most famous fiction publishing house was benignly parasitic on the English trade. When Tauchnitz in 1841, at the age of twenty-five, brought out his first 'Tauchnitz Edition' (Lytton's *Pelham* —that ubiquitous bestseller) he started a list which by 1860 had grown to 500 volumes. Using Leipsig's distributive skills Tauchnitz managed to establish a firm hold on the

English-speaking market abroad, so denying it to home-based business.

Again, there were features of the American publishing scene which made it quite distinct. Contracts were more sophisticated and payments were usually by royalty much earlier than in England.[75] There also operated, among the better houses, something known as 'trade courtesy' (or sometimes 'The Harper Rule'). By this self-regulation, publishing houses would not compete for authors, unless invited to do so by the author himself. Bentley's approaches to Dickens while he was writing *Pickwick* for Chapman and Hall would thus have been frowned on in America. This 'genteel tradition' as practised by the top houses made for longer, less turbulent author-publisher relationships.

But the main difference between America and England was the size and speed of operations. America with her continental spaces tended to concentrate publishing in a number of cities rather than one metropolis. Like Germany the semi-annual trade fairs were used to funnel books to the trade, though there was, as well, plentiful use of travellers and mail order. With a population not much less than Britain's and a reading public more literate it is, above all, the scale of publishing operations which is different. Much larger sale and much lower per-volume prices were the rule. Ten thousand copies of *The Mill on the Floss*, at $1 apiece, went in the first four days. In Britain Blackwood's were overjoyed to clear 6,500 of the same novel at 31s. 6d. in a year. When Ticknor and Fields brought out *Westward Ho!* in the same week as Macmillan's, they printed 3,000 and charged $1.25 (about 7s.).[76] Macmillan's published 1,250 and charged the purchaser 31s. 6d. Three or four times the size of edition and a third or quarter of the cost is a fairly good rule of thumb with which to measure the difference between the markets in this period.

Not surprisingly the biggest American firms dwarfed their transatlantic equivalents. There was nothing in London to rival Harper and Brothers in 1850 who had seven five-storey buildings and turned out over 2,000,000 volumes a year.[77] And yet the astonishing fact remains that the huge and technologically sophisticated American industry drew on the superabundance of English fiction. Thus Harper's first catalogue contained 234 titles of which 90 per cent were English reprints.[78] Since copyright was not legally enforced until 1891 the rich harvest of English fiction was open to piracy. Even the honourable houses who paid for early sheets tended to give much lower prices to the English authors who were almost always selling more for less in America than they were at home (Charles Kingsley got £50 for his American edition of *Westward Ho!*, a seventh of what Macmillan's gave him). Still they took what they were offered for, as Trollope pointed out, the alternative was nothing at all.[79]

Traditionally everything in America was larger, faster, cheaper and earlier. In 1823, for example, the firm of Carey and Son produced 1,500 copies of Scott's *Quentin Durward*, ready for the shop, in twenty-eight hours. Harper's reckoned to sell 100,000 copies of Lytton's *The Last of the Barons* in a fortnight.[80] Harper's *New Monthly Magazine* was selling 130,000 copies a month a decade before the *Cornhill* was doing it in England and retailing at something under the shilling (since the nominal price of 25 cents was rarely charged in full). In the 1860s and 70s the biggest single customer for English fiction in the world was Harper's *Weekly* which sold at 5 cents and had an annual circulation of almost 5,000,000 in 1860. The paper's advertisement for January of that year indicates its staple content:

> HARPER'S WEEKLY will continue, as heretofore, to publish the best tales that are written by native and foreign authors. It has already published *A Tale of Two Cities* by CHARLES DICKENS (with original illustrations drawn for *Harper's Weekly*); *What Will He Do With It?* by Sir EDWARD LYTTON BULWER; *The Dead Secret* by WILKIE COLLINS; *Lois the Witch* by Mrs GASKELL; *A Good Fight* by CHARLES READE; it is now publishing *Trumps* by GEORGE WILLIAM CURTIS, and *The Woman in White* by WILKIE COLLINS.

These are certainly the 'best tales' of the period though the 'native' element is hardly very pronounced.

3

Craft versus Trade: Novelists and Publishers

Despite all the upheaval of the 1840s and 50s the spirit of English fiction publishing continued to be characterised by a tension between innovation and a usually victorious entrenched conservatism. The attitude of the trade indeed seems to verge at times on what one can only call blindness to economic fact. In 1869, for example, when *Lorna Doone* was published in three volumes it was totally unsuccessful. When Sampson Low, against their commercial instincts ('we have lost a lot of money by her; I don't care if we lose some more' declared the firm's director) put out a cheap, one-volume version the book took off to become one of the very best sellers of the century. Could not someone read the signs—that the country was ready for the cheap first-form publication of fiction? And why did not some enterprising publisher take full advantage of the million-or-so purchasers revealed by the *Uncle Tom's Cabin* bonanza of 1852? Richard Altick, the leading authority on the Victorian book trade, has lamented this impercipience, timidity or obtuseness as a lost opportunity:

> It is fascinating to speculate what would have happened to the reading public, and to literature in general, if the firms which published most of the age's great writers—the Smith Elders, the Chapman and Halls, the Macmillans and Murrays and Longmans—had seriously attempted a policy of cheap original editions.[1]

Against this literary speculation one can set the practical wisdom of the trade: 'it is easy to become a publisher, but difficult to remain one.'[2] All the houses Altick lists were perennials, and largely they remained publishers by not rushing into change.

Everyone, of course, realised that there was too much fat on the 31s. 6d. novel. But how much to carve off, and when? In October 1853 Richard Bentley grandly announced his 'New Plan' to bring out new three-volume novels at 10s. 6d. Technically this was now possible, assuming that readers bought in sufficient numbers and Bentley declared himself confident of 'such an increase of sale of the Works as will repay...the boldness of the enterprise'. In fact the enterprise was bolder than simply providing new novels at a third of their traditional price. Bentley simultaneously boosted his 'Railway' series and initiated his 'Parlour Bookcase'. He was thus taking on not just his rival producers of library novels but Routledge's 'Railway Library' and Simms M'Intyre's 'Parlour Library'. Boldness indeed.

In the autumn Bentley issued seven volumes of the 'Railway' series and nineteen of the 'Parlour Bookcase'. Since he had a quantity of old copyrights still assigned to him there was no great problem about finding these. New novels posed greater difficulty. Between January and September the house had brought out seven three-volume novels at 31s. 6d., three two-volume novels at 21s. and two one-volume novels at 10s. 6d. In October there emerged the first of the works under the new plan: *Margaret*, two-volumes, 7s. This was, in fact the only work for which Bentley managed to adhere to the 3s. 6d. per volume scale. In November the house issued two three-deckers at 12s. (instead of 10s. 6d.) and two double-deckers at 8s. (instead of 7s.). This was as far as Bentley chanced his luck. In December he had returned to the old practice with *The Cardinal* at 31s. 6d. Over the next year the 'Railway' series languished as did the 'Parlour Bookcase' (four volumes of the one, two volumes of the other in 1854) and thereafter no more is heard of them.[3]

In the event it was not a very impressive show of publishing boldness. But Bentley's timidity finally turned out to be wisdom. In 1854 the Crimean War paralysed the trade in books, especially fiction. In July 1854 Bentley wrote despairingly: 'with regard to novels, their sale is now nearly (*nil*) gone.'[4] Bentley was hard put to survive. Had he embarked full sail into cheap fiction intending to keep it up for a year, as success demanded he should do, he would surely have gone under in 1854. As it was

Bentley, and all his trade colleagues, left it to the libraries and especially the vigorous Arthur Mudie to kill the three-decker.

A publisher did not need many such warnings not to meddle with what worked very well if left alone. Most houses had some such experience. Blackwood had survived the Constable crash, which was particularly severe on other Edinburgh firms, because in the period of heady speculativeness preceding the catastrophe he had been 'rash like the others but not so rash'.[5] Consequently, when Constable was ruined together with James Ballantyne, William Blackwood found himself, by the elimination of his main competitor, the leading publisher outside London. Caution could thus be ambition's best help. When the young John Blackwood began to take over the reins of the firm in 1840 his guardians were pleased to see that his distinguishing quality was 'prudence'.[6]

Resistance to premature change arose, then, from the quite understandable desire to find stability in a notoriously chancy business. The trading conventions of the publishing world, its preoccupation with losers and winners, the discretionary advance which publishers might stake on a book, often made it seem like a kind of gambling. Unlucky speculators were ruined and even great houses had to hold on tight during long periods of war, depression or misfortune. As Trollope pointed out, 'the author wants no capital and encounters no risks.'[7] Publishers often wanted capital and could not be but aware that, as their agreements stated, books were published 'at their sole risk and cost'. The risks were real and unpredictable. In 1841 a hard-up Charles Lever was complaining of his publishers: 'I *know* Curry and Co are making close to £12,000 by me.'[8] By 1850 Curry and Co. were under the hammer and Lever, though still hard-up, was still turning out his yearly Irish novel.

It is easy to forget how much more bankruptcy was a fact of Victorian business life than it is of ours. (One may calculate how many classics are based on it: *Dombey*, *The Newcomes*, *Middlemarch*, *Hard Cash*, *The Mayor of Casterbridge*.) Hanging over the publishing profession in particular was the traumatic example of Constable. And Constable, it was remembered, had dreamed of bringing fiction to the millions. Again and again in literary and publishing circles one comes across a fear of cheap literature because it is thought that it will somehow release forces which will be beyond the trade's control: 'our cheap literature', wrote Lever in a letter, 'and our copious [?] writing —like our low priced cottons and our cheap pen knives—will ultimately disparage our wares, both at home and abroad.'[9] In this the publishing trade's apprehensions were rather like those of otherwise liberal politicians of the age who feared universal suffrage—these were the edged tools that wise men did not give away too lightly. This professional caution probably explains also why at every point during the nineteenth century one can find some dismal publisher complaining that business is 'at the moment' particularly depressed and no new ventures can be undertaken.

As it affected the novelists institutional conservatism—or 'prudence'—was felt as a complex set of pressures, direct and indirect. Most publishers were, consciously or unconsciously, looking for some system which would reduce the gambler's risk, and novelists were pulled along in the same endeavour. It is instructive, in this context, to look at the century's bestseller lists, for all books.[10] Topping them are grammars, encyclopaedias (especially part-issue cyclopaedias like Chambers' Penny series) and cookery books. The biggest totals were gathered by steady, recurrent and predictable sellers which sold year in and year out. Novels are things of a season and do not have the stamina of, say, text-books. Neither do they have the infinite extendability of particle encyclopaedias.

In a sense the cheap collective issue and serialisation may be seen as adaptations by fiction to the proven forms of success. Another way of reducing risk was for publishing houses to mix their lists. Houses that specialised in novels would often have another specialism which offered a more calculable return. With Macmillan's it was educational and children's books. Bentley must have financed innumerable unprofitable novels with his books of travels, memoirs and cookery books. The seven houses we are concentrating on here were all, in this way, general publishers with a more or less strong line in fiction. Generality made for durability unlike the more specialised, yet shorter-lived, continental publishing firms. Even in England there is evidence to show that fiction alone was a precarious foundation for a house to build on. Tinsley Brothers made a fortune out of selling three-volume fiction to the circulating libraries. (Their very best seller, *Lady Audley's Secret,* a terrific tale of bigamy, murder and detection, sold eight three-volume editions in three months and inspired one brother to build a villa out of the profits blatantly called 'Audley Lodge'.)[11] In 1865 the brothers, with an annual profit of £5,000 a year and ten years' trading behind them, were confident enough to offer to buy out Chapman and Hall for £50,000. Five years later, with the slump in the library trade, William Tinsley (Edward died in 1866 leaving £4,000 debts)[12] was fighting to stave off bankruptcy. The firm did not survive, like Chapman and Hall, to celebrate its centenary.

II

Once an author had made his name he would experience the surrounding urge for stability as an insidious coercion to turn out recurrent bestsellers according to a proven successful formula. The model in most publishing minds was Scott's 'Waverley Novels'. Given a bestseller, a publisher's instinct was to use it as the foundation to set up a series of 'Vanity Fair Novels', 'Pickwick Paper Novels', 'Barchester Novels' on the same lines. Sometimes this was unconscious. John Blackwood's evident feeling, for example, that George Eliot was at her best in stories of English provincial life may well have been an attempt, unrecognised by him, to induce the author to reproduce *Adam Bede* in her later work.

A similar publisher's predisposition may be seen in the contract George Smith drew up for Thackeray when he took over the *Cornhill,* at a salary of £1,000 a year. Thackeray was at this time the second most famous novelist in England and Smith was prepared to pay an editorial stipend which was, even by his standards, 'princely'. Yet into the contract he had written:

Mr. Thackeray in consideration of the engagements of Smith, Elder and Co. contained in this agreement agrees to write two novels the scenes of which are to be descriptive of contemporary English life society and manners, each novel to form as much printed matter as is contained in sixteen numbers of thirty two pages each of Mr. Thackeray's work entitled 'The Virginians.'[13]

Thackeray's last novel before joining Smith had been *The Virginians: A Tale of the Last Century* and had lost a lot of money for Bradbury and Evans. Smith wanted no such historical fiction from his editor. He was to go back to his first success *Vanity Fair: Pen and Pencil Sketches of English Society*—the work which had entranced Smith as a youth when he first decided to have Thackeray on his list.

Even at the peak of fame, therefore, a Victorian novelist was not always free to write what he wanted. Often the pressure on him was direct and unequivocal. Chapman and Hall's terms for *Martin Chuzzlewit* specified: 'the new work shall be, in form size and price, precisely similar to the *Pickwick Papers* and *Nicholas Nickleby*...'[14] By the terms of this agreement Dickens was prohibited from writing a novel as different from *Pickwick Papers* as was the serial *Pickwick Papers* from its predecessors. 'New' here means a fresh supply of the same, known commodity. And in their advance publicity Chapman and Hall released that *Chuzzlewit* would comprise 'matter in the true Pickwickian style'.[15] The effect of this kind of pressure is impossible to measure but it surely had some influence in conditioning the novelist to think about his future work in terms of past models. At least in Dickens's case they were his own models. But so attractive was his apparently sure-fire formula for success that publishers, in an almost talismanic way, would use his novels for the contractual definition of works by Lever, Ainsworth, Lytton and presumably many others.[16]

The numerous progeny which certain outstandingly successful novels had probably owes something to the derivative nature of the second-rate literary mind. But publisher's demand must also have had something to do with it. The way in which a talented, but minor, author could bend herself to the prevailing demands of the age is evident from the example of Mrs Henry Wood. This lady began her career in fiction with *Danesbury House*, a novel submitted for the prize offered by the Scottish Temperance League for a work of fiction illustrative of the evils of drink. Mrs Wood wrote the novel, apparently within a month, and was 'unanimously awarded' the £100 by the adjudicators. The book sold powerfully in the evangelical market, usually barred to fiction. ('I am told,—in fact I know', wrote the author, 'that no work of fiction has ever been so popular in Scotland.')[17] Following this success she went on to write *East Lynne*, a scandalously amoral book by the standards of the age ('foul' Meredith called it)[18] but to the taste of metropolitan library patrons who liked adultery, elopement, divorce and nemesis in their novels. Mrs Wood, it would appear, could write good books for Edinburgh or bad books for London as required. There was clearly more money in the second kind, however, and she was careful not to 'frighten...light readers' with religion in her later fiction.[19]

III

According to Thackeray, 'the rewards of the profession are not to be measured by the money standard.'[20] In some important respects this would seem to have been an empty piety. Literature, and novel-writing especially, was very much a ready-money affair in the nineteenth century. The whole question of an author's independence was bound up with how much he earned. One of the first things to be asked of any Victorian novel is—how much was the novelist his own man in the arrangement he made with the publisher? Some writers, like Dickens and George Eliot, achieved artistic autonomy early and kept it. For others, like Thackeray and Trollope, it was harder to come by and to hold on to. Still others, like Wilkie Collins, achieved independence only to see it gradually slip away. And most novelists never achieved it at all.

It was a moment of supreme importance in his career when the Victorian novelist earned the complete unaccountability which John Blackwood, reverentially, observed in George Eliot: 'The simple fact is, she is so great a giant that there is nothing for it but to accept her inspirations and leave criticism alone.'[21] (Blackwood had no scruples about offering Trollope six pages of advice on how to change *John Caldigate*, this at a period when the once great novelist had lost the protective grandeur of automatic sales success.)

For the autonomous novelist contracts would be blanks in

which he undertook to provide a novel before writing (sometimes before conception) with no more specification than that it would be a commodity of such-and-such a length; and the publisher would be glad to take it as a blind bargain. The novelist could expect publishers to dance attendance on him. This was the condition of Dickens in 1856 when an envious Lever saw him in London: 'living out of the world in solitary grandeur, fanned and peacock feathered by Bradbury and Evans & Co., their wives and daughters'.[22] The price for such an author, especially after the 1850s, would be significantly over the £1,000 mark. One frequently detects in the bargaining that went into the sealing of such contracts an element of reversal—the novelist is, it appears, employing the publisher to handle his wares. Take the following letter of invitation Dickens sent to Chapman and Hall when he was thinking of a new novel in numbers in the 1860s:

In reference to a new work in 20 monthly Nos. as of old, I have carefully considered past figures and future reasonable possibilities. You have the means of doing the like in the main and no doubt will do so before replying to this letter.

I propose you to pay me £6000 for the half copyright throughout and outright at the times mentioned in your last letter to me on the subject. For that consideration I am ready to enter into articles of agreement with you securing you the publication of the work when I shall be ready to begin publishing and the half share.

As I must be rid of the Xmas No. here (i.e. *All the Year Round*) and the Uncommercial Traveller before I can work to any great purpose, and as I must be well on before the first No. is published, I cannot bind myself to time of commencement as yet. But I am really anxious to get into the field before next spring is out; and our interests cannot fail to be alike as to all such points, if we become partners in the story.

Of course, you will understand that I do not press you to give the sum I have here mentioned, and that you will not in the least inconvenience or offend me by preferring me to make other arrangements. If you should have any misgiving on this head, let my assurance that you need have none set it at rest.[23]

It is a cunningly provocative letter (note the appeal to 'old times') and there is no mistaking as to who calls the tune: terms of payment, date of delivery are uncompromisingly laid down; any clue as to what the story will be about withheld. Moreover Dickens knew that he had a trading advantage in that Chapman and Hall was in a state of interregnum. Edward was handing over to the younger, relatively inexperienced, Fred Chapman who would certainly want to inaugurate his period of command with a novel of the century's greatest novelist.

The contract which resulted from the above letter contains all the provisions which Dickens demanded.[24] He had £6,000 advance and £4,611 on half profits. All that Chapman managed to impose on his part was a lengthy and rather macabre death clause which decided on compensation in the event of Dickens's predeceasing the novel's completion. (What this did for the mood of the novel one can only conjecture.)

When a novelist was unfettered in this way he would often try out a long-nursed project, something quite different from what had gone before. For George Eliot, Reade and Thackeray it was an historical novel (*Romola*, *The Cloister and the Hearth*, *Esmond*). For Charlotte Brontë it was the social problem novel (*Shirley*) which attracted her when she had a completely free hand with her publisher. Trollope embarked on the ambitious parliamentary sequence of Palliser novels at the highest paid and correspondingly least controlled phase of his career. Dickens, as in *Our Mutual Friend*, experimented with increasingly plotted fiction. Complexity was a luxury earlier success had entitled him to.

Holding onto this independence was often difficult. Those who managed to do so showed considerable skill and sense of tactics. Usually it required not becoming too attached, by friendship or financial ties, to any one publisher. Dickens, for example, was prone to rupturing differences with his partners, feeling 'netted' if he stayed with one too long. Thus Macrone and Bentley in the thirties, Chapman and Hall in the forties, Bradbury and Evans in the fifties and Sampson Low in the sixties were all fallen out with. In these separations there was offence given and taken and sufficient provocation on both sides. But it was not simple conflict of interest and temperamental fractiousness. Dickens seems seriously to have felt that his self preservation as an artist was involved. The famous declaration he made on breaking with Bentley indicates his conviction on this point; after speaking of the 'net that has been wound about me', he went on to state that 'I do most solemnly swear that morally, before God and man, I hold myself released from such hard bargains as these, after I have done so much for those who drove them.'[25] This is not the language of a man merely embarrassed by business entanglements. The underlying image in Dickens's mind seems to have been that of Samson breaking out of the bonds of the Philistines. There is a sense communicated of the artist's awareness of his own power, and the prime responsibility of looking after it. Dickens seems to have realised from the first that this kind of uncompromising toughness was a necessary part of his equipment for dealing with the publishers. That he was right, in one case at least, is evident from a memorandum by Bentley's manager to his chief, warning him against fraternising with 'the craft':

I am as much concerned as yourself about Mr. Dickens and agree with you that he has been inflated by Forster and Co—but has it never occurred to you that someone else is also to blame? Has *he* not hugged Master Boz and patted him on the back a little too much? All this costs money. Fas est ab hosti doceri...The 'Craft' are all alike, if they set out in innocence, they soon become corrupted by 'evil communications.'[26]

It is an interestingly frank admission by the trade that the only way to handle authors is as the publisher's natural enemies.

Dickens was a hard, stiff-necked man in his dealings and invariably, when pushed, adopted an imperative tone. It is likely, however, that a more ductile writer would have 'bust the boiler' if he had stood by his word and tried to keep up the pace which, between 1836 and 1838, induced him to put his name to a dozen or more contracts. No less than the Romantic poet, the Victorian novelist needed a good measure of resolution and independence to ensure his survival.

Dickens's later differences with Chapman and Hall show a greater tact, though no less underlying mettle. His links were, for one thing, stronger. He had pledged himself that they should be 'his periodical publishers, until he should be advertised in the daily press, as having been compressed into his last edition—one volume, boards with brass plates'.[27] This compact did not last, however. The break was precipitated by the publishers' mild threats to operate a penal clause in their contract for *Martin Chuzzlewit* should sales not reach the high figure hoped for. This was too much for Dickens who took his business elsewhere. But although for a dozen years thereafter he gave his new novels to Bradbury and Evans he left with Chapman and Hall his cheap reprints—thus keeping a presence in both camps. Doubtless this playing one against another helped negotiate the minimal share (75–25 per cent on new, 50–50 per cent on reprint fiction with no dictation on what he should write) which either publisher came to be allowed from Dickens's unprecedented earning capacity. Even with this fractionalised profit any firm with Dickens on its list tended, in spite of itself, to become a one-author affair. After the break with Bradbury and Evans in 1859 Charles Lever glumly foresaw his own prospects with the other firm fade:

> Chapman is quite cocky about having got Dickens again in his hands, he is to publish his next new book...The return of Dickens to C[hapman] and H[all] (which is now arranged finally) must make them so entirely *his* as to leave no margin to attend to any other interests.[28]

An ability to contest and master publishers in this way was a useful asset to a novelist. Thackeray, with his Charterhouse, Cambridge and Athenaeum background was a more diplomatic customer than Dickens. But a similar bargaining toughness to that of the other author is evident in an early threat to 'strike' against *Fraser's Magazine*:

> I hereby give notice that I shall strike for wages...I won't work under prices...I am a better workman than most in your crew and deserve a better price. You must not, I repeat, be angry or because we differ as tradesmen break off our connection as friends.[29]

In later life Thackeray would tease publishers with half-given assurances like the following to Smith where with a double negative he lets the cherry bob against the buyer's lips, then draws it back:

PS. this is a secret. *Next* year I am not pledged not to write a book about the United States, with wh. and the Warringtons of Virginia and the 4 Georges I see a tolerable amount of work before both of us.[30]

In fact *The Virginians* went to Bradbury and Evans, who gave Thackeray the highest price he was ever to have for a novel, £250 a monthly number. As he once said at the *Punch* table Thackeray clearly thought 'Free Trade is the right policy in literature...[a] man takes his work where he's best paid for it.'[31]

Trollope, in his simpler way, seems to have been another Free Trader, changing his publisher with almost every turn of his career and insisting on the kind of money down payment which would expedite the early dissolution of partnership: 'a lump sum' he observed to be 'more pleasant than a deferred annuity'.[32] He lost money, but his professional life was a lot simpler than that of many of his colleagues in fiction. It was also, in its way, a lot more honest. In the contracts he made one finds revisions and additions in Trollope's hand—aftermarks of the tough haggling which he brought to the drawing up of an agreement. He would hold publishers to their side of bargains in a way unequalled among his contemporaries, nagging at them if they did not bring out his books when they said they would, chiding them savagely if they brought them out in a different form so as to make more volumes.

Bulwer Lytton's dealings also had a disarming simplicity. Like the lord he was he would, when dealing time came, treat the publisher as some kind of superior tradesman. Thus he would write a letter to Blackwood airily dismissing any consideration of '*vile argentum*' but beginning: 'I think I before stated to you that I had some very large offers for any work of fiction by me volunteered by two parties?' and ending, 'Perhaps the best plan, however, would be for you to turn the matter over in your mind and say what you think you could venture to propose. I shall await your reply.'[33] Needless to say the reply contained an appropriate handsome offer to the superfine novelist.

Like Dickens, Charles Reade was disputatious and in addition to his substantial earnings as a novelist had a private income.[34] This allowed him such flamboyant gestures as sacrificing £1,000 to put out a book on the 'Eighth Commandment' (THOU SHALT NOT STEAL except from authors). George Eliot, Mrs Gaskell and Charlotte Brontë had longer associations with single publishers than their male counterparts but all seem to have been able to dig their heels in and be eminently unbiddable on occasions. Charlotte Brontë, for example, while writing *Shirley* forbade any 'consultation about plan, subject, characters or incidents'.[35] These ladies prohibited publishers from entering the privacy of their writing processes as they might have banned a man from their boudoir. Indeed their imagery when describing literary creation aften suggests sexual mysteries. 'The whole tale grew up in my mind as imperceptibly as a seed germinates in the earth,' wrote Mrs Gaskell of *Mary Barton*.[36] Charlotte Brontë had to 'fabricate [*Shirley*] darkly in the silent workshop of [my] own brain'.[37] George Eliot talked of being possessed by something 'not herself' when writing *Middlemarch*. Conversely, women authors often affected a charmingly feminine ignorance of the practicalities of publishing which they left exclusively to the man's world: '*Please* let me pay for the horrid old stereotypes, or whatever they are,' Mrs Gaskell once told George Smith.[38]

Of all the women novelists Charlotte Brontë was the most loyal, never taking her novels elsewhere than to Smith, Elder. Her relationship with George Smith, was however, oddly paradoxical. While she might insist on her absolute autonomy as a novelist she would, in the next letter, entrust the £500 paid for the novel (she would, incidentally, take no more) back to Smith to invest for her.[39] The strange compound of independence and dependence worked in this case. It might not have done so with another publisher. Mrs Wood was wise to fend for herself with Bentley who, although he might not stoop to any 'dirty action'[40] would probably have found some use in his firm for any spare £500s offered him. Mrs Wood joined Bentley with *East Lynne* in early 1861 after the novel had been turned down by Chapman and by Smith. Bentley gave it the treatment he normally reserved for novels he was not quite sure of—half profits on a very tentative first edition of 750 in the three-volume form.[41] But as an addendum to the standard printed form of agreement Mrs Wood had put the codicil: 'that the interest of [Bentley]...shall extend to two editions, each edition not to exceed one thousand copies, after the sale of which copies any future editions shall be the subject of fresh arrangement'. It was a happy afterthought. *East Lynne* promptly ran through four editions in the first six months, then had a fabulous career as a reprint (an edition of May 1862 was for 5,000 copies); in the long run it went on to reach thirty-six editions in twenty years and six-figure sales while Bentley had the copyright.[42] In the wake of this success Mrs Wood went on to become one of fiction's toughest negotiators producing agreements prickly with clauses and conditions beneficial to the author. 'I can now command *very* different terms,' she told Bentley in February 1862, as the fifth edition of *East Lynne* became imminent.[43]

IV

While it was a feature of nineteenth-century business generally that as it expanded the managerial functions tended to separate from the manufacturing, this was not the case with publishing. Authors and printers could expect personal attention from a publisher, even the greatest. Novelists and publishers of the period were cultivated and charming people in the main; not surprisingly when business threw them together they tended to stay together as friends. Often such friendships were intimate. In the nature of things a publisher came to know a lot about the personal and financial privacies of an author and he was entrusted with confidences. Conviviality seems to have been the rule. Thackeray introduced Smith into his club (the Reform); Ainsworth did the same for Bentley (the Conservative); Charles Kingsley was godfather to Alexander and Daniel Macmillan's children; Edward Marston named his daughter 'Lorna' in deference to his best friend, R. D. Blackmore; George Eliot was on visiting terms with the Blackwood family; Trollope bought his son a partnership in Chapman and Hall; Dickens's son married his publisher's daughter. Much literary activity centred round dinner nights, 'tobacco parliaments', shared clubs and various social functions. 'You would scarcely believe', grumbled Lever, who lived abroad, 'how much I have sacrificed in not being a regular author of the Guild of Letters—dining at the

Athenaeum—getting drunk at the Garrick—supping with Punch and steaming down to a whitebait feed at Blackheath.'[44] But this friendliness was characteristically complicated by the conflicts bred by business. It is not hard to see how, in terms of pure economics, cross purposes might arise. Success, for example, meant something different to either party. Charles Reade told an interested publisher in 1858:

> You will find that every work of fiction I produce will succeed *more* or *less*; this in a world crammed with feeble scribblers is a sufficient basis for a treaty. As to the exact measure of success no man can pronounce on it beforehand.[45]

In fact it was very much the publisher's interest to pronounce on such matters beforehand and to reduce the 'more or less' aspect of things. The high price of new novels meant profits for everyone on items sold. But on the other hand unsold copies hung very heavily and it did not need many such, sold off at the common remainder price of 9d., to ruin an unlucky producer.

Yet for a novelist success frequently meant what the readers and critics, rather than the ledgers, reported. Mrs Oliphant, speaking with the rueful authority of personal experience, describes the ensuing sense of contradiction well:

> A man finds himself praised on all sides even perhaps with a kind of enthusiasm by the lips of his publisher himself: he is told (but this not generally by the lips of the publisher) that his book is read everywhere, and that the opinion of the general public coincides with that of his literary friends. To be a little elated, to hold his head in the air, and to expect wealth and distinction to follow, are very natural things; but it must be allowed that in a great many instances they do not follow to any great extent, and the author stands bewildered, hearing perhaps (as happens in some cases) that the publisher has even lost by this successful publication of his. What does it mean?[46]

What it means, of course, is that publishers and authors have different notions very often of what constitutes 'success'.

In other ways the two sides tended to view things from conflicting standpoints which gave a quite contrary outlook on events. When, for example, Bentley exploited his two years' right in an agreement with Charles Reade by bringing out *It's*

Never too late to Mend in a cheap version he felt justified in venturing a benignly agrarian image:

I have the copyright for two years only. After that period the property will revert to you, when it will have been planted before the public so carefully that what I shall have done will be only like sowing the seeds of a rich annual harvest to you and yours for nearly the third of a century.[47]

Reade's imagery for the same was was less flattering:

Since then an honourable understanding is nothing to you...and to have made honestly £3,000 from a book for which the author has received £300 is nothing to you unless you can also squeeze one more miserable hundred pounds out and ruin the property to your benefactor, suck the orange dry by all means.[48]

Was Bentley sowing the ground or plundering the crop? If one looks a little into the background of the case it is hard to reach a clear verdict. The disagreement between the two men can be traced back to November 1852 when Reade signed a half profits agreement with Bentley for *Peg Woffington*. The agreement quite specifically stated itself to be binding 'for every edition' of the work that there might be. Since Reade was an unknown at this period a perpetual restriction seemed to hold no great dangers. In fact the edition of 500 copies yielded £10 12s. 8d. of half-profit to the author. By 1857, however, Reade had come up in the literary world and his copyrights were worth much more than £10 to him. In March of this year he took Bentley to court, contending that the original agreement extended to one edition only and that his objection, tendered in February, cancelled the five-year-old contract. The court disagreed and Reade had to bear the costs of the proceedings.[49] With *It's Never too late to Mend* he had been more circumspect and, as he thought, restrained Bentley by allowing him the novel's copyright for two years only. The publisher slipped this noose by printing three-volume editions in August and September 1856, cheap 5s. editions in January, February March, and May 1857 (9,000 advertised as having been sold) and a 'seventh and cheaper edition' in June 1857 (58,000 advertised as having been sold by March 1858) together with an 'Illustrated edition' in the same month. Not surprisingly the author felt that this cascade of editions exhausted the subsequent value of the copyright and remonstrated as we have seen. On his part Bentley could undoubtedly claim that he had launched Reade's career and that the huge popularity he achieved with the house in the late 1850s enabled him to extract huge sums from other publishers in the 1860s. It is possible to feel some sympathy both with Reade's anger at being exploited and Bentley's self righteousness about publicity.

Another factor crossing the course of novelist-publisher relations was that they were, perforce, regularly suspended for the contract which each individual novel required. This meant that every year or so friends had to regard themselves as 'parties' with interests which might or might not coincide. It was hardly surprising that this legal ceremony tended to disestablish friendships. If husbands and wives were called on to renew their union every year instead of making it once for a lifetime there would be, one imagines, many fewer golden weddings. It was extremely rare that novelists had standing orders for anything they might produce. Such blank cheques were too dangerous for the publisher. G. P. R. James, for example, contrived to make an agreement with the twenty-year-old George Smith, just after he had taken over the family firm and was still very green, for £600 for every new work he should turn out. James, an author afflicted with *cacoethes scribendi* as one contemporary put it, then proceeded to pour out three-volume novels at the rate of three a year.[50] Finally Smith had to break his side of the agreement in order to stem the Niagara of mediocre historical romance.

The conflict between author and publisher may be examined in detail through one perennial bone of contention, the joint-profits system. By this kind of agreement, which was very popular with publishers in the middle years of the century, expenses of production were shared and profits on sales after expenses equally divided. It was clearly a useful form of contract with writers of whom not much was expected, or about whom it was difficult to know what to expect. Such was particularly the case with first novels.

On the face of it the system was fair enough but in the working it led to abuses. Publishers made up accounts of cost, which opened the way to invisible surcharging. As Charles Reade put it, 'the accounts, rendered by the trading partner to the other partner, the creator of the copyright, are seldom bona fide accounts as between partner and partner being generally adulterated with secret and disloyal profits on the paper, the printing and the advertisements.'[51] Reade was something of a theorist on this subject and the kind of treaty he favoured was the American commission, or royalty type (a percentage of the retail price of sales rather than a share of the profits).

I have proposed to you [he wrote to the American publisher Fields in 1855] to treat me...as a Boston Author, i.e. allow me what you consider just upon each volume sold. I think no arrangement can be so just or so wise as this. By it the Author is paid according to his deserts: and is encouraged to write his very best; and we all need this encouragement.[52]

This needful encouragement, which came from a sense of genuine alliance, was often missing with the half-profits system. By it, as Frederic Chapman put it, an artful publisher could manipulate costs to make the author 'a partner in everything save profits'.[53] This likelihood Douglas Jerrold made the subject of one of his famous *mots*: personally he liked the half-profits system, Jerrold said, 'because it never leads to division between author and publisher'. This suspicion was never absent for as long as the joint-profits agreement was standard and it was the nagging conviction that most, if not all, publishers falsified their statements of cost that led to the setting up of the Society of Authors in the 1880s under the presidency of George Meredith and through this society the ascendancy of the royalty agreement and the widespread use of literary agents. Their language on the subject of publishers' ethics was immoderate: 'robbery... pillage...plundering' are prominent terms in the Society's manifesto. But above all it was the publisher's account which could not be audited that raised their anger and 'NO SECRET PROFITS' became their battle cry.

Not surprisingly most authors who could, would avoid this kind of contract and as time went by it came to be associated with the lower kind of hack writers. This process is shown by Bentley's normal practice; valued clients would have a contract specially made up for them; less valued but still relatively important authors would have a printed pro-forma half-profits agreement with addenda recording advances or special terms. The least important authors would just have the simple half-profits form.

Such novelists were morbidly suspicious of how their profit share was calculated. It was not always the publisher's double dealing which was at fault, however. Authors had difficulty in understanding the system of bookseller's commission, cash discounts and the necessity for the widespread distribution of free copies. 'Unfortunately for us', Bentley patiently explained to one grumbler, 'all publishers are obliged to employ the use of booksellers who expect also a living.'[54] In fact the half-profits system was probably inevitable in view of the chronic shortage of capital which affected publishing more or less acutely at different periods of the nineteenth century. The ideal situation was one in which the publisher paid the printer in cash, the retailer paid the publisher in cash, the reader (or library purchaser) paid the bookseller cash. But this state of affairs rarely obtained. What usually happened was that payment was deferred (and a commission incurred) and one way of passing the deferred payment along was not to pay the author until all receipts were in.

Nonetheless there were some sharper grounds than this for complaint against the half-profits agreement. The way in which it could be used to mulct an author of his rights may be shown by the experience of Charles Lever in the 1840s. At this period Lever decided to move his literary base from Dublin to London. As part of this move he resolved to wind up his affairs with his Irish publisher Curry and transfer his business to Chapman and Hall.[55] The situation with Curry was complicated, however, and involved the copyright of five novels: *Charles O'Malley* and *Harry Lorrequer* had been sold to Curry outright; *Tom Burke*, *Jack Hinton* and *The O'Donoghue* were sold to Curry on half-profits after surplus sales—i.e. anything after the sale of 11,000 would be divided as net profit between author and publisher. This arrangement was tangled even more by the fact that Lever took an advance payment of something over £1,000 on the three shared novels.[56]

The problem in fact arose with this last novel, *Hinton*, which oversold the threshold at which half-profits began. Of this novel Curry produced 20,000 copies and sold 16,000.[57] At first the publisher managed to juggle the figures in such a way that Lever was 'brought in a debtor' for £134 4s. 7d.[58] Clearly the novelist had been cheated: 'I have been fearfully walked into by that firm,' he wrote to a friend, 'terribly shaken.'[59] But exactly how he was cheated he did not know. For another disadvantage of the half-profits system was that an author had often to wait a long time before costs were covered. In the interval Lever had lost his copy of the agreement and could not clearly remember the details—most importantly the point at which half-profits began. To remedy this there was no way in which Lever could make Curry bring out regular accounts. When he did at last provide some figures they conveniently dropped a thousand here or there and on 16,000 copies of *Hinton* Lever was now allowed £136 4s. 1d.[60] To be in the black rather than the red was something but it was still scandalously little for 5,000 copies.

After a lot of badgering, Lever discovered that Curry was working something of an embezzlement. The novelist was being charged in the accounts for the eleventh part of the original expenses of all the copies of *Hinton* printed, that is for moulding stereotyping, engraving, advertising, materials and printing.[61] In fact he should only have been charged for paper and the working of the copies that had been sold. By this means Curry had contrived to bring the manufacturing cost of the books to 4s., so denying Lever any substantial profit.

Lever was absolutely 'rogued and robbed' as he put it. Curry would not furnish regular, clear accounts because of 'the very natural dislike to expose a broad statement of iniquity to men whose eyes, accustomed to figures, would at once detect the base robbery he would practise'.[62] Lever's freedom of movement was further restricted by a virtual blackmailer's hold which the Irish publisher had over him. When Lever moved his business to London Chapman and Hall took him up enthusiastically. They had just lost Dickens and the Irish novelist seemed a likely replacement. In 1846, when their opinion of Lever was at its highest, they dangled in front of him the prospect of a collective edition of his works. ('People's edition or some such blackguard epithet—being the taste of the day,' the novelist observed privately.)[63] This would mean sales as high as 30,000 on some of his more popular volumes in the English market, with the backing of the most experienced firm in this kind of publishing. But first he would have to recover his half copyright from Curry of the three titles in which the Dublin publisher had an interest.

Curry, with infuriating insolence, offered Lever £200 for his (Lever's) moiety while informing Chapman and Hall that they could buy his (Curry's) half share for £2,500.[64] The fair price was, the London publishers judged, £600–£800. Nor could Lever take Curry to court. The publisher let him know that if he started legal proceedings he would 'swamp' the market with a cheap reissue of Lever's novels, trading ruthlessly on possession while he had it, so killing any future 'People's Edition'. To let Lever know he meant business he sold off 1,000 copies of *Hinton* at virtually no profit.[65]

In this situation Lever had no way of restraining Curry. Charles Reade, as we have seen, once took Richard Bentley to court with the intention of 'handcuffing him'[66] but could get no legal satisfaction and the case was set aside. (Bentley punished the claimant by promptly printing 24,000 cheap copies of Reade's novels.) It was impossible to limit a publisher in the number of copies printed once he was assigned the licence to produce an edition—in fact with stereotyping the whole notion of a limited edition became inoperative. If there was a time limit the author would have the option of buying the unsold stock on expiry day, but what was he to do with 5,000 or so copies of his work? He had no warehouse in which to keep them, no shop through which to sell them.

Time was all important to Lever and Curry's half-interest gave him as much obstructive power as he wanted to stretch negotiations out indefinitely. In desperation Lever, foolishly, made a clandestine approach to Curry; would *he*, instead, like to bring out a new collective issue of the novels?[67] With consummate Macchiavellianism Curry informed Chapman and Hall of Lever's secret overture. The aim was, as the novelist correctly perceived, 'to make me, when cast adrift, an easier prey'.[68]

In the long delay Chapman and Hall gradually cooled towards

Lever.[69] His novels for them did not do well. ('Chapman never reaped the large profits from me that he hoped,' Lever noted sadly.)[70] His 'want of positiveness' made them uneasy. There was a rapprochement with Dickens and the cheap edition went to him.[71] By the end of August 1847 Lever was 'poor as a church mouse'[72] and getting poorer every week. Bad luck worsened. The lawyer whom Lever entrusted to conduct his business with Curry absconded with the novelist's money.[73] When Lever finally thought to return to his line of fiction to the Irish market he found that the Great Hunger had killed the book trade. 'Books are ever the easiest luxury to go without,' he observed bitterly.[74] Lever's kind of fiction was not the only casualty. In the summer of 1847 Curry himself went under after staving off ruin for a year—and Lever was thus prevented from getting his copyrights until 1850, when he paid £600.

Lever's protracted anguish arose directly from the half-profits system and the complicated treacheries it allowed. Curry by padding accounts, stalling, not answering correspondence and fudging statements was able to do Lever a material damage at a period of his life when the ability to move quickly might have done him a lot of good. As it was the novelist was kept out of the lucrative collective reissue market until 1857. What the episode demonstrated was how the balance of power normally lay with the publisher. Occasionally an author would find himself in the position of being able to blackmail a publisher—serialisation was one such situation when a writer could withhold an instalment. (Both Ainsworth and Shirley Brooks did this to Bentley, driving the poor man almost to distraction.) But such power was rare. The extremely successful novelist like Dickens or Mrs Wood (after *East Lynne*) could drive the publisher down to a quarter or a third share of the profits and make other beneficial arrangements for themselves. But this was only a minority of novelists and then, very often, only for a short period in their writing career. In general it seems that unless a novelist could tyrannise over the publisher, the publisher was in a strong position to tyrannise over him. 'I would say to a young writer,' declared Walter Besant, 'when you enter a publisher's shop; when you send him a MS.; you become, like all other persons engaged in the production of a book, a man to be "bested".' It was in the breed, Besant felt, and to clinch his point he would cite the case of the Society for the Propagation of Christian Knowledge gouging a quite unchristian degree of profit from its authors.

On their part publishers could muster their grievances and cautionary tales. 'Calamities of Authors indeed!' Richard Bentley ejaculated in his diary: 'what a huge but painfully interesting volume could be easily prepared on the rascality of authors.'[75] True, doubtless, but one cannot help feeling that on the whole the employers had the better of things.

V

In the final analysis it all came down to property and proprietorial rights. A novel belongs to its author by blood, but a publisher takes it over by adoption. After he has bought it, often at more than it is worth, he feels it is his to do as he likes with. In this situation authors were not unnaturally prone to think that as Reade vividly put it: 'a Briton's literary property is less safe than his house, hovel, haystack and dunghill.'[76]

The key issue was one which was never satisfactorily resolved; namely did an agreement between author and publisher constitute a 'sale of copyright' or merely the assignation of a 'privilege to print and publish'. This had the baffling complexity of a metaphysical problem for literary minds of the day. Who actually 'owned' literary property was never actually stated on contracts after the Copyright Amendment Act of 1842. Before this a publisher might well talk of a novel as 'my exclusive property'. In the 1830s ownership would be put with unequivocal directness, as in an agreement between Bentley and Frank Reynolds where the novelist 'On consideration of... payment...binds himself to assign said novel to [Bentley and Co.] and their heirs for ever.'[77] In this same period it was common for publishers to trade in a living novelist's copyrights without him ever being a penny the better off for it. While Marryat, for example, was getting £500 a novel from Bentley in the late 1830s the publisher was simultaneously negotiating with Saunders and Otley to buy seven of the author's copyrights for £1,500 or a bit more. From these Bentley reckoned to get £6,000; Marryat would get nothing. In fact the deal turned out to be the money-spinner Bentley hoped and the Marryat property continued to make profits for the publisher for twenty years. It would have gone on still longer but that the firm's Inspectors (notably 'that ruffian Evans'[78] whom Bentley suspected of professional malice) insisted that the copyrights be sold off to Routledge. The memory of this 'infamous transfer' of his Marryat property infuriated Bentley to the end of his life.

As the century progressed, and particularly after the tighter definitions of 1842, this kind of horse trading died out. The tendency of the new copyright act was further to shift the law's protection from printer and publisher (for whom copyright legislation was originally devised) to the author, to whom it gave longer possession. Novelists too, as a profession, had become wiser over the years and more of them followed the trade adage—never part with a copyright. Nonetheless it was still advisable to be wary. Nineteenth-century publishing had more than its share of sharp operators; 'an honest bookseller and a prompt paymaster', the experienced Lever observed, 'are among the black swans of literature.'[79] A chronic, and often justifiable, suspiciousness on the author's part explains what seems an almost invariable sequence of events in publisher-novelist relationships of the period. First the connection would be warm and friendly then, after a while, it would be strained sometimes to breaking point, by professional difference. Most writers would have said with Lever, 'I detest the hacknied fightings of booksellers and author.'[80] But equally most were brought to the point of fighting—or at least of looking rather carefully to their weapons. With novelists of fiery tempers like Reade and Dickens, and publishers who were litigious like Bentley, differences would be spectacular with law suits, huffy letters and bad blood which poisoned the atmosphere for years. As befitted the leading historical romancer, G. P. R. James went to the length of challenging his publisher to a duel.[81] In other cases the process was subterranean, often detectable only through an increasingly punctilious attention paid by the author to his benefit and advantage in any agreement.

Mrs Gaskell illustrates the growth of this second kind of hostility well. For *Mary Barton* she received £100.[82] It was a small enough sum for a 'firebrand' bestseller but her aim, as she fervently informed her publisher, was to do good by reaching the widest possible circulation. 'I am (above every other consideration) desirous that it should be *read*,' she told Chapman.[83] Money was one of these inferior considerations. She offered to forego payment rather than add material which she felt might cushion the impact of the novel. And with endearing benevolence she wrote to Chapman after the successful figures of her sales for *Mary Barton* were totted up, 'not the least agreeable part of your letter is that in which you speak of the book, "being a source of profit to the publisher." I am truly glad to hear of it.'[84]

This easy, entirely unsuspicious, conduct was continued in her next major production *Ruth*, the story of a fallen woman. The contract for this work was drafted as casually and simply as could be:

> Memorandum of an agreement entered into this 23rd. day of August 1852 between Mrs. Gaskell of Plymouth Grove Manchester and Mr. Edward Chapman of 193 Piccadilly London. Mr. Chapman agrees to purchase the copyright of a tale by Mrs. Gaskell called *Ruth* for the sum of £500, to be paid to Mrs. Gaskell on the day of publication. Mr. Chapman at the same time undertaking that the publication shall take place either in the form of two or three volumes as he may determine within the month after the completed manuscript of the tale has been forwarded to him.[85]

(The last clause is explained by the fact that Mrs Gaskell was never very reliable as to length.) Again the figure for an author who had proved herself with a bestseller was not all that high, but clearly she was happy with this easy-going relationship, and did not think twice about signing away her interest in the novel for ever.

In the years 1853–55 Mrs Gaskell came increasingly into contact with Dickens and Forster, both of whom were skilled and militant professionals. When *Cranford* (first published in *Household Words*) was put up to Chapman for volume publication a distinctly business-like touch begins to enter Mrs Gaskell's tone of negotiation. Agreement was postponed until she could have 'a little talk' on the subject with her husband.[86] She directed some searching prior questions to the publishers: 'what number [would you] propose to publish in the first instance? and how soon do you think the returns on that number are likely to be made?' In addition she requested a 'form of agreement' rather than the informal memoranda which had hitherto served.

The ensuing agreement, three weeks later, exists in two versions. There is Chapman's rough draft, listing heads and sharpening up definitions. Following this is the formally agreed document, copied out in a clerk's handwriting:

> Memorandum of Agreement betewen the Revd. William Gaskell and Messrs. Chapman and Hall for the publication in a cheap form (at two shillings) of 'Cranford' and a Volume of selected tales both by Mrs. Gaskell.
>
> Messrs. Chapman and Hall to be at the entire cost of printing, binding and advertising the two books, and to pay Mrs. Gaskell a Royalty of Threepence on each copy sold.
>
> This agreement to be binding for two years from the date of publication after which time either party to be at liberty to put an end to it by giving three months notice.
>
> The Accounts to be made up at Midsummer and Christmas and the Royalty due to be paid by the end of February for the Christmas account and the end of August for the Midsummer account...[87]

The precision, angularity and formality of this agreement is unlikely to have arisen from Edward Chapman. He tended to let agreements be formal or not according to the author's wishes. What seems to have happened is that Mrs Gaskell had changed into a more self-consciously professional writer. Inevitably this meant a colder, if clearer, air of business between her and her publisher. This new Mrs Gaskell could write pettishly to Chapman, hinting broadly that he was not advertising her work sufficiently:

> Please to remember that August is drawing very near to a close, and that you have confessed yourself 'very much ashamed of the small amount you had to hand over etc.' the last time; so that *this* time I am hoping for some improvement in either you or the undiscerning

public, which, if they won't buy should be made to buy CRANFORD & LIZZIE LEIGH.[88]

Confronted with this scold Chapman must have longed for the docile lady of five years earlier, so unconcerned with money, forms and sales.

PART TWO

Novelists, Novels and their Publishers 1830–1870

4

'Henry Esmond' The Shaping Power of Contract

In his reminiscences, *Glances Back through Seventy Years*, Henry Vizetelly recalls meeting Thackeray in the 1840s carrying a 'small brown paper parcel with him'. It emerged from conversation that the parcel contained the opening of a story. The writer was off to see the publishers Bradbury and Evans with his sample and

> In little more than half an hour Mr. Thackeray again made his appearance and with a beaming face gleefully informed me that he had settled the business. 'B & E' said he, 'accepted so readily that I am deuced sorry I didn't ask them another tenner. I am certain they would have given it.' He then explained to me that he had named fifty guineas per part, including the two sheets of letterpress a couple of etchings and the initials at the commencement of the chapters. He reckoned the text, I remember, at no more than five and twenty shillings a page, the two etchings at six guineas each, while, as for the few initials at the beginning of the chapters, he threw these in. Such was Mr. Thackeray's own estimate of his commercial value as an author and illustrator A.D. 1846.[1]

Thackeray had some right to be pleased with the price he eventually got. Sixty pounds a month with the prospect of half-profit to follow was good money for a first novel by one whose name meant nothing to the public. But the terms Bradbury and Evans imposed were stringent. Neither in the agreement nor in advertisements were the number of issues *Vanity Fair* was to run specified. This meant that the publishers reserved a right to terminate whenever the work became a financial risk—as it almost did at the third number. As late as the fifteenth number it was uncertain whether *Vanity Fair* was to complete in eighteen or twenty instalments.[2] In the same spirit of precaution

Bradbury and Evans paid their £60 'on the publication of the Number'.[3] But they gave nothing for copy delivered in advance. This held out no cash incentive for Thackeray to run more than one month ahead with his composition, nor did he once the novel was into its stride.

This arrangement was a common enough safety net. In the previous year, for example, Charles Lever was contracted to produce a novel for Chapman and Hall 'in not less than twelve numbers. But if after the publication of the fifth number Chapman and Hall should express such a desire, it is to be extended to twenty or any less quantity of numbers.'[4] The difference here is that Lever, as well as twice Thackeray's fee (£130), had a *quid pro quo*. He was guaranteed at least a dozen numbers and was thus encouraged to design something of a long-term plan for his narrative. Thackeray might well think that any long-term planning would be wasted labour since he could not be sure of the scale of his finished (or unfinished) work.

If Thackeray was at a disadvantage in comparison with Lever he was doubly so with Dickens whose *Dombey and Son* (also brought out by Bradbury and Evans in 1846) was predefined 'to be completed in 20 monthly parts, uniform with *Martin Chuzzlewit*', and paid for accordingly. All Dickens's pronouncements on fiction from his earliest addresses to the reader in *Pickwick* onwards indicate an author thinking in terms of wholeness and structure. His secure, far-seeing relationship with Bradbury and Evans fostered this yearning towards constructiveness. The brown paper parcel Thackeray carried when he called on the publishers was potentially a magazine story, a three-volume novel, or a monthly serial of indeterminate length. *His* relationship with Bradbury and Evans, initially at least, did not encourage foregoing this elasticity or the drawing up of any detailed blueprint for the story. Temperamentally, too, Thackeray at this stage of his life belonged to the class of what Carlyle called 'ready writers', artists who could throw their fiction off with the perfect spontaneity of Giotto's 'O'. It is unlikely that he felt to the same degree as Dickens the need for a mind-held structure to direct his composition. He was more of Lever's party who merrily told his publisher in the penultimate stages of *The O'Donoghue*:

I can wind up with Demosthenic abruptness in eleven numbers, the curtain falling amid the blue lightning and thunder that scattered the French fleet; or I can go on to a more Colburn and Bentley ending with love and marriage licenses in thirteen numbers. You have paid your money and you may take your choice.[5]

Vanity Fair was, it is famous, a wonderful and unexpected success for Thackeray. Bradbury and Evans cleared 10,500 copies; not a Dickensian figure but a brilliant showing for a first novel in numbers. With the significant difference that he was now to be paid £100 a number, Thackeray wrote *Pendennis* in much the same way as its predecessor, *Vanity Fair*. After that novel's success he was in no danger of premature termination. He could now be sure of running to twenty numbers if he wanted to and in fact decided at the half way point to overrun to a massive twenty-four. But no more than in *Vanity Fair* does he seem to have written ahead of monthly deadlines and some critics were hard on what they considered to be the 'inconsistency' of the novel's construction.[6]

Like *Vanity Fair*, *Pendennis* is a brilliant novel. But the mode of publication confirmed in Thackeray a kind of narrative opportunism. One always feels that he has reserved the right to switch the course of his narrative whenever and however it suits him. He alludes jokingly to the arbitrariness of his power over plot in the preface:

Perhaps the lovers of 'excitement' may care to know that this book began with a very precise plan, which was entirely put aside. Ladies and gentlemen, you were to have been treated and the writer's and publisher's pocket benefited, by the recital of the most active horrors ...Nay, up to nine o'clock this very morning, my poor friend, Colonel Altamont, was doomed to execution, and the author only relented when his victim was actually at the window.

This is high-spirited nonsense, though it embodies an element of truth about Thackeray's serialised fiction. Another analogy used in the same preface is closer to the actuality; the relationship between author and reader over the course of a two-year serial is, Thackeray observes, 'a sort of confidential talk'. *Pendennis* has all the strengths of good conversation; it is flexible, easy, spontaneous, responsive to its interlocutor and apparently unpremeditated. But conversational strengths can be a corresponding narrative weakness. Serialisation had a palpably relaxing effect on Thackeray's artistic concentration. Trollope, a harsh critic, compared the other novelist unfavourably with himself in this respect:

I knew, from what I read from month to month, that this hurried publication of incompleted work was frequently, I might perhaps say always, adopted by the leading novelists of the day. That such has been the case, is proved by the fact that Dickens, Thackeray, and Mrs. Gaskell died with unfinished novels, of which portions had been already published. I had not yet entered upon the system of publishing novels in parts, and therefore had never been tempted. But I was aware that an artist should keep in his hand the power of fitting the beginning of his work to the end. No doubt it is his first duty to fit the end to the beginning, and he will endeavour to do so. But he should still keep in his hands the power of remedying any defect in this respect.

Servetur ad imum
Qualis ab incepto processerit,

should be kept in view as to every character and every string of action.[7]

It can be no accident that the Latin tag Trollope introduces here is the epigraph from *Henry Esmond*, the hero's motto. For by general consent this, Thackeray's third full-length novel, is one which escapes any criticism of its structure. It is also the only full-length novel that Thackeray published not in monthly numbers but in three volumes, according to the old pattern.

Most commentators have recognised in *Esmond* a work which is finely made, *unified*. It is not generally realised, however, how much this was due to the predefinition and controls exercised by Thackeray's publisher. The godfather to *Esmond* was George Smith (though as a twenty-six-year-old, as he then was, he still deserved his title 'boy cyclone'). The connection between Smith and Thackeray had come originally through Charlotte Brontë's desire to meet the other novelist, whom she admired immensely. This was followed up by a Christmas book, *The Kickleburys on the Rhine*, in 1850. In March 1850 Charlotte Brontë wrote to Smith about the pressure she felt serialisation imposed on Thackeray and how it was deteriorating his fiction:

The last two or three numbers of *Pendennis* will not, I dare say, be generally thought sufficiently exciting, yet I like them. Though the story lingers (for me) the interest does not flag. Here and there we feel that the pen has been guided by a tired hand, that the mind of the writer has been somewhat chafed and depressed by his recent illness, or by some other cause; but Thackeray still proves himself greater when he is weary than other writers are when they are fresh. The public, of course, will have no compassion for his fatigue, and make no allowance for the ebb of inspiration; but some true hearted readers here and there, while grieving that such a man should be obliged to write when he is not in the mood, will wonder that, under such circumstances, he should write so well.[8]

This may have put it into Smith's mind to change those circumstances. His initiative in contracting Thackeray for *Pendennis*'s successor is remembered by the novelist's daughter:

We used to do our lessons, or sit sewing and reading in the front room with the bow window to the street; and one day, as we were there with our governess, my father came in, in great excitement. 'There's a young fellow just come,' said he; 'he has brought a thousand pounds in his pocket; he has made me an offer for my book, it's the most spirited, handsome offer, I scarcely like to take him at his word; he's hardly more than a boy, his name is George Smith; he is waiting there now, and I must go back': and then, after walking once up and down the room, my father went away.[9]

The action tells us much about Smith. He was very much a publisher who went shopping with his purse open, and who looked for what he wanted rather than waiting for authors to solicit him. Nor did he stint payments. It was he who paid George Eliot £7,000 for *Romola* (so winning her from Blackwood) and Wilkie Collins £5,000 for *Armadale* (so winning him from Dickens). Where money was concerned he was what Charlotte Brontë called a 'practical man',[10] and he spent liberally. He liked the shock tactic; once he offered to 'toss' Trollope for an extra thousand which the novelist wanted. It was quite in character for him to have a thousand pounds in his pocket wherewith to sway Thackeray. And yet, with all this flamboyance, he was a thoroughly honourable businessman. He always waited until a novelist had served out his present contract before making his dazzling overtures, unlike Bentley who rather more schemingly made approaches clandestinely while a novelist was still bound elsewhere.

Especially in his younger days Smith conceived of himself as the assistant of genius. It would not humiliate him to wait in a great writer's hall. His subsequent social intercourse with Thackeray was marked by an easy assumption of seniority on the author's part and an engaging submissiveness on the publisher's. When it came to drawing up contracts, however, Smith was Thackeray's equal. That for *Esmond* was, in the circumstances, an unusually sensitive and procreative act of publishing. Yet, as we shall see, it exercised a necessary measure of tough disciplinary control over the author:

AGREEMENT BETWEEN W. M. THACKERAY AND MR. GEORGE SMITH FOR COPYRIGHT OF A NOVEL IN THREE VOLUMES. JUNE 27, 1851

Memorandum of Agreement between William Makepeace Thackeray Esq....and Mr. George Smith publisher...[Thackeray] agrees in consideration of the sum of Four Hundred pounds the receipt of which he hereby acknowledges to write an original work of fiction forming a continuous narrative in three volumes Post 8vo. to consist of not less than One thousand pages of the usual novel size and to place the Manuscript of the same in the hands of [Smith] complete and ready for publication on or before the first day of ['November' deleted] December [inserted in a different and presumably later ink] next ensuing.

[Smith] agrees to print and publish the said work and on receipt of the Manuscript thereof to pay to [Thackeray] another sum of Four Hundred Pounds and on the publication of the said work to pay to [Thackeray] a further sum of Four Hundred Pounds.

It is agreed between [Thackeray] and [Smith] that the first impression printed of the said work shall consist either of 2500 or 2750 copies at the option of [Smith] and that such impression may be published in one edition or divided into two or three editions as he may consider expedient. In the event of [Smith] printing 2,750 copies he agrees to pay to [Thackeray] One Hundred Pounds if the whole of such impression be sold within eighteen months from the date of publication of the first edition.

It is further agreed that in consideration of the above mentioned payments [that there will be a half-profits agreement on any editions after the first 2,500 or 2,750—all publishing decisions to be left with Smith].

It is also agreed by [Thackeray] that he will not print or publish any serial or other work within six months of the date of publication of the above mentioned work and that any profit that may be derived from the sale of early proof sheets for publication in America shall belong to [Smith].

Stamped London, 1.7.51

The first point that stands out from this document—and a rather startling one—is that Thackeray was agreeing, initially at least, to a drop in income. Bradbury and Evans had paid him £60 for the twenty instalments of *Vanity Fair* (total £1,200) and £100 each for the twenty-four installments of *Pendennis* (total £2,400). He was now settling for £1,200 in three equal instalments.

Clearly, in spite of the £1,000 in Smith's pocket, money was not Thackeray's first consideration, at least not after the initial surprise of having it waved under his nose. Nor, if Thackeray wanted immediate wide circulation for his novel, would he have published it in the expensive, three-volume form. There was no alternative. Smith's firm did not go in for part-issue at this time which, on the face of it, was another reason for declining the young man's flattering bid. But, perhaps stimulated by Smith's obeisance, Thackeray seems from the first to have conceived of *Esmond* as caviare for the general, an artistic opportunity rather than a money-spinner. For such a work the three-decker was quite in order.

On his part, the publisher, in the contract at least, gave the novelist *carte blanche*. There is no specification as to period or subject matter. Thackeray had his first £400 merely on his known ability to write. That Smith would allow historical fiction at all is, in fact, a testament to his faith in Thackeray. The form was in low critical esteem and Smith was badly out of pocket on a rash deal he had made with the veteran historical novelist G. P. R. James a couple of years before.[11] And as his later dealings with Thackeray show he was quite capable of prohibiting the novelist from supplying him with historical fiction.[12] There were other ponderables. In 1851 Smith turned down a novel from Harriet Martineau on the grounds that it dealt too favourably with Catholicism during a period of 'Papal Aggression'.[13] *Esmond* was to offer a once Catholic struggling to restore a Catholic monarchy, so we may assume that no such injunction was laid on Thackeray.

Thackeray had a few ideas 'biling up' in his mind, as he put it. Among other things he was toying with the scheme for 'A Novel with a Hero' for a change. His lectures on the English Humourists, undertaken in 1851, suggested both period and characters like Mohun, Webb and Hamilton. But as regards essentials his mind was, apparently, blank. He left proof of this in a little doodle he made on 1 October 1851, while trying out a new 'anastatic' stylus. For demonstration he sketched a small drawing of a young man in eighteenth-century costume under a tree taking the hand of a pretty young girl, evidently in the act of farewell. In the background is a country house.

> I have drawn this at hazard. You see it represents the beginning of my story. The young hero is taking leave of the young heroine, and about to go forth on his travels. Surely plenty of pretty nonsense might be manufactured in this way...I really think something may come out of this ¼ of an hour's scribbling.[14]

If we are to believe this Thackeray had no great preconception of his new story. Other evidence may be found in the publisher's handout which the *Publishers' Circular* printed in their issue of 15 October 1851: 'the scene of Thackeray's New Novel is laid in England of the eighteenth century, and the stage will be crossed by many of the illustrious of the time, such as Bolingbroke, Swift and Pope. Dick Steele will also play a prominent part'. This suggests that Thackeray had only the scenery of his novel set in his mind (and not even that very clearly: Pope does not cross the fictional stage, nor does Steele play a prominent part after the first chapters). From this evidence we may assume that Thackeray was being paid by Smith to await inspiration. Nor was inspiration prompt in coming: the *Publishers' Circular* announced the new novel as a title for January 1852; in the event it did not appear until November.

When he did come to write Thackeray set to with more urgency and emotional intensity than the above sally with the new pen would suggest. *Esmond* was given a peculiarly sombre cast by the Brookfield involvement. The novelist fell in love with his best friend's wife in 1851; there was an estrangement;

Thackeray recoiled wounded and desperately unhappy. The unhappiness colours the novel which has a power lacking in Thackeray's earlier fiction and rarely recovered in his later.[15]

The strong emotions contained in *Esmond* are, however, contained in an aesthetic sense. The novel is a work of art not a *cri du coeur*. The structural integrity of the narrative and its solidity of historical specification control what might otherwise have been fatally disturbing passions. The agreement was made some time before the Brookfield imbroglio but there is little doubt that, albeit unconsciously, Smith had played an important part in letting Thackeray control his work in this way. Most importantly the terms of the agreement allowed the novelist to reserve his manuscript for many months before letting another pair of eyes see any part of it. But in return the contract made a notable stipulation. Thackeray must provide 'an original work of fiction, forming a continuous narrative in three volumes post 8vo. to consist of not less than one thousand pages of the usual novel size'. The one term here which is unusual (I cannot remember it on any other contract of the period) is 'continuous'. As it is phrased the prescription has an echo of the Aristotelian formula for tragedy—that it should be of a certain size and complete in itself with a beginning, a middle and an end.

What the contract desiderated was a literary virtue which had hitherto been in somewhat short supply with Thackeray. One remembers that *Vanity Fair* began as discontinuous 'Pen and Pencil Sketches of English Society' and was paid for month by month. With *Esmond* Thackeray would get the second helping of money not for the part but the whole. This would give the publisher a chance to review the complete work and to get second opinions on it. (Smith used Charlotte Brontë for this purpose feeding her one volume at a time so as to get the library reader's response.) The third payment would be made over on publication. This third postponement it is that explains why *Esmond* is the most carefully prepared for press and proof read of Thackeray's novels (by no means an easy task since it was set up in Queen Anne period type). Thackeray was willing to undertake this arduous task because he was still in the employ of Smith.

In fact Smith relaxed, and Thackeray bent, the conditions considerably both as to delivery dates and the completeness of the manuscript expected by November, December and then well into the new year. But the important effect on Thackeray remained. He was forced, from the first, to think in terms of wholeness and unity. His cast of mind was thus quite different from that which preceded the composition of *Vanity Fair* or *Pendennis*.

In other ways Smith was careful to guard against possible dissipation of creative energy. Take the clause: 'It is also agreed by [Thackeray] that he will not print or publish any serial or other work within six months of the date of publication of the above mentioned work.' This was a far-sighted prohibition. Thackeray had gone straight from *Vanity Fair* to *Pendennis* with hardly a break. Three-volume *Esmond* would require longer to sell itself through several editions and interest might be drained off if Thackeray began a serial straight after. But in a less obvious way Smith was protecting his literary property. It was only too easy for a popular novelist like Thackeray to put too many irons in the fire. Dickens's overwhelming himself with work enough for five novelists during the course of *Pickwick* is a spectacular example of this tendency. The amount of extra writing Thackeray undertook while writing *Vanity Fair* tells a similar story. During the course of that work he contributed to *Punch* alone nine numbers of the 'Snob Papers', twenty-one numbers of 'Novels by Eminent Hands', fifteen 'Spec' papers, four instalments from 'The Fat Contributor'. At the same time he wrote *A Little Dinner at Timmins's*, completed a Christmas Book and turned out a wealth of incidental journalism and magazine illustration.

There was, of course, nothing to stop Thackeray from writing serials *pari passu* with *Esmond* and holding them six months before publication, but this was not his way of doing things. Smith was safe enough on this score. On the other hand a clause like this was, surely, unenforceable in law. It is more in the nature of a gentleman's agreement and the publisher's security was only the author's moral integrity. Here again Smith was safe; Thackeray prided himself on acting like a gentleman in business affairs. (When, for example, he found himself unable to deliver the manuscript on time he called on Smith to offer him back his advance.)

As an immediate result of Smith's restrictive clause Thackeray's bibliography for 1852–3 is thinner than for any other year of his writing life.[16] Was it necessary? Probably it was. *Vanity Fair* had not been much deteriorated by Thackeray's extra-curricular publications but during the course of *Pendennis* the novelist suffered a near fatal illness; thereafter his health was never strong again. He might take on as much work as before but there was a likelihood that a lot of it would be substandard.

In the long run nothing was lost by Smith's ban. The mode of payment and restriction was as intelligent as it was unusual. Thackeray was persuaded by it to think in the long term about income. Thus the £400 advance (together with some incidental journalism and a lot of lecturing) would keep him until the second installment at the end of the year. We find him writing to Smith in August 1852 in a way which suggests that he is putting his life into very methodical order: 'My present plan is to prepare 4 or 5 extra lectures previous to the American campaign—and, I think, when in the States, to make a book...'[17] At the same time the scheme of the 'American continuation' to *Esmond* (i.e. *The Virginians*) was forming in his mind. He would be able to gather material and ideas for this sequel while touring in the new world.

Altogether Thackeray was led by the terms of his arrangement for *Esmond* to do two things which were unusual for him personally and the Victorian novelist generally. These were to think in terms of 'plans' for his career, and to pay attention to the completeness of the work in hand. Circumstances usually conspired against the novelist doing either. If he was at the bottom of the tree he was writing for his life. If he was at the top he was swamped with more work than he could reasonably manage. This was made worse by the hefty advances which a name author could command from his publisher. If these were indiscriminate they tended merely to speed up the writer's treadmill. It was no favour to an author to keep him living a year or so ahead of his earnings. 'For my sake', pleaded Lever with one publisher in the 1860s, 'don't give me any money till I ask for it.'[18]

An extreme example of what indiscriminate advances could do to an author is afforded by G. A. Lawrence. After the success of *Guy Livingstone*, the most muscular of the muscular Christianity novels, Lawrence was promoted to the £1,000-a-novel grade. His publisher records that he would take his £500 advance, rush off to Homburg and lose it on the gaming tables in less than a week. He would then write back for more.[19] Not surprisingly his manuscript always arrived promptly on time. Even less surprisingly, perhaps, his succeeding novels were all in the same mould and show no improvement over *Guy Livingstone*.

This situation might well be exacerbated by the fact that the novelist was indebted to his publisher, or publishers, on other scores. It was common to run up charge accounts for books which publishers could get at trade price, or to borrow cash from one's publisher. Thackeray, for a long period in the 1850s, owed Smith £200 which he offered to pay off 'in kind'.[20] Disraeli went up to £900 with his publishers in the same period.[21] In 1866 Lever was so much overdrawn with Chapman and Hall that they were in a position to demand, and get, the assignment of *all* the novelist's copyrights in return for the £2,500 owed.[22]

Thackeray was made of sterner stuff than Lever and Lawrence and had better novels in him than Disraeli. But the pressures on him were no less. These pressures were, for *Esmond* at least, remitted. Smith had helped create a rational economic framework for its composition.

II

For the reader the immediate outcome in *Esmond* from the agreement is the novel's handsome, dignified appearance. Few three-deckers can have been so well worth 31s. 6d. It is, in every sense, a book. The tendency of the monthly number was to sink to the condition of the periodical. Thus *Vanity Fair* appeared escorted by advertisements for the Invisible Ventilating Peruke, Keating's Cough Lozenges and the Improved Elastic Chest Expander. Even the illustration of the monthly number tended to diminish its dignity by affirming a family link with the comic almanac. (*Esmond* was unillustrated.)

For many in the nineteenth century the three-volume novel

had an inherited grandeur that could not be replaced. The publisher Tinsley put what was a widespread prejudice for the traditional form of fiction: 'A book rich in talent or genius, has as much or more right to good dress as a rich man. Where is the intellectual man or woman who is not proud to possess the glorious octavos of Thackeray, Dickens, Lever...'[23] *Esmond* is an elegant book, a possession for a gentleman's library not a ware for the bookstall. With its antique, Queen Anne print, its witty running titles, its fine binding and paper, *Esmond* has the appearance of an *edition de luxe.* (It would be interesting to know how much more than the average work it cost Smith, Elder to produce.)

If he spared no pains in production Smith was equally open-handed with advertisement. 'The History of Henry Esmond' stands out in large print everywhere in the literary journals. The line the advertisements take indicate a tactical decision to promote Thackeray as something more than a run-of-the-mill fiction writer. *Esmond* was advertised as a package together with his lectures on the *English Humourists* to which was to be added a bulky *apparatus historicus* by James Hannay; also offered at two guineas was a reproduction of Laurence's portrait of the great author (commissioned and paid for by Smith). In pushing *Vanity Fair* and *Pendennis* Bradbury and Evans had made much of Thackeray's *Punch* connection. For Smith Thackeray was not a comic magazine writer but a great historian. The promotional campaign for *Esmond* was modelled on Macaulay's phenomenal success with his recent *History of England* (1849). It was as a reputable historian of the eighteenth century, not as Michaelangelo Titmarsh, that Thackeray was now put before the English public. It was a successful campaign; the second edition was advertised a month after publication and Mudie took 430 copies of the first—a higher figure than for any other novel of the period.

III

Turning to the novel itself one is struck by a notable control of phase, sequence and unit, what Trollope calls the 'string of action'. Its narrative conforms neatly to the three volumes with each 'book' starting on a new era of the hero's career (I childhood, II military, III Jacobite) and finishing on a low point (I in prison, II jilted by Beatrix, III betrayed by King and betrothed). Like *Vanity Fair* and *Pendennis*, *Esmond* has a double-heroine plot. But in *Esmond* it is much more complex and tense. Amelia and Becky proceed in a kind of see-saw relationship; the one goes up as the other goes down and they both come to rest in ironic equilibrium as respectable women in *Vanity Fair*. *Pendennis* has a tug-of-war shape, Blanche and Laura (as on the novel's cover) contending for Pen's love. It is, however, quite clear from the first that Blanche is unworthy and it is, we feel, only a matter of time before Pen finds this out. No-one, I fancy, hurries through the final chapters of these two novels in eagerness to find out what happens on the last page.

In *Esmond*, by contrast, there is real surprise and suspense about whom the hero will marry and how his choice will finally go. Everything works to a tremendous climax in the third volume. At this stage, it will be remembered, to take advantage of the situation Esmond has engineered, the Pretender should be in London to ingratiate himself with the dying queen and recover the English throne for the Stuarts. But, instead, he has lecherously pursued Beatrix to Castlewood. Esmond and Frank chase down to the country house after him to save the honour of the family. Esmond all the while is consumed with injured pride, love, baffled loyalty and a disturbing awareness of his growing love for Rachel. Finally the pursuers manage to force an entry through the priest's secret window and confront the guilty prince. There is a duel, Beatrix appears and in a final purgative moment Esmond is simultaneously rid of his love for his unworthy mistress and his allegiance to an unworthy king:

'Will it please the King to breakfast before he goes?' was all Beatrix could say. The roses had shuddered out of her cheeks; her eyes were glaring; she looked quite old. She came up to Esmond and hissed out a word or two:—'If I did not love you before, cousin,' says she, 'think how I love you now.' If words could stab, no doubt she would have killed Esmond; she looked at him as if she could.

But her keen words gave no wound to Mr. Esmond; his heart was too hard. As he looked at her, he wondered that he could ever have loved her. His love of ten years was over; it fell down dead on the spot, at the Kensington Tavern, where Frank brought him the note out of Eikon Basilike. The Prince blushed and bowed low, as she gazed at him, and quitted the chamber. I have never seen her from that day (III, xiii).

The lapse into the first person in the last sentence is masterful. Even after forty years the event has power enough to shock Esmond out of his habitual reserve.

This episode has been managed throughout at a near melodramatic pitch with rising excitement, pace and climax. The final moment has both surprise and logic to it. It combines the two Aristotelian constituents of the complex plot—downfall and enlightenment. The hero has lost everything, but he has gained an insight which in its way is a bitter reward and which enables him to turn now to Rachel. The whole structure of the novel reinforces the local situation to create a sense of genuine culmination. There is, for example, a significant circularity in this last climactic scene. Esmond has entered Castlewood by the window which Holt the Jesuit showed him as a young boy. The scene of disappointment with Beatrix matches the scene of initial enchantment when, in the same place, the young Harry first saw Rachel:

...coming back to the lad, with a look of infinite pity and tenderness in her eyes, she took his hand again, placing her other fair hand on his head, and saying some words to him, which were so kind and said in a voice so sweet, that the boy, who had never looked on so much beauty before, felt as if the touch of a superior being or angel smote him down to the ground, and kissed the fair protecting hand as he knelt on one knee. To the very last hour of his life, Esmond remembered the lady as she then spoke and looked, the rings on her fair hands, the very scent of her robe, the beam of her eyes lighting up with surprise and kindness, her lips blooming in a smile, the sun making a golden halo round her hair (I, i).

In the mind of the reader the whole novel telescopes at such moments, starting and finishing points merge. It was not unusual for Victorians, who had a voracious appetite for fiction, to read a three-volume novel at one go—Thackeray, for example, did so with *The Woman in White*. One is tempted to think that to be fully successful moments like the foregoing in *Esmond* have to be read while the whole novel is resonating in the mind, as one single experience. Had *Esmond* been serialised the early days at Castlewood would (for the first readers) have been experienced some eighteen months before the final scene with the Pretender and Beatrix. The kind of resonance which requires a simultaneous awareness of the whole novel would have been lost.

Smith, I have argued, deserves some credit for the glories of *Esmond.* His terms allowed the novel to come into existence in its complete form. During the composition he was tolerant of Thackeray's difficulties in coming up to the line. The date on the contract was changed from November to December and Thackeray was allowed to over-run the second date. Even so Smith did not manage to get the work out until November 1852.[24] Thackeray, it must be said, fell back on many of the serialist's habits he had developed. This was not altogether a bad thing. The novel combines the best of Thackeray as he normally was and as he could be when trying his hardest. The novel has both plotting in depth and facile improvisation. One may only regret that after this brief experiment with Smith Thackeray found that such departures from his usual writing habits were too expensive to be repeated. He returned, therefore, to Bradbury and Evans and the frantic round of hand-to-mouth serial writing.

5

'Westward Ho!'

'A Popularly Successful Book'

During the Crimean War Thackeray, now a great man of letters, made a speech on the condition of literature. The speech, which was probably in reply to a toast, is not recorded but the novelist's notes survive:

Glad to hear literature mentioned at all
book trade frozen up [illegible]
The reason—reality more interesting than novels
The novel heroine and wag
Heroines and heroes what are they compared to the Crimea?[1]

The dispirited tone of these jottings reflects what was a widespread feeling of malaise. After an initial flush of bellicosity the war was not generally popular, nor thought glorious; among other things it was hideously mismanaged and brought about a justified demand for administrative reform. As well as making speeches more powerful than Thackeray's, Dickens was inspired by his sense of governmental bungling to write his most disgusted of novels about English life, *Little Dorrit*, with its parasitic tribe of maladministering Barnacles. In addition the book trade was indeed 'frozen up'. (Thackeray's image, incidentally, is taken from the situation of the British troops stalled outside Sebastopol that winter.) The economic situation was not propitious for either novelist or publisher. In times of distress books, especially novels, were luxuries easily sacrificed. 'With regard to novels', complained Bentley in 1854, 'their sale is now nearly...gone...business is well nigh paralyzed by this cruel war.'[2] Things did not seem much brighter to the practising writer: 'if this war continues', Wilkie Collins noted, 'the prospects of Fiction are likely to be very uncertain to say the least of it'.[3]

One novelist, it would appear, was not inclined to take a jaundiced view. This was the pugnacious rector of Eversley, Charles Kingsley, a man grimly convinced that 'war in some shape or other is the normal condition of the world'.[4] Neither was Kingsley inclined to see fiction as irrelevant or superfluous during this particular war-time. Rather he conceived of the novel as the social tonic the country needed and set about administering it. As chance would have it he was meditating an Elizabethan romance when the hostilities which had long been threatening broke out. This work, which later became *Westward Ho!* was adapted as a stimulus 'to make others fight', and to 'put into people's heads some brave thoughts about the present war'.[5] In an age lacking developed mass communication other than the newspaper the best-selling novel was a handy medium for propaganda of that sort, although to be fully effective such a novel would have to be, as Kingsley realised, 'immediately popular'.

Kingsley was not a born popular novelist. A friend explained the failure of *Westward Ho!*'s predecessor to him in just these terms: 'you fire over the heads of the public...the pigmies of the circulating libraries.'[6] Nor was he at home in Grub Street, or comfortable with its ways. His association with Macmillan's, who were to publish his war novel, had come about through his relationship with the group of high-powered Cambridge intellectuals and dons who formed the nucleus of that house's extremely select early lists, and who gave it its long connection with muscular Christianity and universities. Kingsley had, in fact, written fiction before *Westward Ho!*, but not for them. To other publishers he had proved a difficult novelist to handle, obstinate and prone to pick 'unpleasant' subjects like Chartism or the afflictions of the working class. *Alton Locke*, which was eventually taken by Chapman, had been turned down by his regular publisher. (The Macmillans also saw the manuscript but they apparently did not want it.) As a reputedly rabid socialist tract it enjoyed a certain *succès de scandale*, although it was almost universally deplored by the critics. At an early stage in the negotiations for *Westward Ho!*, however, Macmillan's were assured that their novel would be an apolitical work, safely set in the Elizabethan past.[7] Its ideology was to be one of muscular Christianity, not Christian socialism. Yet it would have the topical appeal necessary for a book to succeed in these war times.

II

The Macmillans began as publishers on £500 working capital borrowed from Archdeacon Hare. In 1855 their firm had been in existence for some dozen years and had never seen fit to publish a novel.[8] Nor had they ever looked like the kind of house who might handle fiction and emphatically not, like Bentley or Bradbury, *popular* fiction. This was a point they were particularly keen to impress on Kingsley. *Westward Ho!* must, they pleaded, be a 'respectable book',—'Don't let it go out like a Minerva press novel.'[9] The bestsellers Macmillan's had handled immediately before *Westward Ho!* were Smith's *Arithmetic*, the Bishop of New Zealand's *Sermons* and Maurice's *Sermons on Sacrifice* (an author who influenced Kingsley considerably). Todhunter's *Treatise on Analytical Statics* took up a lot of office time at this period as did correspondence with clergymen on various topics. Kingsley's preceding work with Macmillan's was the publication of his sanitary reform *Lectures* in 1853. When he had become interested in the scandal of sweat-shop tailoring in the late forties they had published his 4d. pamphlet on the subject (*Cheap Clothes and Nasty*) leaving the sensational novel he wrote on the same subject for Chapman and Hall to bring out.

The character of Macmillan's as formed by the founders' origins and the Cambridge connection was one of high minded religious and educational concern allied with a desire to prosper. 'The Macmillans', their annalist records, 'would serve their God and make their fortune because, as it happened, they believed in both.'[10] On the basis of their first decade's performance one would have guessed them to go on to develop like Bell's, or possibly Chambers', rather than becoming, as they did, a great fiction-publishing concern. Such a move was not to be made lightly: at Cassell's, for example, it was a resigning matter for one of the partners when the publishing of novels became the firm's policy.[11] This is not to say that the Macmillan brothers had anything against novels on principle. They read them and were intelligent critics of them. (Alexander, incidentally, lost his first job with a strict Glasgow bookseller for having a Minerva Press novel about his person.)[12] But caution was the rule in making a decision that would transform the character of the house. The Macmillans' affairs, moreover, were in a delicate state. They were cumbered with an awkward partnership arrangement from which they were trying to free themselves and they were looking forward to the opening of a London branch. With all this in mind it is the more surprising that the suggestion that Kingsley should bring his novel to Macmillan's was their initiative rather than his.[13]

As it turned out the conscientious tone of Macmillan's operations by no means impeded the production of *Westward Ho!* It was a work which came to be nurtured by the evangelical sense of mission which the publishers shared with their author. Their favourite epithet in pushing the novel with booksellers throughout the country was 'spirit stirring' and they were insistent about the 'high moral tone' which was, they urged, 'sure to do good'.[14] On his part, Daniel assured the author: 'we feel sure it will be a right brave and noble book, and do good to England.'[15] The publishers, like the author, were fired with a sense of national emergency: 'we are all fully taken up with Sebastopol here,' wrote Alexander in November, 'it is fearful to think on all the misery this war is causing...we ought to be proud and thankful to our noble army.'[16] Patriotic appeal meant that the Macmillans could fully approve the attempt for mass readership: 'the subject', Daniel predicted, 'will make it more popular than anything [Kingsley] has done before—and I think it will be a better book.'[17] Mass appeal was *Westward Ho!*'s *raison d'être* for it was to use the novel as a form of national communication; 'the whole book', declared Daniel, 'will be reproof enough to the present generation from the statesman to scavenger.'[18]

'Popularity' and 'high moral tone' were thus, for once, mutually uplifting principles. As it happened this mixture of morality and commerce made good business sense in the mood of the times. George Bentley noted in 1854, 'to the excitement attending Russian matters is greatly to be attributed the want of success this season of all works that do not touch upon the war, or on the countries in which it is performing.'[19] But Bentley's reaction was to put in hand a spate of books about Russia, Asia minor and accounts of the War. This was not how Macmillan's played the market. Theirs must be a 'good' book as well as a popular one.

The sense of combined enterprise between novelist and publishers was reinforced by social links. While writing *Westward Ho!* Kingsley became godfather to Alexander's son. He was deeply affected by the failing health of the consumptive Daniel, an unusually loveable man, apparently. Conversely the Macmillans concerned themselves about the illness of Mrs Kingsley that forced the couple to Devon. Novelist and publishers were equally upset at Maurice's losing his professorship (precipitated by the *Theological Essays* which Macmillan's published in 1853). To each other in discussing these and other matters they were 'Dear Kingsley' and 'Dear Macmillan', there was none of the formal sparring that marked the usual novelist-publisher intercourse.

There was, however, more than friendly co-operation behind *Westward Ho!*. It is unlikely that many publishers could have entered wholeheartedly, as did the Macmillans, into the spirit of Kingsley's endeavour. He was not an easy man to be congenial with. As well as a natural prickliness he brought to the historical novel a sense of divine accountability which is, as one looks at it today, terrifying in its intensity. *Westward Ho!* was to be read elsewhere than in English parlours. 'I expect to have every page that I ever penned *reviewed*', wrote Kingsley, 'in a very awful way, when I stand before my Maker in the life to come.' In this he felt a sense of separation, not just from hack romancers like Ainsworth and G. P. R. James, but from the very fountainhead of the nineteenth-century novel, Scott himself:

> He was an honest man at heart—none honester, but the sense of power, the love of fame, and the love of money, allured him to play with truth—to write historical novels which he ought to have known were untrue pictures; and the mischief which Kenilworth, the Abbot, and one or two more have done, is incalculable. But it did not pay him, Sir. The heavens are just—you may laugh at me as superstitious: but if you ask me—why did God let that noble soul end in

ruin and decrepitude—I must answer because he fancied that the great Walter Scott was great enough to play with impunity with the things which *are*, because God has done them, and falsify God's dealings with His people. Mind, Scott was not a bad man: if he had been he would probably have escaped with impunity: but because God loved him (as who would not?) he chastened him, that he might be saved in the day of the Lord.[20]

It is not facetious to say that Kingsley saw his Maker as one of the parties involved in the publishing of *Westward Ho!*—just as He had brought poor Constable to ruin so as to 'chasten' Scott. God, it would seem, had a short way with publishers who brought out books He did not like.

III

These, then, were the preconditions for a joint venture. *Westward Ho!* was concocted between publishers and novelist as a popular, regenerative work of fiction which would inspirit the English people with war readiness. The result of the collaboration was one of the most remarkable bestsellers of the century. For the publishers its success entailed a major change of direction. After *Westward Ho!* Macmillan's became one of the great fiction publishing houses, later going on to handle such writers as Hardy, Hughes, Henry James, Kipling and Morgan. Much of the capital required for expanding, and most of the confidence, must have come from the single success of *Westward Ho!*.

Macmillan's, however, did not rush into this new area. They were not at all sure about *Westward Ho!*'s prospective sales and made up their first printing with truly Scottish canniness. Before giving any order they asked their printer, Clay, to estimate for composition and press work for 1,000, 1,250, 1,750 and 2,000 copies.[21] Finally they went for 1,250, an extremely modest figure by the standards of 1855 and 750 below their own premeditated ceiling. (One may compare this printing with the 1,500 which they ordered at the same time for the second series of Butler's *Sermons.*) Similarly modest was the remuneration offered Kingsley, £300 and £250 on reprinting.[22] This was a quarter of what Thackeray had for *Esmond*, the novel on which, in other respects, Macmillan's modelled *Westward Ho!*.

If they were excessively cautious as regards numbers Macmillan's were, by compensation, unusually energetic in getting the novel launched. Actual bookselling was an area in which they excelled. Alexander, especially, was indefatigable in jollying along booksellers into buying more advance copies at the special rate. He recommended *Westward Ho!*'s regional appeal to Devon retailers, its high moral tone to Scottish. He handled Mudie with the toughness required to get any advantage in dealings with that notoriously sharp businessman:

> Sir,
> 'Westward Ho!' is a work of fiction and a very spirit stirring one it is —just fit for these War Times.
> If you take 300 copies we shall let you have them at *10 percent off-sale* but conditions with the author will not enable us to do better than this. We only allow our agents 5 percent commission. We hope therefore that the 10 percent will meet your wishes.
>
> We remain sir, your respectful servants,
> Macmillan & Co.[23]

Mudie in fact was persuaded to take 350, a third of the first edition, though as Alexander reported, 'he screwed us down a good deal, but we are glad to get so many off at once.'[24] It was probably the Macmillans' first major transaction with the 'Leviathan'.

There was no difficulty in getting the other 900 off. Macmillan's moved the first impression with a despatch Bentley himself would have envied. Two weeks after publication on 5 April 1855, Alexander informed the novelist's wife that 'Westward Ho! is going on very swimmingly. We have sold above 900.'[25] Encouraged by these figures, he was thinking of a reprint in May. With a punctiliousness extremely rare among nineteenth-century publishers, however, Macmillan was against exploiting the market with a low-price edition because a cheap reprint too soon would be unfair to the purchasers of the three-volume edition.[26]

They did not lose much by this scrupulosity. *Westward Ho!* outlasted the war which gave it birth. One is tempted to surmise that its blazing popularity branded it indelibly on the national mind, where it has remained as a kind of folk memory. Until quite recently most schoolboys, many of whom would have had difficulty in saying exactly where the Crimea was, could recite a bit of the Charge of the Light Brigade and tell you something about Amyas Leigh.

Macmillan's believed in what their historian calls 'long-term publishing'—that is steady, long-serving sellers. For them the high sales of *Westward Ho!* (by 'Professor' Kingsley, as they preferred to call him) must have been less gratifying than its stamina as an earner for the house over many decades. The following table shows the novel's remarkable sales career:

February 1855, 3 vols. at 31s. 6d.

May 1855, 3 vols. at 31s. 6d. (750 copies only; a 'few copies' were advertised as left on hand when the third edition came out.)

1857, issued in one vol. at 7s. 6d., reprinted 1861, 1865, 1869 at 6s., 1871, 1872, 1873, 1874, 1875, February and November 1876, March and December 1877, 1878 (sales stimulated by Kingsley's death, 1875), February and November 1879, 1880.

Fourth edn 1881, reprinted seven times by 1889.

6d. edition, 1889, reprinted twice October 1889.[27]

It is small wonder Macmillan's felt pleased with their first novel. And they had a bonus in that the popularity of the muscular Christianity doctrine propagated by *Westward Ho!* boosted the subsequent sales of *Tom Brown's Schooldays* (28,000 in its first four years) and Henry Kingsley's early works.

IV

While writing his novel Kingsley kept in close collaborative touch with his publishers. In February 1854 he wrote them the outline of the projected action:

> The autobiography of a knight of Queen Elizabeth's time, a pet of Grenville and Raleigh, who goes out with Drake to the West Indies, has to do with Caribs, the Inquisition, the Spaniards, and all the rest of it, and finishes by helping to fight the Armada.[28]

By 1 June the work was, he reported, 'complete in my head'.

On 18 June he promised to 'send you some bits in a few days... and I assure you that I shall take advice when given, for it is very important to me to write a popularly successful book'.[29] By July he was sending the Macmillans substantial installments for inspection. Kingsley, who was normally a stiff-necked, proud man, insisted that he was amenable to advice; nay that he welcomed it:

> Pray get any one's opinion you can...I am aiming altogether at popularity, and am willing to alter or expunge wherever aught is likely to hurt the *sale* of the book.[30]

The Macmillans took him at his word. Kingsley was apparently persuaded to drop the autobiographical form in which the first draft was begun. Alexander (always the more outspoken of the brothers) suggested that the egoistic quality of the book should be further reduced by cutting the numerous 'preachments'.[31] Most readers would, I think, see the criticism as just. Kingsley was ever prone to take any halt in the narrative as a wayside pulpit from which to preach on Crimean heroism, sanitary reform or Jesuit malefactions. It was Kingsley's besetting vice. In 1850 he apologised to Chapman about *Alton Locke* on just this weakness in himself: 'I am afraid the book meddles with too many questions—that it is too political here and there, too theological in other places—too—everything at times.'[32] The Macmillans contrived to make *Westward Ho!* a little less 'everything'. He dropped scenes; jointly they decided against the pastiche archaism of *Esmond*'s presentation—the obsolete idiom and old-fashioned looking print might, they thought, work against the book's 'popularity'. (They took the trouble to enquire of Thackeray himself on this point.)[33] As Kingsley despatched his manuscript piecemeal to Macmillan's, Macmillan's despatched it piecemeal to Clay. This 'feeding the printer' is another indication of the high degree of trust that existed between parties. Bentley, for example, resolutely refused to 'embark my capital upon a book which may possibly never be completed'.[34]

The conveyor belt mode of production meant that the period between first thoughts and printed text was short; under the year saw it complete. (The actual composition of *Westward*

Ho!'s quarter of a million words took only seven months.) Haste and Kingsley's 'plan of printing as we go on'[35] led to the suspicion that the work was perhaps patchy. Daniel complained mildly of what looked like 'chasms in the text'. Kingsley reassured him that 'the gaps...are physical only, and come from my habit of writing a bit here and a bit there.'[36] It seems to have satisfied the brothers. There was no real objection by them against the hasty provision of copy. They appreciated the urgency of the work and the need to take time by the forelock. *Westward Ho!* might easily find itself an anachronism if events on the battlefield overtook it. Together with Kingsley the publishers 'kicked up'[37] Clay ('that snail' as the novelist called him), bullying him into faster printing. Even so Kingsley was disappointed. He had hoped to get the novel out at first by Christmas, then by January (i.e. from first penstroke to bookseller's window in six months).

In general, publishers of novels, unlike publishers of journals, do not like this kind of pressure since it leads to errors both of judgement and production; there are optimum times of the year to publish (January 1855 was not one of them)[38] and very few novels are the worse for careful preparation. As it was Macmillan's suffered from not having time to sort out copyright affairs and so forestall the inevitable 'Yankee dodges'. The unorthodox process of writing and printing in tandem made casting off impossible and resulted in over-running which was not pleasant for Macmillan's at a time of economic stringency. (*Westward Ho!* came out 60,000 words longer than *Esmond*, itself a substantial three-decker.)

V

Westward Ho! undoubtedly benefited from the moderating effect of the Macmillans' collaboration but it remains very much an idiosyncratic novel, propelled by Kingsley's phobias, enthusiasms and shifting moods. Many readers found the ferment of propaganda, muscular Christianity, chauvinism and emotional extremism repellent. Above all the pathology of the work is distasteful. Its violence offended the first readers, the Macmillans, and Alexander complained:

Couldn't you leave out two incidents.
1. Amyas' breaking poor old Brimblecombe's scull—excuse me but it does not look like the act of a brave boy to hurt a poor old man even though he was a dominie and
2. Old Salterne's beating his daughter.
—they are the fly in the ointment to me. I daresay I am squeamish.[39]

For many others they have also proved the fly in the ointment. The scene Alexander mentions bears quoting at length in support of his objection:

The old gentleman jumped up, ferula in hand, and darted across the school, and saw himself upon the fatal slate.

'Proh flagitium! what have we here, villain?' and in clutching at his victim, he raised the cane. Whereupon with a serene and cheerful countenance, up rose the mighty form of Amyas Leigh, a head and shoulders above his tormentor, and that slate descended on the bald coxcomb of Sir Vindex Brimblecombe, with so shrewd a blow that slate and pate cracked at the same instant, and the poor pedagogue dropped to the floor (II).

When she hears what her son has done Amyas's mother can 'hardly help laughing' and Sir Richard 'laughed till he cried'. Kingsley's description of the assault is like the act itself, callously 'cheerful'. (One notes the facetious assonance and alliteration.) Whenever Amyas's juvenile boisterousness is introduced the narrative tone assumes an approving heartiness in this way. The early parts of the novel abound in cracked sconces, broken bones and lusty buffets all handled in this same falsetto jollity.

Worse is the physical violence of the middle and later sections where Kingsley concentrates on the tortures and rapine the Spaniards inflict on their Indian and heretic victims. Kingsley's narrative comes alive with suspicious metaphorical vividness when he describes scars left by the strapado, the galleys 'with their sickening musky smell, as of a pack of kennelled hounds' (XX), death by slow burning or the description of Spaniards using Indians as human bearers:

three or four drivers, armed with whips, lingered up and down the slowly staggering file of Indians, and avenged every moment's lagging, even every stumble, by a blow of the cruel manati-hide, which cracked like a pistol-shot against the naked limbs of the silent and uncomplaining victim (xxv).

(By the kind of contradiction that never seems to have bothered Kingsley, *Westward Ho!* was dedicated to Rajah Brooke, himself notorious for maltreating natives under his governorship.)

Often it requires no great penetrative power to detect an ambivalence towards violence in Kingsley. Following the description quoted above, for example, one of the Indian porters falls, is beaten and when he cannot be tormented into going on his Spanish master steps back, flourishes his 'toledo blade' and brings it down 'not on the chain, but on the wrist which it fettered. There was a shriek—a crimson flash—and the chain and its prisoner were parted.' At the time when he wrote this Kingsley was confiding to Hughes: 'Oh for one hour's skirmishing in those Inkerman ravines, and five minutes butt and bayonet as a bonne bouche to finish with.'[40] Is he, one wonders in *Westward Ho!*, with Amyas in ambush watching in horror or with the Spaniard slashing mercilessly at his victim?

It would be dishonest to claim that the work is less readable for its 'sanguinary' elements. There are more than enough rosewater Victorian novels. But it hardly accords with some of Kingsley's pronouncements about 'brave thoughts'. Undoubtedly too the violence of *Westward Ho!* accounted for much of its success with first readers and its subsequent popularity with schoolboys. As Trollope put it 'the artist who paints for the million must use glaring colours.'[41] Blood red was one of the more effective tints on the novelist's palette in 1855.

While considering the novel's shortcomings, one should also note that it is not a masterpiece of construction. The breakneck provision of copy took a heavy toll in terms of organisation. Macmillan's were worried continuously about 'proportion' and as late as October they were unsure about 'the shape and type and number of volumes'.[42] Kingsley's view on the matter was 'when one is going the pace, one cannot always *stop to see how it all looks*... and a good deal was left as it ran out of the tap.'[43] To protect international copyright it was necessary to have a title but for a long time everyone was ignorant as to whether the book was to be named after the hero 'or by some fancy name'.[44] This reflects an uncertainty about just what the centre of action was to be. In the first volume Amyas is offstage for long periods and distantly handled in the narrative. In the second and third volumes the author is increasingly inward with the hero and for these sections 'Amyas Leigh' would not have been an inappropriate title.

There are other disproportions in the novel. Kingsley seemed strangely reluctant to take his narrative to sea, probably because he had not finished his research into nautical history. Hence not until chapter 17 do we follow Amyas on board ship. The early chapters in Devon, although they contain some fine descriptive passages, retard the action. In this early section the narrative tap flows at very low pressure, with digressions, inset narratives and verbose shows at style. It is not until the half-way mark that the abduction of Rose gets the main plot line underway. This was a serious dereliction; library readers demanded a lively first volume to induce them to order the other two. (Thackeray noted as the novel's shortcoming that the first volume was 'too prolix'.)[45] Early dilatoriness exacts a heavy price later on when the build-up to the Armada battle has to be cramped into one chapter. ('We always require a little dodging at the end of a story' Kingsley once told his publisher consolingly.)[46]

Shapeliness was further hindered by the writer's hobby-horsical tendencies which, although they could lessen, the Macmillans could not altogether bridle. Kingsley the preacher, essayist, social scientist and biologist constantly distract the novelist in him. He is forever likely to launch into a description of what the jellyfish are doing below the wave while Briton fights Don above, or while in the tropics to give an incidental disquisition on the ceiba tree, the Areca palm, Guazu-puti deer or pirai fish. Amyas's quest is suspended while the author lashes out at 'shallow anthropologic theories' that suggest man is descended from 'some sort of two-handed apes' (XXIV). More forgivable in terms of the novel's originating impulse are the frequent interventions of Alma, Balaclava, and Inkerman and such instructions as he gives the authorities on the 'simple laws' (XXI) of preventing cholera epidemics among serving troops. And Kingsley is nothing if not generous in the sideshows he offers the reader. As well as the Crimean enemy he loses no opportunity to counterattack papal aggression, and anti-jesuit tirades are numerous, as are Jesuit bogeymen incorporated into the action. In *Westward Ho!* the war lust of 1854 is combined with the sectarian paranoia of 1851 to keep the novelist's blood up during the narrative.

As time went on it needed some keeping up. The novel was begun in a heady war excitement which seems to have infected the whole country:

> ...the people were intoxicated. Memories of past victories went to their heads, the names of Waterloo and Trafalgar were on every lip, crowds paraded the streets delirious with excitement, inflated with national pride. 'When people are inflamed in that way they are no better than mad dogs,' wrote Cobbett; and so in March 1854, shouting, cheering, singing the nation swept into war.[47]

And Kingsley swept into his novel celebrating the martial and manly virtues of Elizabeth's glorious reign. He began writing with 'virulence' and the first half of the novel is, as the novelist called it, 'wolfish'—a fierce exultation of physical force. In July Kingsley reported that he had a hundred pages of manuscript and in September that the work was half written and three-parts done in the rough.[48] Amyas's expedition to the Caribbean was thus composed simultaneously with the allies' invasion of the Crimea in August. Between summer 1854 and February 1855 when all copy was finally delivered there intervened the glorious victory at Alma, the dubious successes at Balaclava and Inkerman and the terrible winter siege of Sebastopol. At this time opinion in Britain began to be influenced by an entirely new factor; the Crimean war was the first to be journalistically reported (notably by Delane's *Times* which sent William Howard Russell to the front). The eyewitness accounts, printed in the daily press, let the British Public know for the first time what a modern war was like, and in this case how ineffectively it was being run. The cumulative result was first to contradict, finally to annihilate the heady martial afflatus which we find in the early pages of *Westward Ho!*

As the winter drew on Kingsley's spirits fell. 'I am a poor queasy, hysterical half baked sort of fellow,' he complained in

October. The book he felt, was 'only half as good...as I could have written and only one hundredth as good...as ought to be written on the matter.'[49] In December as he was finishing his gloominess darkened even further: 'I have been all but stopped the last fortnight...whether what remains to be done will be as good as what has been done, I know not, so poorly am I.'[50] This dejection mixes oddly with the brash militarism of the 'Battle Pieces' which Kingsley turned out for Macmillan's in February while writing the last stages of the novel. On the whole one is inclined to believe the private sentiment rather than the public: Kingsley was always prone to whistle in the dark.

Kingsley was oppressed by a number of worries as he completed the novel. He was extremely short of money. (He needed the sale of a second edition, he told Macmillan, 'to pay my bills'.)[51] He was bereaved in February. Above all 'the Crimean War weighed on him like a nightmare.'[52] When he had first thought of the work in February 1854 it was as a celebration of Elizabethan virility. The war, which began in the same month and the naval successes in March filled Kingsley with a fierce 'joy'. When Kingsley finished the novel all joy was spent; the Allies were still in stalemate outside Sebastopol and were to remain there until summer. The furore over the charge of the Light Brigade and Raglan's handling of the war was growing. It was no longer the time for brave thoughts.

Kingsley's growing sense of uncertainty is accompanied by a complication of his hero. From being a simple, healthy male animal with a 'monocular' view of the universe, Amyas is warped by the lust for vengeance into a tormented, baffled giant. The most powerful moment in the novel is when he stands, *Amyas agonistes*, watching Guzman snatched by the storm from his vengeance and is betrayed into cursing God:

> 'Shame!' cried Amyas, hurling his sword far into the sea, 'to lose my right, my right! when it was in my very grasp! Unmerciful!'
>
> A crack which rent the sky, and made the granite ring and quiver; a bright world of flame, and then a blank of utter darkness, against which stood out, glowing red-hot, every mast and sail, and rock, and Salvation Yeo as he stood just in front of Amyas, the tiller in his hand. All red-hot, transfigured into fire; and behind the black, black night (XXXII).

Edward Fitzgerald's comment on this moment in the novel voices an admiration which many, otherwise antipathetic to Kingsley, must feel:

I think a really *sublime* thing is the end of Kingsley's *Westward Ho!* (which I never could read through). The Chase of the Ships: the Hero's being struck blind at the moment of revenge; then his being taken to *see* his rival and crew at the bottom of the sea. Kingsley is a distressing writer to me, but I must think this (the inspiration of it) of a piece with Homer and the Gods.[53]

As is often the case, mixed, unresolved emotions in the author produce fiction greater than any simple-minded certainty could have done. Had the Allies marched on from Alma to capture Sebastopol and enforced peace by spring 1855, *Westward Ho!* would doubtless all have been of a piece with its first volume, a brazen glorying in the physical power that imposed England's sovereign will on lesser peoples. As it is, Amyas, the blind impotent warrior, may well have reflected the mixed feeling of the nation about the indeterminate war in spring 1855, just as Amyas, proud and omnipotent, embodied the national mood of the previous spring.

Kingsley and the Macmillans had their 'popularly successful book' although it finally turned out to be rather different from what was foreseen. Macmillan's, moreover, had set the pattern for many more popular and successful books to come out under their name.

6

Trollope
Making the First Rank

The longest and most hazardous step for any Victorian novelist was that which took him out of the second into the first rank of fiction. For a few, like Charlotte Brontë or Dickens, the elevation happened overnight: they woke and found themselves famous. For most it meant a years-long slog in which luck, talent, pertinacity and ruthlessness all played a part. In this chapter we examine Trollope and his publishers over the crucial years 1858–60 which saw his rewards rise from a few hundred per novel to the £4,500 a year which he averaged during the twelve years of his zenith. Only two other novelists, Dickens and George Eliot, equalled the consistent magnitude of this income, and they were geniuses. Trollope was not and knew he was not. Moreover his achievement was made without any runaway successes like *Pickwick* or *Adam Bede*. Trollope never received more than £3,200 for a single novel and probably none of his works sold more than 30,000 copies in book form.[1] Any number of novelists could claim higher figures than these, but very few managed to keep up with Trollope over the years. It can hardly be said that he had a secret of success since in his *Autobiography* he went out of his way to publicise his working methods as aggressively as he could. Nonetheless by looking closely at these formative years, in which his character as a novelist was cast, one sees the emergence of the *modus operandi* by which Trollope raised himself to equal the greatest writers of the age.

In 1859 Trollope began what promised to be an ambitious novel. He had been a post-office employee in Ireland during that country's unhappiest years, 1845–7 when two millions of the native population were either starved to death or driven to emigration. Trollope decided to use this national catastrophe as the background to his new work, *Castle Richmond*. It was matter that no other major author had had either the temerity or the competence to tackle in fiction. The materials lay about Trollope who was still in Ireland at this date, though by now his tour of duty with the G.P.O. was coming to an end and he was preparing for the move back to England.

Trollope engaged 'to deliver the MS. of the work complete by the end of March 1860'[2] in return for which Chapman and Hall had undertaken to pay him £600. It was a comfortable enough arrangement by mid-century standards, though by no means exceptional. Nonetheless Trollope must have been pleased with himself when he signed the agreement in August 1859. His rise to this respectable income bracket had been gradual and anything but inexorable. His first novel, *The Macdermots of Ballycloran* had netted nothing and the bulk of its 400 copies was pulped.[3] Its successor, *The Kellys and The O'Kellys*, not only failed to make money (196 of its 375 copies were left on hand), it earned its author a letter from Henry Colburn solemnly advising the tyro not 'to proceed in novel writing'. He proceeded with *La Vendée*, a historical romance and another dud. Trollope, who later wrote a thousand-page story in praise of 'doggedness' soldiered on with *The Warden*. This short pilot for the Barchester series returned a moderate success: 'the novel reading world', he recalled, 'did not go mad about *The Warden*; but I soon felt that it had not failed as the others had failed.'[4] One reason for its relative success was that Longman's were prepared to put a larger stake on the novelist's chances of success—1,000 copies as opposed to the 500 or less that previous publishers had ventured. This gave *The Warden* a chance to get through to discriminating readers.

Another reason was its unassuming subject matter. In his first three abortive novels Trollope's strategy had been clear enough. He was aiming at a large market by exploiting cataclysmic current events. The first two Irish novels were written in the terrible aftermath of the potato famine. Their topicality was realised by Colburn who wrote in March 1848 of the *O'Kellys*: 'considering the work is illustrative of Irish society, it should appear as soon as it could be printed.'[5] *La Vendée*, a novel about the first French Revolution was written shortly after the second in 1848, a social convulsion which shook the whole of Europe and about which Carlyle waxed terribly lyrical in his *Latter-Day Pamphlets*. In the event it was not with these novels of great social and historical affairs that Trollope struck public acclaim but a short narrative of quiet, provincial, ecclesiastical infighting.

The Warden was followed by a sequel, *Barchester Towers*; this related Barsetshire novel notched up another small increment of success and remuneration. It was nothing startling in the way of *Pickwick*, *Adam Bede* or *Vanity Fair* but increasingly comfortable to both author and publisher. Trollope was on his way. Next came *The Three Clerks*, a story of the trials of a young man in the civil service. More comic than anything he had hitherto attempted it achieved a respectable sale. Trollope followed it with another Barsetshire novel, *Doctor Thorne*, which also did well.

These three moderate successes were followed by a social satire, *The Bertrams*. 'It failed', Trollope reports bleakly in his *Autobiography*.[6] This then is the account as it stood between novelist and the publishers in 1859; the figures are taken from the novelist's own table, drawn up in later life:[7]

	By whom published	*on what date*	*what terms*	*what money received*
The Macdermots of Ballycloran Novel, 3 vols.	Newby	1846	Half profits	No proceeds
The Kellys and The O'Kellys Novel, 3 vols.	Colburn	1848	Half profits	No proceeds
La Vendée Novel, 3 vols.	Colburn	1850	Half profits with £20 paid in advance	£20—on publication

	By whom published	*on what date*	*what terms*	*what money received*
The Warden Novel, 1 vol.	Longman	1855	Half profits	In 1856 £9 8s. 8d.
Barchester Towers Novel, 3 vols.	Longman	1857	Half profits £100 to be paid in advance	In 1857 £100
The Three Clerks Novel, 3 vols.	Bentley	Nov. 1857	sold out and out	£250 Dec. 1857
Dr Thorne Novel, 3 vols.	Chapman and Hall	May 1858	sold out and out	£400 May 1858
The Bertrams Novel, 3 vols.	Chapman and Hall	March 1859	sold for three years and half possession	£400 March 1859

As well as a somewhat indecisive advance in his profession this ten year run up to *Castle Richmond* reveals a notable artistic restlessness. By 1859 Trollope had tried his hand at Irish, historical, English rural, institutional and metropolitan settings. He had written thesis novels, comedies, romances, satires and, on the side, travel journals and guide books, a play and a novel-length critique of English society, *The New Zealander*, which defies categorisation. Now with *Castle Richmond* he was going into the social problem novel. On the evidence it is safe to assume that after fifteen years of writing Trollope had yet to find his groove.

Nor it would seem, had he found a publisher who agreed with him. Trollope is the most nomadic of the great Victorian novelists. On the title pages of his novels sixteen different publishers' names are to be found, evidence of the restless relationship he enjoyed with the trade during his long career. It was usual for novelists, once they had made a name for themselves, to settle down to long-term relationships with one particular house. Trollope, however, made no such alliance during his career.

Looking at the table of early publications the obvious place for such an alliance to be formed was with Longman's, or Bentley—both of whom handled promisingly popular works by the young novelist. The process by which these houses lost him to Chapman and Hall, and Chapman and Hall went on to lose him to Smith, Elder throws some interesting light on the way business was done at the period and, more particularly, how Trollope liked to do business—which was not always the same thing.

We may begin in 1857. Buoyed up by the moderately encouraging reception of his Barchester novels, Trollope offered Longman's the copyright of *The Three Clerks* for two hundred advance and half profits (i.e. twice what he had obtained for *Barchester Towers*). Longman's were an extremely prudent firm. (They had even found parts of *The Warden* too 'strong' and the innocuous *Barchester Towers* too 'warm' and wanted it radically changed.) *The Three Clerks* was satirical, it attacked some aspects of the civil service and introduced identifiable personalities. The public was still reeling from the shock waves of Dickens's *Little Dorrit* and its satire on the 'Circumlocution Office'. Dickens's impertinence had been bitterly repudiated by Fitzjames Stephen in the *Edinburgh Review*, a journal with which Longman's had the strongest connections.

Longman's did not see the manuscript but they probably got wind of its contents. Anyway they seemed disinclined to be enthusiastic and offered Trollope a paltry £100 advance. Trollope's reply was typically uncompromising:

> I am sure you do not regard £100 as adequate payment for a 3 vol. novel. Of course an unsuccessful novel may be worth much less—worth indeed less than nothing. And it may very likely be that I cannot write a successful novel, but if I cannot obtain moderate success I will give over, and leave the business alone. I certainly will not willingly go on working at such a rate of pay.[8]

Trollope could scarcely not have known when he made his modest claim that Longman's had lavished £20,000 on Macaulay in March 1856, on account for the second two volumes of the *History of England*. However this might be Longman's were not going to be dictated to by an obscure novelist. They intimated to Trollope that Longman's name on his title page was reward in itself. Trollope demurred and broke off his connection with the firm.

The novelist then went with his manuscript to the office of the lesser publisher, Hurst and Blackett. He waited there in vain for one of the partners who did not bother to keep an appointment with an unimportant novelist. The occasion is immortalised by the comment of one of the firm's employees filling time with an enquiry about the work in question: 'I hope it's not historical Mr Trollope...Whatever you do, don't be historical; your historical novel is not worth a damn'.[9]

Meeting with no success in this quarter Trollope went to Richard Bentley in New Burlington Street where he finally found a buyer prepared to pay his price (in ready money). Bentley had the novel 'for his sole use and benefit'[10] in return for £250, payable in two months' time. Trollope's only concern subsequently was for the way in which the money was to be delivered. Bentley's note of hand was, he decided rather unflatteringly, preferable to a banker's draft. He does not seem to have cared what Bentley did with his new property after the purchase price had been paid over in the form he desired.

The Three Clerks was by no means a failure. Of the first 1,000, 710 were sold straight off. Bentley enquired about *Barchester Towers*—did Trollope, he wondered, have the copyright of that work? But he was wary a few months later when Trollope demanded £400 (the demand had again been nearly doubled) for the absolute copyright of his present work, *Dr Thorne*. The publisher decided he must consult his ledgers. At this point the two men seem to have been temperamentally at odds. Bentley expected intricate dealing, scheme and tactic. Trollope passionately preferred straightforwardness, even if it cost him money. Bentley, after the first interview sent the following letter to the novelist, reversing what had clearly been a hopeful discussion in which, evidently, the £400 was practically assured:

Jan. 25 1858

Dear Sir

To my regret I find I miscalculated the extent of sale of the 'Three Clerks.' The sale of that work will not enable me to give more than £300 for the new story. To give more would leave me wholly without profit. I send this off at once that you should be informed of this without delay. Yours faithfully, R.B.[11]

Now in this letter Bentley was simply feinting. According to his own figures he had made some £74 on *The Three Clerks* which seems modest enough when Trollope wanted an extra £150. But the reason that the profit was so low was that he had desired to get a quick sale, and so had sold Mudie's 500 copies, a month or so earlier, for the knock-down price of 12s. a three-volume copy. On the face of it this was a very strange piece of business indeed. Bentley's costs for the manufacture and advertising of the first edition of 1,000 were; £268 16s. 3d. plus £63 7s. 8d. If one adds to this the author's fee of £250 one ends up with a per copy cost of a shadow under 12s. Bentley, in other words, after he had paid package, carriage and production overhead was losing money on the deal. And a novel published on 30 November would hardly have seemed ripe for remaindering in December.

It was not such a suicidal move as it might have seemed. Bentley wanted to clear the three-volume edition so quickly in order to get on to the cheap reprints. Since Trollope had given him the novel unconditionally there was a killing to be made in this form. Just how big a killing may be gathered from the fact that in January 1859 he brought out a one-volume *Three Clerks* for 5s. In March 1860 he brought out a 3s. 6d. edition. In 1865 it was profitable to bring out a 6s. version and thereafter the cheap edition was reprinted in 1866, 1872, 1874, 1878, 1883 and 1890.[12] From none of these (some 8,000 copies in all) did Trollope get a single penny. Forty years later, when Bentley's were being wound up, the copyright still had a residual value of £125, half what the publisher originally paid.

Bentley evidently got a dusty answer from Trollope to his offer of 25 January. According to the novelist he came down to the G.P.O. to see him in person which argues a certain interest. And on the 27th he made a radically improved bid:

Dear Sir

I am willing to give for the copyright of [the] new work of fiction Dr. Thorne in three vols. the sum of Four Hundred and Fifty Pounds in manner following:

£300 on going to press with an edition of 1250 copies, £50 more on sale of this edition and £100 on going to press with another edition.

Yours faithfully, R.B.[13]

What happened next is not entirely clear. According to Trollope he turned down Bentley's offer out of hand, even though it had been raised 50 per cent in two days. He was not going to be played with by any publisher. Once more he took to the streets with his manuscript and flounced down to Piccadilly. The 'same afternoon' he sold the novel to Edward Chapman, the good natured publisher looking at the infuriated novelist 'as he might have done at a highway robber who had stopped him on Hounslow Heath'.[14] The agreement, signed on 29 January, precisely identifies the novelist's transitional stature at this stage in his career, the extent and limitations of his power with publishers:

Memorandum of Agreement...for the publishing of a novel by Anthony Trollope in three volumes to be called Dr. Thorne. Mr. Trollope engages to deliver the MS. of volumes 1 and 2 complete for the press by the middle of March next, and the MS. of the third volume by the middle of April, and to sell the copyright and all the rights attaching thereto at home and abroad for the sum of Four Hundred Pounds.

Mr. Chapman engages to pay the sum of £400 for the entire copyright on the fifteenth day of May 1858, and to bring the work out as early in May as can be accomplished.[15]

Trollope's growing power is indicated by the fact that he could prospect by selling a novel in this way while it was still on the stocks. (*Dr Thorne* was something over half written in January.) Four hundred pounds was a good sum. Not long before Trollope had been working for a quarter of that, per annum, at the Post Office. On the other hand he had been obliged to attend in person at Chapman and Hall's office. Personal salesmanship was not required of the great novelists. The way in which a writer at the top of the tree did business with Chapman and Hall is evident from the kind of lordly summons sent by Lytton:

Sir Edward Bulwer Lytton presents his Compts. to Messrs Chapman and Hall, and would be glad to have some conversation with either of these gentlemen on Thursday next about eleven O'clock, if not inconvenient to pass this way about that hour.

19 James St. Buckmn. Gate. April 26 1846[16]

Trollope's relatively subordinate position is further indicated by the fact that *Dr Thorne* is so named in the contract. This implies that the work had been subject to some kind of verbal definition and physical examination before the parties agreed on terms. In the palmy time soon to come, when Trollope could command his terms, specification would be as vague as in the agreement signed on 3 July 1860 '...for the publishing of a serial to be completed in twenty monthly parts'.[17] (It is a measure of the distance covered between 1857 and 1860 that Trollope had £2,500 for 10,000 copies of this work, which turned out to be *Orley Farm*.)

One notes in the *Dr Thorne* agreement that Trollope was bound by an inspection clause. Trollope was to submit two volumes by March for Chapman to ensure that the work was in order. In this and other respects the novelist was held to firm dates and ones which would hurry him along. A volume a month was brisk going, even by his standards. Moreover much of it had to be written on board ship during a stormy voyage to Egypt on official business by a traveller who discovered himself prone to sea sickness. Nonetheless he managed, as always, to deliver the goods and Chapman paid over the £400 on May 15.

Dr Thorne was, as has been said, a middling success and encouraged an improvement in the terms Chapman and Hall gave for *The Bertrams*. Trollope again had £400, but he was also allowed joint ownership of the copyright after three years.[18] *Castle Richmond*'s contract was drawn up on the same lines as those for *Dr Thorne* and *The Bertrams* with the exception that Trollope succeeded in jacking the remuneration up once more, this time to £600—partly on the strength of some free publicity which he gained from controversy over his book on the *West*

Indies which had just come out. All in all 1859 was a good year for the novelist; a second edition of *The Bertrams* came out at 31s. 6d., a fourth edition of *Dr Thorne* at 5s., a new edition of the *Kellys* at 5s., a new edition of *The Three Clerks* at 5s., a new edition of *The Warden* at 3s. 6d. and a second edition of *The West Indies* at 15s. Trollope was everywhere in the bookshops, libraries and trade lists. And he was beginning to acquire the professional reputation which was later to become a legend. In its issue of 15 October 1859 the *Publishers' Circular* wondered at the energy of 'the most industrious of post-office officials and the most prolific of novelists'.

Chapman and Hall's offer of £600 was Trollope's most considerable reward yet. The gross sum indicates that he had now attained some standing in his profession. So do certain other details in the contract. The space for the amount to be paid, for instance, was left blank by the copying clerk and filled in later in a different ink. The author's ability to negotiate terms in the office testifies to a growing independence of publisher's dictation.

It is conceivable that given success with *Castle Richmond* Trollope might have gone on to become a novelist of social conscience and he might have formed a long-standing alliance with Chapman and Hall. But circumstances intervened. On 23 October 1859 he floated the idea of some short stories he had written for Smith's and Thackeray's new periodical, the *Cornhill*, which was due to come out in January 1860. Twenty pounds each was what he had in mind for these modest pieces. To his surprise Thackeray put himself out to write back a charmingly flattering letter to the younger novelist. To his fellow editor Smith he scribbled a note: 'I will write to Trollope saying how we want to have him—you on your side please write offering the cash.'[19] And as it happened he had made his application at a critical moment. Thackeray it appeared was unable to come through with the necessary front-running serial and time was getting very short. Trollope, who had merely been scouting for some work on the side, found himself offered the chance of opening the splendid new magazine with a full-length work. It was the chance of a lifetime. Six months later and the *Cornhill* would have no more use for Trollope than for any other £600-a-novel writer. 'It was', he realised, 'my readiness that was needed, rather than any other gift.'[20]

Typically Smith despatched to Trollope an immediate bid of £1,000 for a three-volume-sized novel, sight unseen, the first part to be delivered for publication in six weeks. This, of course, clashed with *Castle Richmond*, the work in progress for Chapman and Hall demanded in March next. It must have been a moment of keen introspection for Trollope. His three contracts with Chapman and Hall indicated that his star was in the ascendant. If it kept rising at the present rate he might expect £750 or so from them for his next work. But the offer from Smith would carry him straight into the top flight of novelists. One hundred thousand copies of his novel would be sold with the *Cornhill*, he would earn an initial £1,000 with more to come. These were temptingly large and round figures, the kind Thackeray and Dickens dealt in. But to accept Smith's offer might mean breaking faith with Chapman and Hall. Even a novelist of Trollope's stamina might find it hard going to produce two full-length novels by the new year, earn his £800 per annum at the G.P.O. and move house.

Thackeray's praise was pleasant to Trollope. Pleasant too was Smith's money: 'the price...was more than double what I had yet received, and nearly double that which I was about to receive from Messrs Chapman and Hall.'[21] This seems to have decided it. Trollope accepted Smith's offer, apparently without any great feelings of guilt. He must have known, however, that it might be impossible to fulfil both contracts to the best of his ability, and that he might have to give one of his employers inferior goods or delayed service. It need not be assumed, on the other hand, that he was merely mercenary and selling out to the highest bidder. He was almost certainly swayed by Smith and Thackeray's carefully diplomatic handling and the implicit artistic recognition in their overtures. The tone of their address to the as yet undistinguished, if hardly fledgeling, novelist may be gathered from the opening of Smith's letter and its almost oriental courtesy:

Dear Sir,

Mr. Thackeray having informed us that we might hope for your cooperation in our new Magazine if we could make satisfactory business arrangements with you, we have the pleasure of addressing you on the subject.[22]

This was very different from waiting attendance in publishers' offices and making small talk with the clerks.

Protocol weighed with Trollope. It had, for example, been a point of honour with him to squeeze £100 advance from Longman's for *Barchester Towers*—not because he needed the money but because he felt it was due to him as a professional entitlement: 'It seems to me', he wrote, 'that if a three vol. novel be worth anything it must be worth that.'[23] For the same reason he had been mortally affronted by the indignities of the half-profits system inflicted on him by his early publishers. Now, at last, he was being treated as a novelist of his abilities should be.

II

Having accepted Smith's offer Trollope at first fondly hoped that he could simply transfer the half-finished *Castle Richmond* to his new paymaster. Chapman and Hall, good natured as ever, agreed to waive their interest; Trollope might break his contract with them if he wished. Smith, however, had other ideas. The *Cornhill*, with its 100,000 circulation and family readership, was not interested in such strong meat as *Castle Richmond*.[24] Starving Irishmen might do very well for social problem novels of the hungry forties, they would not do for the *Cornhill* in 1860. Smith wanted a new novel and 'suggested the church as though it were my peculiar subject'. His suggestion was accompanied by 'some interesting little details' as to payment which Trollope found particularly persuasive. 'The details were so interesting', he reports, 'that had a couple of archbishops been demanded I should have produced them.'[25] Cash, as always, spoke eloquently with Trollope. He therefore undertook the heroic task of bringing out a three-volume novel for each publisher.

Smith's account of the crucial interview is slightly contradictory as to details but worth quoting for the stress it puts on the power of his money and the way in which he would use it to overwhelm an author:

Trollope came to see me and naturally asked what was my scale of payment. I replied that we had no fixed scale for such works as his; would he mind telling me what was the largest sum he had ever received for a novel? when he mentioned £500, I offered him double the amount if he would write one of his clerical novels for the *Cornhill*. He at first proposed to give me an Irish novel which he had on the stocks, but to this I demurred; an Irish novel would not suit my public. His genius shone in delineating clerical life and character, and I wanted a clerical novel. The result was *Framley Parsonage* which proved an attraction in the *Cornhill* and had a large sale afterwards.[26]

Smith had his finger on the public pulse. Publishing lists of 1859–60 reveal that there was a small vogue for clerical novels in this period. (Mrs Oliphant was soon to ride to success on the same vogue with her Carlingford novels.) Smith seems to have realised what generations of later readers have confirmed—that Trollope's 'genius' was for the chronicles of Hardings, Proudies and Grantlys. The publisher's intuition was vindicated when *Castle Richmond* made its appearance and despite Trollope's best efforts 'certainly was not a success'. *Framley Parsonage*, by contrast, after a successful run in the *Cornhill* went on to sell mightily for Smith. It was still doing well in a 2s. 6d. edition when Trollope repossessed it in 1878. Also vindicated was Trollope's opportunism. Had he reluctantly declined Smith's offer on the ground that he had a prior engagement with Chapman he might never have got beyond £600 a novel, or have struck the vein of popularity which made him a rich man and the leading novelist of the 1860s. As it was he won himself a pleasant bonus for fulfilling both contracts to his employers' satisfactions. He had £600 from Chapman and £1,000 from Smith and through the convivial *Cornhill* table he had an *entrée* to the literary world of London, an inestimable asset in furthering his career over the subsequent years. From this point his place in the first rank was assured. Chapman gave him £2,500 for his next novel (ten times what Bentley had paid for *The Three Clerks*, and 125 times what Colburn had advanced for *La Vendée*). Having attained this level of earning Trollope did not drop below it for the next ten years.

III

How did he do it? Trollope has left a graphic record in the work schedules he drew up for the period. We can make a precise quantitative account of what it meant for the novelist to take on two three-deckers in nine months. The figures below are abstracted from the calendars he drew up for himself and religiously fulfilled.

2 August: agreement with Chapman for *Castle Richmond*
4–10 August: 84 pages *Castle Richmond*
11–17 August: 84 pages *Castle Richmond*
18–24 August: 32 pages *Castle Richmond*
25–31 August: 78 pages *Castle Richmond*
1 September–29 October: 'Pyrenees, Five Tales.' These were the tales Trollope offered Smith for the *Cornhill*.
23 October: Trollope writes to Thackeray about the tales.
26 October: Smith writes back, offering £1,000 for a full-length novel.
2–7 November: 38 pages *Framley Parsonage*
3 November: agreement with Smith for *Framley Parsonage*
8–14 November: 70 pages *Framley Parsonage*. Tells Smith the title for the first time.
15–21 November: 84 pages *Framley Parsonage*
22–8 November: 17 pages *Framley Parsonage*. Trollope in England to hand over the first number.
29 November–5 December: 51 pages *Framley Parsonage*
6–12 December: 44 pages *Framley Parsonage*
13–19 December: 52 pages *Framley Parsonage*
20–3 December: 28 pages *Framley Parsonage*
8 Numbers written, i.e. half the novel.
Leaves Ireland to settle in Waltham Cross.
29 December–4 January: 30 pages *Castle Richmond*. First number of *Framley Parsonage* published.
5–11 January: 45 pages *Castle Richmond*
12–18 January: 45 pages *Castle Richmond*
19–25 January: 49 pages *Castle Richmond*
26 January–1 February: 46 pages *Castle Richmond*. Second number of *Framley Parsonage* published.

2–8 February: 45 pages *Castle Richmond*
9–15 February: 40 pages *Castle Richmond*
16–22 February: 44 pages *Castle Richmond*
23–9 February: 46 pages *Castle Richmond*
1–7 March: 45 pages *Castle Richmond*. Third number of *Framley Parsonage* published.
8–14 March: 45 pages *Castle Richmond*
15–21 March: 45 pages *Castle Richmond*
22–8 March: 33 pages *Castle Richmond*
By 31 March *Castle Richmond* was finished.
3–9 April: 44 pages *Framley Parsonage*. Fourth number of *Framley Parsonage* published. Proofs of *Castle Richmond*.
10–16 April: 4 pages *Framley Parsonage*
17–23 April: 8 Pages *Framley Parsonage*
Over this period Trollope notes 'Committee' and 'sore throat' as distracting factors. They hamper him until 24 April. His proof-reading of *Castle Richmond* suffered accordingly: the work in its first edition had what Trollope's biographer calls an 'appalling' number of errors.
24–30 April: 40 pages *Framley Parsonage*
1–7 May: 48 pages *Framley Parsonage*. Fifth number of *Framley Parsonage* published. Chapman and Hall published *Castle Richmond*.
8–14 May: 0 'up in London'
15–21 May: 48 pages *Framley Parsonage*
22–8 May: 23 pages *Framley Parsonage*
29–31 May: 25 pages *Framley Parsonage*
1–7 June: 'Spanish Story'. Sixth number of *Framley Parsonage* published.
8–11 June: 26 pages *Framley Parsonage*
12–18 June: 70 pages *Framley Parsonage*
19–25 June: 38 pages *Framley Parsonage*
26–7 June: 10 pages *Framley Parsonage*
'*Finis*'
July: starts *Orley Farm*

In appreciating this feat it is worth noting that the writing problem was compounded by Trollope's having so little in hand when he started. It was not his habit to go naked to the publisher this way. The contract for *The Three Clerks* was signed on 15 October 1857, the writing took place from 15 February to 18 August 1857. When he sold *Dr Thorne* he had 367 of its 624 pages written. The contract for *The Bertrams* was signed 10 November 1858, the novel was written 1 April to 20 December 1858. For *Castle Richmond* and *Framley Parsonage* Trollope was adopting new and unpremeditated mode of composition.

IV

This *Cornhill* episode touches what is, famously, the basic tenet of Trollope's artistic creed and one which, in later life, he never tired of reiterating: 'A labourer must measure his work by his pay or he cannot live.'[27] Measuring is important, so is pay; the image is that of the journeyman who sells his labour day by day to the employer who will pay best, allowing no ties of loyalty to interfere. The simplicity of the transaction was important to Trollope. This it was that made him turn down Bentley's intricate £450 for *Dr Thorne* in favour of Chapman's £400 with no strings attached. This creed in turn justified the desertion from Chapman who had stood loyally by him and given that £400 when he needed it, without question. Others might perhaps have seen Trollope as a mere commercial adventurer and although he could doubtless justify his actions to himself the prospect of breaking his contract with Chapman or giving poor goods must have worried him a little. The worry spills over into the narrative he devised for Smith. Mark Robarts, the Framley Parson, becomes involved in a series of moral tangles through having countersigned for Nat Sowerby a £400 bill (later raised to £900). Although he is not morally responsible for the debt Mark's signature involves him in endless agony of spirit. The name 'Sowerby' is unusual and not, apparently, accidental. On the agreement for *Castle Richmond* stands one signature other than Anthony Trollope's, that of J. Sowerby who signed for Chapman and Hall. Consciously, or unconsciously, Trollope seems to have dramatised his anxiety in his new novel.

Apart from this private idiosyncrasy *Framley Parsonage* was conceived as a formula novel, written to order. The title was not altogether fresh: Hurst and Blackett brought out a *Framleigh*

Hall in 1858. Trollope worked out the main ingredients on the train as he left London after his interview with Smith:

The story was thoroughly English. There was a little fox-hunting and a little tuft-hunting, some Christian virtue and some Christian cant. There was no heroism and no villainy. There was much Church, but more love-making.[28]

Trollope here uses the language of the cooking recipe—adding love-making, for example, as one might add sugar to a cake. It was always one of his foibles to degrade fiction in this way, confusing art with trade, aesthetic activity with manual crafts. In so doing his motives were not, as is sometimes assumed, mere debunking philistinism. This reductive habit of mind relates to what was, in fact, a seriously thought-out theory of novel-writing. He was given the chance to expound the theory three months after *Framley Parsonage* opened in the *Cornhill*. Trollope, now riding high for the first time in his career, received a letter requesting his professional advice. The tribute to his new stature was probably sweet, and he took the trouble to write back at some length. (From the figures mentioned it will be seen too that already he was embroidering some myths about his recent past.)

All trades are now uphill work, and require a man to suffer much disappointment, and this trade more almost than any other. I was at it for years and wrote ten volumes before I made a shilling—, I say all this, which is very much in the guise of a sermon, because I must endeavour to make you understand that a man or woman must learn the tricks of his trade before he can *make money* by writing.[29]

It was in the same letter that Trollope, for the first time apparently, made the comparison: 'my belief of book writing is very much the same as my belief as to shoemaking.' The shoemaking analogy has become notorious from the seventh chapter of the *Autobiography*, where Trollope asserts it at length. But it is interesting that he should have introduced it at particularly this juncture in his career, when he was simultaneously engaged to produce two three-volume novels. The important feature of the shoe maker's profession is that he makes the same article with small variations time and again. There is little future for the artisan who dedicates himself to inventing a new kind of shoe; there is a glowing future for the shoemaker who can turn out the same pair of shoes faster or cheaper than his competitors. Trollope's experiences up to the crucial year 1859–60 may be seen as finally reinforcing his conception of himself as a rapidly productive formula novelist. In one sense it was a conception which he had, almost literally, inherited with his mother's milk. Mrs Trollope after her runaway success with *The Domestic Manners of the Americans*, in 1832, produced in the next five years fifteen volumes of fiction and six volumes of travels; moreover two of the novels were set in America and two of the travel books direct copies of her first success. At this time the young Anthony was acting as her secretary. (Bentley's staff would make satirical comments about young Anthony's errands for his 'mamma'.)[30] Such documents as the following between his mother and Richard Bentley must have made a deep impression:

The said Mrs. Trollope hereby undertakes to write and the said Richard Bentley agrees to publish the undermentioned four works upon the terms hereinafter stated—viz first a novel founded on American manners to be entitled 'Jonathan Jefferson Whitlaw'... secondly another work of fiction under the title of 'The Unco' Good' (or by whatever name it may be hereafter called)...Thirdly a work describing Mrs. Trollope's travels in Austria and more particularly her Residence in Vienna to be treated in a similar manner to her recent book called 'Paris and the Parisians'...Fourthly a similar account of her travels and residence in various parts of Italy.[31]

This bulk order was for ten volumes and £1,800. Clearly Bentley wanted from Mrs Trollope in this massive contract known commodities. There is no invitation for the writer to do anything she has not done before—note the 'novel founded on American manners'. Trollope's experience with Smith could not but convince him that in Barsetshire he had found a similarly successful formula. Smith had impressed on him that his value was a worker who could turn out a specified product, to order, in a specified period. It was his 'readiness' Smith was willing to go over the odds for.

Furthermore the experience of ten books, five publishers and twelve years must have convinced Trollope that his career was not going to shape like Dickens's or Thackeray's or Charlotte

Brontë's. He would not break on the world with a *Pickwick* or a *Vanity Fair*. But if he could produce two novels like *Castle Richmond* and *Framley Parsonage* for every one of theirs he would not be far behind at the end of the day.

All these factors combined to confirm Trollope as a great mass producer of fiction. If, as Henry James detected, there is a 'perceptibly mechanical process'[32] in Trollope's work it is there for a reason. As in other kinds of mass production what matters most is not mere speed, which would only produce slapdash work, but efficiency of design. As he seems to have realised in the train carriage where *Framley Parsonage* was conceived—if you have the blueprint worked out quality and delivery dates need present no problem.

It is harder, according to Trollope, to think about a novel than to write it. Formula and method saved him thinking excessively about each novel. With their help he could devise and execute a first-rate novel for Smith in six months. Later they served him in earning sufficient from his novels to belong to the Athenaeum and buy his town house in Montagu Square. But what is interesting, fascinating even, about Trollope is that he combined prolific production with a high level of artistic idealism and achievement. He was not a hack, although he accepted the market conditions that produced the hack novelist. Other writers passed his total of forty-seven novels; none turned out so much good fiction. Trollope, alone of the great Victorian novelists, turned out first-rate novels with the facility of potboilers.

7

Lever and Ainsworth
Missing the First Rank

The Cambridge Bibliography of English Literature divides its nineteenth-century fiction entry very confidently into 'major' and 'minor' novelists of the period. While Victorians would have understood the distinction well enough they might have had difficulty in guessing whose name would appear where. Many contemporaries would have backed Harrison Ainsworth and Charles Lever against Dickens and Thackeray for the very highest literary honours. Yet even during these novelists' life-times it became evident that Ainsworth and Lever, good though they might be, were not *great* writers. In this chapter we examine their careers at that critical moment when their essentially second-rate status was confirmed.

A talented, vigorous writer, Ainsworth had his first success with *Rookwood* which he produced on half-profits with Bentley.[1] In November 1833 the novelist sent the publisher a third of the work as a sample; the contract was signed in March 1834; the three-volume novel came out in May. A historical romance featuring Dick Turpin, *Rookwood* shocked critics, delighted readers with its 'outrageousness' and became the hit of the season. A second edition was called for by August and another in 1835.[2] With *Rookwood*'s triumph Ainsworth plunged into lucrative fiction and magazine work. But he made little effort to move out of the sphere which had brought him his initial fame. The way in which his subsequent fiction was cut from the template of his first success is evident enough from its titles and subtitles: *Crichton* (1837), *Jack Sheppard: A Romance* (1839–40), *The Tower of London: A Historical Romance* (1840), *Guy Fawkes: A Historical Romance* (1840–1), *Old St Pauls: A Tale of the*

Plague and Fire (1841), *The Miser's Daughter: A Tale* (1841), *Windsor Castle: A Historical Romance* (1842–3), *Saint James, Or the Court of Queen Anne: A Historical Romance* (1844), *Revelations of London* (1844).

Ainsworth's success was, at first, extraordinary. *Jack Sheppard* had eight dramatic versions running simultaneously, his novels were all smash hits in multi-volume, serial and one-volume reprint form. He was taken up by Bentley to fill the gap left by the defection of Dickens and by 1837 he had become one of the very select band (others were G. P. R. James, Marryat, Lytton) who had received £1,000 payments for their novels. Bentley, deserted by Dickens, was to some extent at the mercy of his new protégé. 'He thinks that he has become necessary to me,'[3] the publisher fulminated, and indeed he had. So much so that he had to go to law to protect his investment from the pirates, just as he had earlier with Dickens. It was only worth doing this for authors who were 'necessary' to the house's dealings.

Ainsworth gloried in the strength of his youth. On the wrappers of the cheap version of *Rookwood* he had written the account of how he had composed the ride to York, 'a hundred ordinary novel pages', in less than twenty-four hours, so riding his muse as hard as Turpin had Black Bess. Meanwhile he was enjoying a wonderful social success, dazzling the company at Gore and Holland houses as one of London's handsomest young men, 'brilliant with pins and rings and long oiled locks'.[4]

For a while Ainsworth's star was higher than Dickens's. But he broke no new ground in his prime. It is as if Dickens had written in his first five years as a novelist: *Pickwick Papers, Nicholas Nickleby, Peter Pickleton, The Bagwig Club, The Picklington Papers, The Adventures of Harry Hogstock*, etc. As it happens Dickens would have been commercially justified in such a course: in every reissue throughout his life *Pickwick* consistently outsold every other title by as much as two to one. But the danger of this kind of stereotype repetitiousness was that a novelist stunted his development and became so closely associated with one brand of fiction that it was impracticable for him to change. In 1851 Ainsworth had a demonstration of this when he brought out *Mervyn Clitheroe*, something quite different from the run of his earlier fiction, an autobiographical work, lacking the historical setting and adventure plot which were by now his trademarks. Ainsworth himself regarded this 'mere transcript' of his early schooldays as a risky experiment and he had embarked on it only after considering the safer course of a second series of *The Tower of London* with Bentley.[5] Given *Clitheroe*'s date one naturally aligns it with the equally autobiographical *Pendennis* (1848–50) and *David Copperfield* (1849–50); like them, it was announced (in November 1851) 'to be completed in Twenty Monthly Numbers'. But Ainsworth was not to be allowed to change his mode of fiction. *Clitheroe* failed spectacularly with the reading public. His 'story of modern life' was found unexciting by those who had expected something Ainsworthian and issue was suspended after only four parts had been published by Chapman and Hall.[6] So, in 1853, Ainsworth returned to the old groove with *The Star Chamber*.

Mervyn Clitheroe may be seen as a crucial moment in Ainsworth's career, the moment when he failed to break out of the limiting format of the historical romance. If one overlooks Dickens's career one can see, at such junctures, distinct points of new departure. With *Dombey* there emerges an interest in structure; with *Bleak House* a new sombreness in tone; with *Tale of Two Cities* he tries his hand at the novel centred on incident rather than character. A similar discontinuity is evident in the work of Thackeray, particularly in his variation between modern domestic and historical settings. Each of these changes in Dickens's and Thackeray's fiction elicited something of a protest from a reading public whose principal demand was for more of the same—until satiation. An element of resistance was required; take, for example, the sales of *Copperfield* as reflected in Bradbury and Evans's printing figures for the novel: No. 1 30,000; No. 2 24,000; No. 6 22,000.[7] Clearly Dickens's autobiographical novel slumped at about the same point as had *Clitheroe*. But Dickens, fortified perhaps by his greater self confidence, carried on. Thackeray, the first in the field with his autobiographical novel, decided, at the half-way mark, to run *Pendennis* on to a massive twenty-four numbers.

With sixty years, Ainsworth can claim the longest novel-writing career of the century. But it is made up almost entirely of the same historical romances, with the same grandiose action, rousing titles and thin veneer of scholarship. When times and tastes changed, as they inevitably did, he was left beached, his talents exhausted and capable of nothing but increasingly feeble reiteration. This catastrophe occurred relatively late. After the wild successes of the 1830s and 40s Ainsworth held his own through the 1850s. A decline began in the 1860s, however, and thereafter accelerated inexorably. The process is painfully recorded in a series of contracts he made with Chapman and Hall during this decade. The Chapmans were not cruel men, but their treatment of Ainsworth in dealings over these years reads like a subplot from *New Grub Street*.

The sixties started badly for Ainsworth. Bentley deserted him as publisher for *Bentley's Miscellany* and some time after started a competitor magazine which from the first did better.[8] This was sharp practice since Ainsworth had bought *Bentley's Miscellany* for £1,700 from Bentley in 1854 on the understanding that the publisher would not 'publish, carry on or conduct any periodical publication of a like nature to *Bentley's Miscellany*'. Ainsworth meanwhile moved his business to Chapman and Hall—old friends who had run a highly successful collective reissue of his novels in the late 1840s.

The first agreement between these new partners was signed on 26 June 1861 for *The Constable of the Tower*.[9] Chapman agreed to print two editions, 1,000 copies in three volumes to sell at 31s. 6d. and a one-volume edition of 3,000 copies for the firm's 'Standard Editions of Popular Authors'. Ainsworth surrendered his copyright for three years and was paid £400 by publisher's bill at six months. Since he had already had some revenue from the magazine serialisation of the novel this was not a bad price, though Ainsworth could remember many higher.

For *The Lord Mayor of London* Ainsworth drew up the agreement himself on 6 March 1862. Optimistically he made the same terms as for *The Constable of the Tower*—the titles, after all, were similar enough. Chapman remonstrated. He submitted a statement of the previous novel's disappointing sales. In the face of that Ainsworth gave ground.[10] Two editions were taken, but only 750 in three volumes, and 4,000 for the 'Standard

Edition'. For this the novelist received £350 (£400 is crossed out in the agreement) by bill at four months.

In 1864 Edward Chapman, Ainsworth's old friend, retired. His place was taken by his cousin Frederic. Fred Chapman was a sportsman and his taste ran to sporting novels and 'vigorous and open air stories'. Ainsworth's musty romances could scarcely have been to his liking. 'Mr. F.C.', as Ainsworth called him, began harrying the novelist for small sums of money he claimed were owing to the firm.[11] The change of control in the house may well be reflected in the terms the novelist had under the next agreement, signed on 16 April 1864, for *John Law*. The size and number of editions were identical but payment was further reduced to £300. At this stage in his relationship with Chapman and Hall a note of desperation enters Ainsworth's correspondence. About his next novel, *The Spanish Match: Charles Stuart at Madrid*, he wrote:

> It shall not be my fault if the work does not succeed, and I therefore engage to advertise it, if necessary, to the extent of £100—at my own cost. This sum ought to carry off an edition of 750 copies but if you think proper, you need only print 500.
>
> You will also observe that I have given you the right of selling a cheap edition to Messrs. W. H. Smith and Son.[12]

Clearly Ainsworth was pressed for money. 'It will not suit me to postpone the publication of my book to November,' he wrote, 'I must bring it out in June.'

From the agreement signed two days later it is evident that Ainsworth got his June publication date. But only in return for considerable concessions. Chapman had three editions—750 in three volumes, 3,000 for the 'Standard Editions' and in addition a one-volume cheap edition to be stereotyped and distributed via Smith's bookstalls at 2s. These cheap editions, catering for the relatively undiscriminating reader not desperate for the latest thing in fiction were good investments for the publisher. In their compact standardised form, or on easily stored stereotype plates, they could wait years for a sale;[13] whereas the bulky three-volume edition, printed from type kept standing for the hoped for reprints, had to be cleared within a few months or remaindered. But the existence, actual or potential, of many thousands of copies of his novel together with plates which could be sold to another, cut-price producer killed the novel's afterlife from its author's point of view. Ainsworth, moreover, in addition to the usual three-year undertaking had agreed *never* to publish an edition of *The Spanish Match* at under 5s. In the circumstances this meant that he had signed away his interest in the novel in perpetuity, and for this he received £300. The price was not really bad, but the conditions were getting tighter. And it is evident from the terms imposed that Chapman and Hall were chiefly interested in Ainsworth for the reprint market where they could reap long-term profits with the author well out of the way.

As it was Ainsworth was being cut to the bone. He clearly needed the money promptly. This meant he would discount the bill immediately and take a heavy loss. If he did pay for advertising (or give it free in his journal) this would leave him with little more than £100 for a three-volume novel. 'One hundred pounds', as Charlotte Brontë once told George Smith, 'is a small sum for a year's intellectual labour.'[14] But when she made the protest Charlotte Brontë had prospects of higher rewards to come; Ainsworth had none. The days when he could expect £100 for every single number of a novel were ten years behind him.

About this time Ainsworth made a vain attempt to get a new agreement with Bentley to publish his novels at an 8 per cent commission rate.[15] Bentley, however, had too sharp a nose for failure and success and none of Chapman and Hall's regard for old friends. Ainsworth was now indeed old, in his sixtieth year. It was usual for novelists to slow down as they aged. Dickens, George Eliot, Thackeray who all fired off their early books in quick succession took at least a two-year interval between books in later life. It has been noted that the Victorians in fact aged very quickly. Thackeray was white haired at 40; Dickens damaged in health in his early forties; George Eliot emerged from *Romola* suddenly 'an old woman'; 'I was thirty years younger ten years ago' Lever declared in his mid-fifties.[16] Poor Ainsworth was no exception to the general superannuation but for him there was no respite. He was working as hard as he ever had to produce the same historical romances at the rate of one or two a year. In the sixties he wrote eleven novels, edited two magazines and wrote for them. This in spite of the fact that he was a sick man who desperately wanted rest. In 1864 he stoically observed:

For several years I have been obliged to work exceedingly hard, and the strain is almost too much for me and I may break down. It is only prudent, therefore, to relax these excessive exertions, but as I now stand I cannot do so.[17]

Exhaustion is manifest in the very length of the novels he turned out. The usual size of a three-volume work was 'upward of 300 pages', and 22 to 24 lines to a page. For a guinea and a half such materialistic prescriptions were important; a purchaser getting less might well feel cheated. *The Spanish Match* however, came out at 3 × 295 × 21 and the novel that followed it from Ainsworth's pen at 3 × 288 × 20. This was paring the three-decker down to almost fraudulent exiguity.

Ainsworth who liked to present himself as a landed gentleman and had contrived to have his pedigree printed in the 'Supplement to the Landed Gentry' was forced, piece by piece, to sell his property until he, who had lorded it in Kensal Manor over one of the most brilliant salons in the country, was living in a small house in Reigate. Nor was it because he was a fool where publishers were concerned. He had been one himself and appreciated the value of driving hard bargains. He cunningly arranged as many sales for his work in different forms as he could—magazine, multi- and single-volume—never entirely parting with a copyright. In this he was a model man of letters. (He would even write 'all rights reserved' on his manuscripts.)

No degree of astuteness with publishers, however, could mend his manifest unpopularity with readers. He had lost his place. In his downward course his relationship with Chapman and Hall stabilises briefly; *The Constable de Bourbon* (February 1866) commanded the same terms as its predecessor. But then, in March 1867, the slump entered into its final phase. Chapman took only one edition of *Old Court*, 650 copies to be brought out in three volumes, for which he paid £150. Ainsworth gave up the copyright for a year unless (as was extremely unlikely) the first edition sold out. In this eventuality he was free to publish as many copies in whatever form he liked. This 'concession' was Chapman and Hall's way of indicating that they had no interest in the novel after skimming the library market for those few diehard readers who still remembered Harrison Ainsworth. As it was, popular taste was running in quite a different direction; this was the era of the women sensation novelists—Mrs Wood and Miss Braddon and Ouida were sharing the public's favour with the 'manly' Lawrence, Henry Kingsley and Whyte Melville ('Ouida in breeches' as Michael Sadleir unkindly called him).

On 5 September 1867 *Myddleton Pomfret* was taken on the same terms as *Old Court* except that the single three-volume edition was shrunk to 500 copies. A year later Ainsworth was obliged to sell *Bentley's Miscellany* (which he had bought for £1,700 in 1854) back to its nominal proprietors for £250. (Bentley purposed to 'extinguish' the journal.) This broke a link with Chapman and Hall, who had published the *Miscellany* for Ainsworth while he had it. Finally the nadir in the novelist's fortunes was reached on 26 April 1869 when Ainsworth agreed to write *Hilary St Ives* for an edition of 500 copies in the three-volume form for £100. So devalued was Ainsworth's stock that it was felt unnecessary to put in any restricting clause about copyright.

Hilary St Ives was a pathetic attempt to produce a novel set in the present day, a transparent imitation of Collins's *Moonstone* and *Armadale*. It failed miserably. Years of habit had confirmed Ainsworth as the kind of novelist with only one novel in him—his modern characters were always prone to explete 'Zounds' when surprised and give the impression that they would be happier in armour than tweeds. It was now too late to desert historical fiction for sensational. Chapman and Hall, who by now had 20,000 copies of Ainsworth for their cheap library for little more than printing cost, let the author go. He gravitated to Tinsley, a vulgar man who dropped his 'h's' and patronised the proud old dandy. He continued writing with the same desperate facility until he died; exact prices are hard to come by but the scale of his rewards can be guessed. In 1873 we find him haggling with Tinsley for the sale of three copyrights at £50 the lot and in 1875 he produced two full length novels for the same publisher for £40 a volume.[18]

Even in the barefaced terminology of the literary contract there is something tragic in this depreciation. In the ten years of the 1860s Ainsworth's market value had diminished from £400 to £100 a novel. (In twenty years it had diminished from £2,000.) To an elegant, haughty man who affected a *de haut en bas* tone with his publishers it must have been wormwood to sell work which represented a year's effort for a promissory £100. Thirty years before his *Jack Sheppard* had eclipsed *Oliver Twist* with which it shared top billing in *Bentley's Miscellany*. (Ainsworth's novel actually increased circulation by 800–900 a month.)[19] Certainly Dickens felt threatened and from the moment *Jack Sheppard* caught on 'the sword was drawn' between him and Bentley.[20] Bentley valued the novelists equally giving Ainsworth exactly the same as he had Dickens for *Oliver Twist* (£500).[21] It was a good bargain for the publisher, even at this price, who had *Jack Sheppard* running in his magazine (January 1839 to February 1840), sold 3,000 at 25s. in three volumes in a couple of months after publication in October 1839, brought out a one-volume edition at 16s. in March and serialised the work simultaneously in fifteen weekly parts. In 1847 it was worth Ainsworth's while to recover the still valuable copyright for £200.[22] And when he took over Dickens's vacant chair at *Bentley*'s in 1839 it was at a higher salary than his predecessor.[23] In those days it was an event for celebration whenever Ainsworth finished a novel. In 1840, after *The Tower of London*, he threw a banquet attended by all the *illuminati* of the publishing and writing world.

Many would have backed Ainsworth's talent against Dickens's in 1840. In the 1860s Dickens was earning £10,000 a novel, Ainsworth a hundredth of that sum; Dickens was buying Gadshill, Ainsworth was forced to sell his property piecemeal. And while Dickens was a household name in two or more continents Harrison Ainsworth was antediluvian, a literary joke. Percy Fitzgerald reports the following cruel exchange between Browning and Forster at a dinner of Fred Chapman's in the 1860s:

'...a sad, forlorn looking being stopped me today and reminded me of old times. He presently resolved himself into—whom do you think? —Harrison Ainsworth!' 'Good Heavens!' cried Forster, 'is he still alive?'[24]

II

Other novelists with long-spanned careers suffered declines similar to Ainsworth's, if in a less acute form. G. P. R. James, the author of an amazing number of romances, declined from four figure payments in the 1830s to a few hundreds in the 1840s. In 1858, two years before his death, forty-six of his copyrights together with stereo plates could fetch only £2,075 at public auction. (Needless to say, Routledge bought them.) It was what the trade thought the novelist's life-work was worth, and he died broken down and in debt. It could happen to much greater artists than James or Ainsworth. Trollope earned hundreds for his novels in the 1850s, rose to the thousand mark in the 1860s, thence to two or three thousand per novel by the end of the decade. In the 1870s, however, his price first stabilised, then subsided and finally collapsed. At the beginning of the decade Chapman gave him £3,000 for *The Way We Live Now.* A year later the same publisher offered only £2,500 for a similarly long work, *The Prime Minister.* By the end of the 1870s his basic rate for a full-length novel hovered around £1,200. Finally he discovered that his friends, Chapman and Hall, had lost £120 on the £1,000 they agreed on in 1878 for *The Duke's Children* (one of his finest novels, by the way). And even more galling another old friend, John Blackwood, turned down *Ayala's Angel* in 1879.[25] Still, to have stuck around the one-thousand mark was a low point which Ainsworth, from his submerged depths, would have looked up at enviously.

Ainsworth had been caught in a trap set by the system of rewards and incentives by which the nineteenth-century publishing world operated. From the economic facts of his career it is fair to assume that there was a period—in the early 1840s —when he was free to write whatever he wanted, had he cared to exert his authorial will. He chose to submit to pressure and reproduce his best selling work, eventually to the point of public nausea. In the end his margin of freedom was reduced until his style of work was determined by the imperative that he must write historical romances or starve.

What would have happened if, at the critical moment, he had

braced himself and broken away from his fictional stereotypes, writing something deliberately unAinsworthian? There is no guarantee that he would have come to any happier condition in the long run. Alongside Ainsworth's we may put the case of Charles Lever who, at the critically testing point of his career, did make the break for artistic freedom, with unfortunate results.

In 1845 Charles Lever had some reputation as a comic novelist with a good line in Irish *picarós* like Harry Lorrequer, Charles O'Malley and Jack Hinton. Under duress of financial worries he wound up his affairs in Ireland, resigned his editorial place at the *Dublin University Magazine*, sold up his home Templeogue and moved his business abroad. After a brief alliance with the dubious Colburn he was taken up by Chapman and Hall to fill the vacancy left by Dickens who had transferred to Bradbury and Evans after rowing over payments for *Martin Chuzzlewit*. The publishers opened their relationship with Lever through the agency of a mutual friend in late 1844. The outcome of this was a one-volume, 5s. book, *St Patrick's Eve*. Lever was to have £200 for 5,000 copies printed of his work to come out, as the contract specified, 'of the form and size type of "The Chimes" '[26] (Dickens's previous Christmas Book.) The price was not wonderful but Lever was accorded unusually deferential treatment by his new publishers. They consulted him about format, page layout, cost and arranged to have the work published, according to his whim, on St Patrick's day itself.[27] Lever was clearly being groomed for literary greatness.

Like *The Chimes*, *St Patrick's Eve* was socially controversial; like its predecessor also, it was a reasonable success and in May 1845 Lever went on to sign a contract with Chapman and Hall for a monthly serial to rival that currently arranged between Dickens and Bradbury and Evans. The terms were munificent: £130 a monthly number, a sliding provision extending from a minimum of twelve to 'twenty or any less quantity of numbers'.[28] The likely reward for Lever, £2,000 or more, was a sum previously given only to Dickens and exceeded by far anything the Irishman had hitherto earned. Chapman and Hall also planned production on a Dickensian scale. Ten thousand copies of the first monthly number were budgeted for, with the option of an extra £10 to Lever for each thousand additional to the initial figure.

Lever rose to the occasion. This was clearly his great chance. The *Knight of Gwynne* is a complete departure from the rollicking military tales he had hitherto specialised in. A political story centred on the Union between England and Ireland it was designed to reflect current concerns and to contribute something serious to the debate on repeal. (It also indicates an intended challenge to Dickens as the leading novelist of social conscience.) Lever normally held the cheerful doctrine that: 'books write themselves...sitting down with a title...and a well nibbed pen are the only essentials.' But for *The Knight* he took pains; the novel began with a good—one might almost say a foolhardy—resolution:

I am emboldened to hope that I am improving as a writer—one thing I can answer for—No popularity I ever had—have—or shall have will make me trifle with the public—by fast writing—or careless composition. Dickens's last book [i.e. *Martin Chuzzlewit*] has set the gravestone on his fame—and the warning shall not be thrown away.[29]

The resolution was fruitless. Despite all Lever's efforts *The Knight* was a failure. He could not hit the monthly public (whom, incidentally, he secretly despised). By November 1846 he was 'too ashamed and afraid'[30] to enquire about his novel's progress. He fell out with Phiz, his illustrator who would not read the numbers he was hired to illustrate. Chapman and Hall became increasingly restive and tried to interfere with the course of the narrative. Lever was out of the country, wandering around Europe with his family and copy was forever getting lost or delayed in the post. He lost heart: 'I lose all courage', he had once told Chapman, 'if I once feel that I am an unprofitable acquaintance to my publisher.'[31] Unforeseen factors hurt the novel. The cover, for instance, displayed Ireland 'GREAT GLORIOUS AND FREE', with vignettes recording the country's progress 'in the development of her resources in the happiness of her people from Poverty, Misery and Anarchy'. It was cruel luck that the work should have coincided with the potato famine which starved Ireland's population and plunged the country into a misery, poverty and anarchy unequalled in modern times.

The Knight came to an end amid a general feeling of gloom and mortification. 'I always believed it better than I suppose it was found by the Public,'[32] Lever concluded sadly. At least he had his £130 a number. The publishers not only stood the loss but they saw Bradbury and Evans score a great hit with *Dombey and Son* (1846–7) and bring out a serial, *Vanity Fair*, by a beginner novelist which after a shaky start took the reading public by storm. Lever was thus not only run down by 'the great Dickens train'[33] he was also overtaken by Thackeray whom he had always slightly looked down on as an impudent cockney. Not surprisingly, perhaps, Lever took refuge in savage, though private, vituperation against the 'Dickens–Thackeray clique'[34] whom he felt had done him down:

> The Times is severe on Dickens's Xmas Book—but what care his readers for criticism! You might as well advise a sow wallowing in his [sic] garbage to read something on dirt! The Atlas praises Thackeray's new serial—if it would wish its subscribers to have the same opinion it should have omitted the extracts...[35]

This pugnacity alternated with maudlin self pity, a pose of better breeding than his victorious opponents:

> I have suffered—I am suffering for the endeavour to supply a healthier more manly and more English sustenance but it may be that before I succeed—if sucess does come at all—the hand will be cold and the heart still—and that I may be only a pioneer to clear the way—for the breaching party. That such a taste must rot out of its own corruption is clear enough—but meanwhile Literature is an unattractive career for those who would use it with higher purpose.[36]

When *The Knight* finished in July 1847 Lever found himself 'really and for the first time—at sea',[37] poor as a church mouse. In desperation he reverted to his old modes of fiction—'rascal autobiographies' of 'very free and easy Paddies'.[38] There was little talk in the succeeding years of 'Literature' or 'higher purposes'. His next book he privately described as 'powerless trash'.[39] Humiliatingly, in July 1850, Chapman and Hall advertised their stocks of his novels for sale reduced from 10s. 6d. to 7s. per volume. By 1859 his 'mainspring' had gone;[40]

for a writer whose appeal was *brio* and dash this was mortal. 'You ask me how I write,' he told John Blackwood in 1863, 'my reply is, just as I live—from hand to mouth.'[41] His letters over the years after 1847 show him more and more concerned with ever smaller amounts of money and pettier concerns. In the end he was reduced to the humiliating condition of petitioner—applying to men who had previously been his equals for favours. One can only hope that time had dulled his sensibilities when in 1861 Thackeray offered him a 'loankin' of £100, or when Dickens intervened with Chapman and Hall to get him £60 a number for *Barrington*, or when Blackwood out of sympathy paid him the thousand that should not properly have been his since *Tony Butler* had not sold sufficiently.

Looking back over Lever's career one is forced to conclude that he did not have greatness in him. *Vanity Fair* had been the making of Thackeray, even though it began less auspiciously than Lever's novel with 3,000 fewer copies printed and the author paid only half as much a month. *The Knight of Gwynne* was, in a like way, the unmaking of Lever. He had been given his chance and could make nothing of it. Ainsworth, on the other hand, had a similar chance proffered but declined to put himself to the test. Whether he would have risen to the challenge like Thackeray or flopped like Lever is a matter for conjecture. At any rate, we may conclude that there are few sadder sights in Victorian literature than the worn-out novelist doomed to produce increasingly unsaleable wares. Lever, for example, lived to envy Thackeray his tragically early death:

> He was fortunate, however, to go down in the full blaze of his genius as so few do. The fate of most is to go on pouring water on the lees, that people at last come to suspect that they have never got honest liquor from the tap at all.[42]

8

Dickens as Publisher

In a presentation copy of *Nicholas Nickleby* (1839) Dickens wrote, as inscription for his publishers, Chapman and Hall:

'How should you like to grow up a clever man and write books?' said the old gentleman.

'I think I would rather read them Sir' replied Oliver.

'What! Wouldn't you like to be a book writer?' said the old gentleman. Oliver considered a little while, and at last said he should think it would be a much better thing to be a bookseller; upon which the old gentleman laughed heartily, and declared he had said a very good thing, which Oliver felt glad to have done, though he by no means knew what it was.[1]

There is an element of hostility in this otherwise good-natured gesture. At an early stage in his career Dickens seems to have been alive to the divisions of labour, and of profit, involved in the book-making process. This reinforced the other impression made by the spectacle of American booksellers and publishers enriching themselves from his work without paying him a penny. He determined not to allow the English trade to do the same.

Dickens's career, viewed from one aspect, emerges as a successful exercise in elbowing aside the booksellers who stood between him and the reader. This he achieved, oratorically, in the public readings of 1858 when he began to deliver his own fiction in his own person to enraptured audiences all over the kingdom, earning a thousand guineas a month in the process.[2] In the literary sphere his prodigious sales power had by the same period enabled him to dictate his terms to any publisher, and get them. His usual 75–25 per cent split represents, apart from anything else, the negligible authority his nominal employers had over their novelist. Dickens reduced the publisher to the purely functionary status of printer—this in fact was one motive in his leaving Chapman and Hall for Bradbury and Evans in the 1840s. 'A printer is better than a bookseller,'[3] he declared, because a printer merely takes orders, he has no will of his own. In the fifties this intractability had grown even more pronounced. 'The only thing Dickens wanted', writes his biographer, 'was that his publishers should not cross any of his desires, and that was the way it was henceforth to be.'[4] To date he had set the lawyers on Macrone, flouted agreements with Bentley, broken with Chapman and Hall when Hall ventured to hint that *Martin Chuzzlewit* might be less than overwhelmingly successful. Every publisher who had to do with him felt Dickens's bite sooner or later.

In 1858 he left Bradbury and Evans over their refusal to carry in *Punch* the announcement of his separation from Mrs Dickens. The novelist angrily started proceedings to buy out the publishers' quarter share in *Household Words* and set up in its place his very own journal *All the Year Round*. This he determined to run himself with W. H. Wills (who 'has no genius', he commented)[5] as business manager and sub-editor. 'There is no publisher whatever associated with All the Year Round', he declared.[6] 'Except Dickens', he might have added.

All the Year Round began with an appropriate flourish.[7] A quarter of a million handbills were distributed through Smith's. One hundred and thirty omnibuses trundled round London with advertisements for the new journal on their panels. Rail travellers looking out of their windows up and down the country would see hoardings with the new journal's name on them and even those who did not care to look at the view would find advertisements in their carriage and on the station.[8]

The advertising campaign paid off. After a month Wills could report: 'Our success here has exceeded the most sanguine expectations. One hundred and twenty thousand of No. 1 have already been sold and we are settling down to a steady current sale of one hundred thousand.'[9] Dickens liked to point out that this circulation was several thousand more than that of *The*

Times. On occasions sales are supposed to have reached 300,000—staggering if true. If we assume that every copy of the 50 per cent that stayed in the metropolis was read by three people this would mean that half the population of London read *All the Year Round.* In fact handling this kind of circulation was the one area where Dickens's independence came unstuck. It was impossible to distribute this many copies to retailers in and out of London unless one had a regular chain of supply and outlets. Consequently he was obliged to use Chapman and Hall as his agents for country sales. So, in the end, there was 'a publisher...associated with All the Year Round'.

The major difference between *Household Words* and *All the Year Round,* however, was the latter's dedication to long fiction. At the end of the first serial (*A Tale of Two Cities*) and the beginning of the second (*The Woman in White*) Dickens declared what was to be the new journal's distinguishing feature:

> We purpose always reserving the first place in these pages for a continuous original work of fiction occupying about the same amount of time in its serial publication as that which is just completed...And it is our hope and aim, while we work hard at every other department of our journal, to produce, in this one, some sustained works of imagination that may become a part of English Literature.

From our standpoint in literary history it does not, perhaps, seem an altogether momentous announcement. But in the context of 1860 it was revolutionary. In its issue of 1 August of that year the *Publishers' Circular* saluted the transformation in fiction publishing practice which Dickens and his journal had brought about:

> A long continuous story appears to be now an established condition of success in a weekly periodical, and it is curious to note the fact, because it is not long since a totally different theory prevailed. For nearly a quarter of a century after its first appearance, Messrs. Chambers, we believe, never admitted into their Journal, without an apology, a story extending even to two numbers, though they were, if we remember rightly, among the first to adopt the new fashion. Mr. Dickens, in *Household Words,* began cautiously with stories in a few portions or chapters. But if anything nowadays can be considered proved, it is that readers will not only follow a thread of fiction week

after week for many months, but demand it as an indispensable feature of their weekly literary entertainment.

In all important respects, then, Dickens was now an unfettered bookseller, and manuscript buyer in the market with other publishers of fiction. He is the only novelist of stature in the period whose name appears on the contracts of other novelists of stature. It was he who read hopeful manuscripts, decided terms, made offers and ratified them. Even Wills's authority in the 'commercial department' was 'subject to powers reserved to Dickens'.[10] As if to demonstrate his power Dickens was arbitrary about prices. Lytton, whom he admired immensely, had £1,500 for an eight-month story; Mrs Gaskell, whom he did not admire immensely, was offered £400 for the same length of narrative at exactly the same period.[11] Who today would agree with that ratio?

In addition to the publisher's proprietorial decisions Dickens retained the editor's powers of close supervision. This allowed him not only to hire a novelist but also, if he felt it necessary, to interfere with the course of a story during publication. Often enough he did feel it necessary. [T. A.] 'Trollope's story is *exceedingly good,*' he wrote in September 1862, 'highly picturesque and full of interest. But he mars the end by over anticipating it, and I have changed it there a good deal.'[12] There is something of the busybody here, but in other ways Dickens's infinite pains with his contributor's work is admirable and distinguishes him from the run of his fellow magazine editors. When, for example, Trollope was offered the editorship of *Temple Bar* in 1861, the terms proposed by the proprietor were £1,000 a year (twice that Dickens took as salary) 'for three or five years with the ostensible editorship of the Magazine...the real work of editorship will be performed as heretofore by Mr. Edmund Yates.'[13] In *All the Year Round* it was Dickens himself, aided by his staff of three, who did the 'real work'. Even when touring with his public readings he examined proofs and considered the layout schemes which Wills sent him. When in London he had rooms over the business premises. Most contributions, and all fiction, which passed under his hand would be carefully scrutinised and often altered.

What kind of partner was Dickens for his 'fellow labourers' on *All the Year Round*? A very good one as it turned out. A case can be made that in the early years of the magazine Dickens presided over something like a truly co-operative novel-publishing venture, that *All the Year Round* offered, for a while at least, a glimpse of the ideal in publisher-novelist relationships. A high degree of cross-fertilisation, the judicious application of authority and sympathetic intervention make the frequent appeal to 'fellowship in labour'[14] something more than a rhetorical flourish on Dickens's part. Nor is it too much to say that in the early years the novelists on *All the Year Round* at times attained to a group creation of fiction. 'If [Wilkie Collins] should break down' Dickens once observed, 'I would go on with his story so that nobody should be any the wiser.'[15]

To illustrate the peculiarly clement conditions which Dickens set up we may examine his handling of three of the novelists who worked for him during the first two years of the journal, Lever, Collins and Lytton.

II

On the face of it one would not suppose Dickens an easy man to write novels for. A name he toyed with for the new periodical—'Charles Dickens's Own'—declares the essential egocentricity of *All the Year Round*. He had hitherto shown little of the pliability which marked the most successful publishers' dealings with respected clients. Had Trollope come to Dickens in 1859, as he did to Chapman, and blandly suggested breaking a contract in favour of a rival publisher he would probably have received a sharp answer.

As a drawer-up of contracts Dickens was frank to the point of offensiveness in including any doubts he had about a novelist. In that with Reade for *Hard Cash*, for example, he put in a clause that would actually penalise the notoriously expansive author for any over-matter. Moreover in the same document he stipulated that he should write 'to the utmost of his skill and ability'[16]—an unflattering allusion to Reade's habit of plagiarising other people's ideas if they appealed to him.[17] No other publisher, it would appear, was capable of taking this kind of high line with a major novelist.

Nor was *All the Year Round* an easy journal to write for. It was designed around a running serial, usually making up three-volume length, by a 'name' author. Its twelve pages were double-column and in small print. It carried no illustrations. In addition to the fiction it usually carried five or so anonymous articles of a miscellaneous nature—pen sketches, reportage, political discussion, gossip of the week; all 'small beer'. Selling at the near give-away price of 2d. (cheaper than *The Times*) the periodical could scarcely be other than drab as a specimen of typography and layout. Even Victorian readers, whose standards were not high in these matters, were somewhat taken aback by the grimness of *All the Year Round*'s appearance. 'I add, at Mr Dickens's special request,' wrote Wills to their printers, 'that the surface appearance of the journal is greatly complained of, even amongst general readers.'[18]

All the Year Round carried relatively few advertisements by modern standards. Its revenue depended almost entirely on high sales, and these in turn depended on the serial. The journal's sales strategy was thus quite different from that of the *Cornhill*, its great rival, which every month for 1s. sported a host of great names. Readers of the *Cornhill* in 1860, if Trollope's serial did not please, could turn to Thackeray's, or to his Roundabout Paper, or Millais' illustrations, or Tennyson's poem, or one of the 'heavy' articles on some topic of the day. Galactic profusion was Smith's method; the single, star turn Dickens's.

Not unnaturally the novelist who had the responsibility for keeping Dickens's sales going all the year round felt the strong glare of a single spotlight on him. If circulation dropped, there was only one person to blame. The serial was always the first item in the paper. It usually ran five pages, though over-runs of up to twice this were allowed so as not to cramp the author (any cuts were made in the following articles). Often at the end of a novel's run the successor would, for one or two issues, run abreast then take the baton himself.

Writing in the dimensions required by *All the Year Round* was not easy. 'The small portions', Dickens complained, 'drive me frantic.'[19] Collins, in *The Woman in White*, he adjudged to have mastered the form best and the image with which he chose to congratulate him is graphic: 'an admirable book...it grips the difficulties of the weekly portion and throws them in a masterly style.'[20] If length posed problems analogous to wrestling, the frequency with which an installment had to be provided and its proof corrected Collins likened to a 'weekly race' and spoke of the 'bucket of sweat' each number cost him.[21]

When he trusted the ability of his novelist Dickens only made some such provision as: 'it is not to be supposed that you would have the whole story completed before the serial publication began; but it *is* to be supposed that you would be sufficiently far advanced to be at ease in the design and to feel safe.'[22] But with authors whom he knew to have difficulty with length, like the overflowing Mrs Gaskell, Dickens would be stricter. From them he would stipulate an allotted proportion of copy in advance, and he would reserve the right to 'interpose' a short story so postponing publication until there was prior evidence of competence with *All the Year Round*'s dimensions.

Whatever the terms agreed the author would at some time or another surely find himself racing just ahead of weekly deadlines, an athletic feat which strained creativity to the utmost and made many feel anything but safe. In a week the novelist would need to devise, in five pages, an installment which both added to the narrative yet was sufficiently barbed with suspense or the promise of good things to come to keep the reader wanting more. If readers were lost it was, as Dickens was not slow to point out, 'very, very difficult' to win them back.[23] And success was a knife edge; 'at present', Wills calculated in 1859, 'we lose one percent to cripple our sale.'[24]

All the Year Round was in many ways the epitome of the furnace-like conditions in which much of the best Victorian fiction was created. It raised to the highest pitch what Thackeray called the 'Life & Death' struggle with the unwritten number. At the same time it was, when handled properly, a superb instrument for fiction. No writer in *All the Year Round* could forget for a moment the mechanics of publication. The pace, narrowness and need for 'incessant condensation'[25] cut away all fat; the responsiveness of the sales to any slackening tension kept the novelist nervous and alert. Weekly intervals meant that a reader came to every installment primed, which was not the case with monthly serialisation where the plot had that much longer to fade in the memory. Readers became very sharp indeed, bringing to the mystery stories *All the Year Round* favoured the keenness of amateur detectives. Wilkie Collins was pulled up for some slight contradictions in the time setting of *The Woman in White*, Lytton for the solecism of having a man tried *in absentia* in an English court. *All the Year Round* came to specialise in fiction that wasted no time in making an impact on the reader. Hence its preference for autobiographical narrative (four out of the first six full-length novels had 'I' narrators) and stories based on crime (five out of the first six had capital crime as the mainspring of their plots).

Saturday publication suggests that the family should employ weekend leisure to read. (One presumes that the prohibition against secular reading on the Sabbath was relaxed in at least 100,000 Victorian homes.) Monthly reissue of all the parts, bound, meant that gaps could be filled, and reissue in volumes meant that whole new novels could be had at a fraction of the standard purchase price by any readers who still had a lingering prejudice against fiction in numbers, or who objected to taking it in 'teaspoonful' doses. About a quarter of *All the Year Round*'s sales in the early years came from the bound-up parts by which a purchaser could buy a whole novel—and much extra—for 8s.

Dickens seems to have been fully occupied with *All the Year Round* only for the early part of the 1860s, and by 1870 he was dead. During the period 1859–64 what is most remarkable about the journal is that its conductor should have managed to maintain such a high standard of fiction satisfactory to such a wide circle of readers. It was by no means easy. When Cassell's magazines, which catered to exactly the same market, tried serials by Charles Reade and Wilkie Collins things always went wrong; circulation was lost; the artistic idealism of the novelist could not run in harness with the commercial practice of the proprietor.[26] Dickens managed discreetly to control his novelist while at the same time raising the intellectual capacity and moral tolerance of his reader.

III

All the Year Round was a test for any novelist and some were simply incapable of the journal's pace. The first two serials, *A Tale of Two Cities* and *The Woman in White*, were up to the mark and well beyond. To follow, Dickens tried for a number of top names, none of whom would firmly commit himself. *All the Year Round* used up contributors at a prodigious rate: 30,000 words a month, a three-volume novel in just over half a year was faster than many could trust themselves to write. And Dickens was in the market with other periodicals. His main competitors, *Once a week*, the *Cornhill* and *Macmillan's*, had the advantage of him in that they could offer higher remuneration. Since these rivals were all affiliates of large publishing houses they could make a bid for serialisation and volume publication combined. If he wanted to attract an author with temptingly large sums Dickens had to offer an awkward brokerage arrangement with an 'unimpeachable publisher' and agreements requiring four signatures (Dickens's, Wills's, author's and publisher's).[27] To contract the kind of contributor he wanted Dickens was always prepared to put out his considerable powers of charm—but often this did not suffice. His disadvantage can be shown in the dealings with Charles Reade for *Hard Cash*. Dickens had long wanted Reade as the 'best man to be got for our purpose'. But Reade's price, £925 for the serial rights, was too high; £800 was the most Dickens felt he could offer. Meanwhile Reade had had a simultaneous offer from Smith: '£2000 for a novel—copyright four years—lowest price 5s. and another £1000 if published in the "Cornhill Magazine".'[28] Smith's was the better offer by hundreds, if not thousands. But Reade's *amour propre* was wounded by the fact that there was no guarantee that his novel would appear in the magazine (the *Cornhill* was between editors).[29] For this reason Dickens got his serial. There is no doubt, however, that, if he had really gone for Reade, Smith could have taken him from Dickens with no trouble at all. As it was, Reade was left with the arduous business of negotiating the best price he could from Sampson Low for volume reissue. He demanded £3,000—the sum Collins had been given for *No Name*. On being offered £2,250 he decided to have his work published on commission and take all the risk himself. None of this complication would have arisen had he taken Smith's offer in the first place.

For *All the Year Round*'s third serial Dickens, in what one imagines was some desperation, turned to his friend Charles Lever. Lever had at least one of the qualities Dickens required—a 'name'—but was sadly lacking in most of the others. He had never been very strong on what he called 'chains' in his narrative (apparently he saw them as a kind of bondage) and what Dickens by contrast called 'the needful strong thread of interest'.[30] It augured ill for *All the Year Round* when Lever before the first issue asked Wills to remind him how the portion of the story he had provided went so far, as it had slipped his mind for the moment.[31] His habit of writing two serials simultaneously, one in the morning and one in the evening, did not make for clear-headedness on these matters.

Lever in the sixties was no longer the boisterous young man who had rattled off *Harry Lorrequer* so merrily: 'I have fallen upon evil days', he told Dickens, 'and can only write one out of every three or four.'[32] Lever had a keen sense of the pathos of his situation and the opening note in a pocket book he started to keep in 1861 records his imaginative bankruptcy well enough: 'Beginning to keep a Notebook at my age—is pretty much like building a stable after your horses have died off—Here is the book—but where are the Notes to come from?'[33]

It is likely that Dickens, out of affection and sympathy, blinded himself to the inevitable difficulties this disability of Lever's would produce. To make things worse Dickens, who had tentatively lodged his order with Lever in January, found himself suddenly wanting the work in July; George Eliot had let him down: 'Adam (or Eve) Bede is terrified by the novel difficulties of serial writing, cannot turn in the space; evidently will not be up to the scratch when Collins's sponge is thrown up.'[34] Lever answered amiably enough to this emergency:

My Dear Dickens,
Here's how it is. I believe by waiting till next year I could have done something creditable enough—but if wanted for July—I'll be up to

time with a rambling sort of autobiography...I have done none of it —save in my head.

With his empty head, unpreparedness, his imperfect energies Lever had, however, one great virtue. He was, as he said, 'convenient':

As to cutting out [he told Dickens]—Lord love you—cut—carve—and insert as you will with me—and always think of your public and not of *me* who have no amour propre about pen work.[35]

Dickens took full advantage of this permission, and would have done, one imagines, if Lever had had the *amour propre* of a peacock. Though he proclaimed publicly in his columns that 'I do not consider myself at liberty to exercise that control over [the novelist's] text which I claim as to other contributors',[36] it is evident that Dickens held his hand only for the most eminent of the novelists who worked for him, and Lever was not of that class.

In spite of Dickens's correcting hand the resulting story, *A Day's Ride* was a disaster for the journal. Lever was used to the monthly number and could not work to the pace or length of the short *All the Year Round* units. The tale he provided was as ambling as its title suggests. On receiving the first proofs Dickens was uneasy about Lever's failure to 'get at the action of the story'.[37] The reason was simply that there was no action to get at, nothing as Dickens complained, to 'take hold of the reader'. (With pardonable mendacity, perhaps, he informed the trade that the first numbers were notable for their 'dash' and 'very careful writing'.)[38] Insofar as it has a plot line the autobiographical narrative concerns an Irish apothecary's son, Algernon Sydney Potts (i.e. 'galleypots'—a representative jest) who gets himself tipsy, wagers away the horse he had hired and thereafter launches into a Quixotic expedition through Europe, involving a series of more or less comic accidents. The story is loose, picaresque and garrulous. It promises occasional Shandean comedy but is generally lame. To compound Dickens's problems Lever, who was living in Italy, proved to be dreadfully irregular with copy and telegrams flew from the *All the Year Round* office. On one occasion when the novelist gave sunstroke as his excuse Wills working through an unseasonably cold August rather surlily wished that 'his flaming Majesty'[39] would strike some of them at the *All the Year Round* office.

It took a few weeks for audience reaction to register. Readers would persevere with a dud story for a number or two; booksellers took a while to change standing orders. Nonetheless by October the signs were unmistakable. Dickens perceived that there was 'no vitality' in the serial: 'we drop', he told Lever, 'rapidly, and continuously, with The Day's Ride.'[40] The story would not, it was evident, keep up sales until Christmas when Dickens himself would come in.

The failure put Dickens in a cruel dilemma of divided loyalty to his journal and to a vulnerable old friend. But 'the property of All the Year Round' he decided 'was far too valuable' to take risks with.[41] Yet he seems genuinely to have felt that Lever was worthy of something other than summary foreclosure. With hindsight we can see, and probably Dickens could see, that he had fallen into what Trollope calls 'that worst of literary quicksands, the publishing of matter not for the sake of the readers, but for that of the writer'. In such circumstances, according to Trollope, the editor *must* steel himself and write, 'My dear friend, my dear friend, this is trash! It is so hard to speak thus—but so necessary for an editor.'[42]

Dickens was not prepared to undertake this necessary editorial brutality. Instead he decided to staunch the flow of readers with his own newly conceived monthly serial, *Great Expectations*. This had to be modified for the new form of weekly serialisation but even so he felt he could 'strike in' with it in December.[43] Generously he did not make Lever terminate: 'we must go on together' he told the other novelist.[44] For once *All the Year Round* carried two serials.

Dickens was particularly gentle in his breaking the unavoidably wounding news to Lever, who was at first mortified. Personally he thought *A Day's Ride* 'the best you ever wrote'.[45] It was a 'lottery' this magazine serialisation, he told Lever: 'some of the best books ever written', he claimed, 'would not bear the mode of publication.' It had been a 'toss up' with Wilkie Collins when he began *The Woman in White* 'on my leaving off'.[46]

Lever, who regularly exploded at the 'cool scoundrelism'[47] of other publishers was stimulated by Dickens's action to reply with rueful grace:

There are desagrémens in life that—by the feelings they elicit—are dearer than successes and believe me—that I am prouder in the friendship you feel for me than sorry for this event that evoked it... I own to you I hadn't thought so ill of the Ride as the Public has, but so submissive am I to that same Public—and so convinced am I of the Talleyrand maxim, that tout le monde a toujours raison—that if told by the same authority I was blind—I'd buy a dog tomorrow to lead me.[48]

Dickens would not hear of Lever 'stabling his beast'. The novelist got his promised payment of £750, even though after *Great Expectations* began they had to sell the American rights of *A Day's Ride* at half price. Lever's novel thus finished its course under the shadow of a much greater work. Nonetheless readers were not entirely pacified and Dickens had to insert an advertisement seven issues before the end of Lever's tale to assure exasperated subscribers that its days were numbered.

IV

Dickens was surely justified in acting as he did when Lever's serial floundered. It was the kind, but authoritative, intervention many publishers must have wished they could make with a failing writer. Dickens did not, however, reserve this solicitous interference for weaker contributors only. As he told Lever, Wilkie Collins's novel had by no means passed unscathed through the *All the Year Round* office (though we may suspect that the 'toss-up' business was an exaggeration designed to soothe Lever's pain).

Dickens, as was usual with him, waited until the introductory phase of *The Woman in White* was complete before commenting. As one reads it now with the whole structure in hand the novel has one of the best openings of any narrative in the language. In five short numbers the reader is introduced to the sensitive artist hero, Walter Hartright, is thrilled by the spectral woman in white he encounters at night in Hampstead, tantalised by the mysterious baronet who pursues her and the strange goings-on at Limmeridge. Each instalment finishes on a brilliantly conceived curtain line which keeps the reader firmly on the hook.

Collins laboured over the opening of this 'longest and most complicated [serial] I have tried yet'.[49] He left London, took a cottage at Broadstairs and sweltered through the summer there working out the opening. After the first two numbers were set up in proof he broke them down so as to perfect the narrative's beginning and abbreviate it to needle sharpness.

On Saturday 7 January, the day when the seventh instalment, in which Walter leaves Limmeridge and Laura to Sir Percival's schemes, was published Dickens wrote to Collins. He began by congratulating the younger artist on his improved 'tenderness' and his 'writing'. Then he went on to level the criticism that was clearly in the forefront of his mind:

> I seem to have noticed, here and there, that the great pains you take express themselves a trifle too much, and you know that I always contest your disposition to give an audience credit for nothing, which necessarily involves the forcing of points upon their attention, and which I have always observed them to resent when they find it out—as they always will and do.[50]

One would think this a little hard to take. The letter conveys a thinly veiled instruction, almost a warning order, against over-ingenuity. As he had told Collins before, Dickens did not like fiction which was 'too elaborately trapped, baited and prepared'.[51]

Dickens's relationship with Collins in other respects was of the warmest. Indeed he seems to have confided and relied on the younger man in the distress produced by the break-up of his marriage. Professionally they had collaborated on various theatrical ventures and Dickens had accepted in good part Collins's criticism of *A Tale of Two Cities*. But with *The Woman in White* there is no doubt who wields the dominant influence. It may not be coincidental that Collins after this communication from Dickens went on to develop the duel between Marian and Fosco at Blackwater, the tensest and most gripping section of the narrative.

Collins was not apparently offended by Dickens's intervention. Even after success had quintupled his salary to an offer of

£5,000 from Smith for his next novel (only Dickens himself had ever been offered as much for *one* work, Collins complacently noted), he continued to supply proofs of his fiction for *All the Year Round* for inspection. And as before Dickens spoke his mind; *No Name* he felt needed some comedy added, and the narrative should be generally relaxed.[52] There is no evidence that Collins made any such offering of his work to Smith for prior examination.

It was not merely a one way current—a mentor-pupil relationship. Dickens affirmed himself Collins's 'obedient disciple' in acknowledgement of the fact that he was learning from his brilliant protégé. Since most of the interchange was oral we cannot know how much each contributed to the other. But it is certain that Dickens read his fiction to the younger novelist, and the general tightening of plot in his last three novels suggests he picked up something from Collins's tightly knit fiction.

V

Bulwer Lytton who took over from *Great Expectations* with *A Strange Story* was an altogether different case from Lever or Collins. Lytton had written best-selling novels years before *Pickwick* and was an author for whom Dickens and the discriminating reading public generally had an enormous respect. No less than Dickens Lytton had shown an ability to progress beyond styles in which he found early fame. He had mastered the historical, 'silver fork', 'Newgate', and lately the domestic novel. For Dickens he was to supply what is probably the first science-fiction work in English.

Dickens played Lytton very carefully. There had been some friendly discussion about *A Tale of Two Cities*, as among equals, about the 'canons of fiction' regarding improbability. Dickens followed this up in August with a request that Lytton might think of contributing to *All the Year Round*. The letter of proposal was delicately laudatory. No inducement other than that of personal friendliness towards the editor could persuade such an august writer. Anticipating some patrician hesitation about association with a twopenny weekly he assured Lytton that 'it has the largest audience to be got that comprehends intelligence and cultivation.' If Lytton could 'reconcile the doing of such a thing with [his] inclination and convenience', it would give Dickens 'unspeakable gratification'.[53]

Lytton was at this period a 'Blackwood's author' and punctiliously he offered the new novel he had in mind to the Edinburgh firm for the same price that Dickens proposed. But *Blackwood's Magazine* (circulation around 7,000 monthly) could not enter the field with the twopenny weekly: 'It may answer to Mr. Dickens to give such a sum as a tale from you will be a great advertisement and stimulus to "All the Year Round" but we could not make such a transaction pay.'[54] Blackwood's would not stand in Lytton's way, so Dickens got his man.

Lytton accepted, eventually, and it is a measure of Dickens's deference that he offered an initial payment of £1,500—two or three times the usual payment. With the £1,200 he would get for the volume publication, £300 for the American rights, odd £50s for European translations and what Routledge would give for the cheap editions (Sampson Low were forbidden by the contract to sell the novel under 7s. 6d.), Lytton stood to make not much less than £5,000 from this one work. Dickens, however, was not alone in thinking his man worth the price. The *Publishers' Circular* for 17 June 1861 hailed the alliance of Lytton and *All the Year Round* as a new era in literature: 'really an important fact, as marking another great step in the progress towards that universal magazine writing which appears to be now rapidly approaching'.

Once he had the novelist signed Dickens carefully explained the technical problems of length and installment to the new recruit. Lytton provided an abstract of his proposed story which it was decided would be begun in August. This was now December and *Great Expectations* was still running, so there was ample time for advance writing and the kind of tutorial discussion Dickens liked to have with contributors who were also close friends. At this stage, when the diplomatic minuet of offer and acceptance were completed, Dickens's manner became much more business-like. 'I have perfect faith in such a master hand as yours' he had assured Lytton;[55] yet he made it quite clear that he was to have what film-makers call the 'final cut'. After recommending a changed ending for the first part he added: 'I think I have become, by dint of necessity and practice, rather cunning in this regard; and perhaps you would not mind my looking closely to such points from week to week.'[56] Similarly it was intimated that Dickens would want to see the story in advance both to relieve the pressure on the hard-pressed printer and so that he could judge the quality of the work with a 'sweep of the story, in front of him'.[57] Lytton was quite amenable on this point and three months before publication Dickens had the earlier part of the story before him, set up in proof.

With the strong sense of coterie that marked *All the Year Round's* proceedings Dickens tried the sample on Wills as representative of the solid, average reader and on Collins, the master of the short unit serial. The consequent advice was substantial and to the point:

—In shortening the conversations, to bring out the immediate human interest, particularly through Isabel.
—To make the vision in the Museum less abstruse, and perhaps to shadow out in Margrave's brain, his part of wickedness in the story.
—Greatly to condense the MS. read by Fenwick at Derval Court.
—To substitute some other terror for the raising of the dead from the Mausoleum.[58]

It is clear from these suggestions that Dickens had the story up to about the fiftieth chapter, as it is in the printed version. It is equally clear that Lytton took the advice. The conversations in the first half of the novel (unlike those in the second) are short and brisk. The vision in the Museum is not abstruse and we are given a picture of the inside of Margrave's brain, 'a moral world, charred and ruined' (ch. 32). The manuscript which Fenwick reads in chapter 39 is quoted only for a page or so, then it is summarised and the whole is condensed into one chapter. The 'terror' in chapter 51 is short, hallucinatory and unspecific. From these few details it is safe to assume that the staff of *All the Year Round* had some important influence in revising Lytton's story.

The most interesting interchange, however, took place over the ending to *A Strange Story*. Dickens did not come to see this in advance as Lytton was still wrestling with it while the novel was coming out in the journal. In September, after the serial had been running a month, Dickens expressed himself 'burning to get at the whole story'.[59] There were, however, difficulties. Lytton was not at all sure how he should wind his story up. At first he was disposed to cap the narrative with a long, explanatory dialogue between the hero Fenwick and his old patron Faber. This would lay out all the meaning of the story for the reader, whom Lytton did not really trust to extricate it for himself. As before with Collins, Dickens was for trusting the reader: 'I counsel you most strongly NOT to append the proposed dialogue between Fenwick and Faber...Decidedly I would not help the reader...Let the book explain itself.'[60] And again a few days later: 'the explanation point...*must be done as a part of the book.*'[61] In this advice Dickens was imposing the house style on his new contributor. *All the Year Round* favoured tight, self-contained narratives which first stimulated then tested the reader's alertness. This was one reason why *The Woman in White* succeeded and *A Day's Ride* failed. Bulwer ought to observe the disciplines of the journal in this matter.

Dickens in fact had a solution to Lytton's problem. He had particularly liked Mrs Poyntz, a tyrannical old snob, who figures in the early part of the narrative. 'Could Mrs. Poyntz', he asked, 'as the representative of The World be brought into it? I fancy I see a loophole of light in that direction.'[62] Lytton replied with 'cordial thanks for your trouble and hints. No doubt every story should contain in itself all that is essential to its own explanation—and to a thinker I hope mine does...I don't see how Mrs. Poyntz can be reintroduced into the story. How could she come to Australia?' (where the story ends, a fair objection). But she might, he thought, be brought into a 'supplementary chapter, as talking over the book'.[63] Dickens approved this suggestion. At the same time he suggested some of the 'laboriously symbolical' touches might be toned down.[64] But at this stage Dickens's influence seems to have waned. There is no reappearance of Mrs Poyntz and the very end of the book, unlike the first two-thirds, is 'laboriously symbolical'.

VI

This interference was something no normal publisher could venture with an author of Lytton's stature. Bentley, for example, had been unable to explain to Lytton in terms sufficiently authoritative or critically persuasive that *Harold* was too portentous and laden with historical erudition. Consequently the work had gone on to be something of a failure. But suggestions offered, as they were, *inter pares* were acceptable to the great man. Where they were incorporated they were beneficial since their overall tendency was to curtail Lytton's besetting weakness for narrative inflation and pomposity of manner.

This is the more surprising when we remember how proud Lytton was. When Wills unwittingly put an intramural advertisement in the journal for the forthcoming *A Strange Story* as by Lord Lytton, the author was infuriated. It had to be advertised anonymously as 'by the author of *My Novel*, *Rienzi*, etc.' His name was not to be bandied about in a twopenny journal. After Dickens's intervention he was mollified but it was not the kind of objection the editor can have been used to. Wills was constrained to write a humble letter thanking the author for his 'handsome' conduct in the matter.

And yet for all his grandiloquence and assumed indifference about 'the common herd'[65] (as he liked to call the reading public) Lytton was chronically nervous about the reception of his work. Might not *A Strange Story*, he feared, be too subtle? In short, were *All the Year Round*'s readers up to appreciating Lytton? In June, coming up to publication day, he wrote to Dickens voicing his fears:

> I must own that my doubts as to the suitableness of this tale to your audience are somewhat increased and trouble me much—so that I should be glad of your thoughtful opinion as soon as more is printed—The doubts are also aggravated by the unexpected discovery that the copy is not sufficient [he goes on to discuss problems of length]...But at present my doubt is on the whole thing—and it is very much this—The moral or physcological [sic] intention being necessarily subtle or somewhat ideal—May not the whole outward

story appear as addressed to a very popular class, like an appeal to superstitions—I fear too that it will be difficult to judge of this thoroughly even from the portion to be printed—only to be judged as a whole.

I am deep in the back numbers of your tale with which I am literally *enchanted*. What freshness and gusto—In point of interest I know of none even of yours more enthralling. I think I remember the old White Woman in her bride dress who must have furnished [Miss Havisham]...[66]

This letter is peculiarly indicative of the unusual give and take relationship Dickens had with his client. In this case reassurance was forthcoming and Lytton's misgivings as to subtlety were soothed. Yet at the same time as he instilled confidence Dickens received commendation—and more than commendation—for his own efforts. Having been willing to put his novel onto the workshop floor for his 'fellow labourers' to criticise and reshape Lytton went on to suggest some 'improvements' to the ending of *Great Expectations*. At the other writer's instigation Dickens changed the proofs of the last number of his tale so as to unite Pip and Estella in the ruin of Satis House. This happy ending replaced one directly opposite in which the lovers meet blankly, years after, in London. It was, Dickens admitted, 'entirely due' to Lytton.[67]

Whether we think *Great Expectations* improved by the happy ending or not, the fact remains that both Lytton's and Dickens's novels were substantially altered. In other circumstances Dickens would probably not have taken it on himself to alter Lytton's work and Lytton would not have directly meddled with Dickens's novel had they not been 'working in company'.[68] As it was, either felt free to tell the other how best to end his story.

It is likely that Lytton got the better in the exchange. *A Strange Story* was reckoned a success and raised circulation by an estimated 1500.[69] Profiting from instruction Lytton went into the 'art of the weekly number' with a 'quite extraordinary constructive skill'[70] that surprised even his admirer Dickens. Lytton is not much read now, apart from the inferior *Last Days of Pompeii*, but *A Strange Story* is a work that deserves to be. It is narrated by a young doctor, 'a stern materialist' who becomes gradually entangled and practically destroyed by the forces of the occult. The action contains a murder hunt, a mysterious villain, a love plot, a climactic Australian setting and plentiful suspense. Most interesting for the modern reader is the use of contemporary scientific reference to authenticate an otherwise wildly romantic action. The result is what *The Times*, fumbling for our modern term, called a 'fairy tale of science'. *A Strange Story*, like its successor *The Coming Race*, originates many of the techniques of science fiction. Working out from the known facts of mesmerism through the more sensational claims of animal magnetism and electrobiology Lytton fantasticates his plot until the Sage of Aleppo, the elixir of life and such lines as 'Down to my feet, miserable sorcerer!' are tolerable. Although the ending is, as Dickens complained, 'laboriously symbolical' and talkative it remains for the most part a sharp little gem of a story from a writer whose fiction is normally loose-knit.

To sum up: in the years that Dickens was giving it his full attention *All the Year Round* brought out more good novels than any comparable house, with the possible exception of Smith at *Cornhill*. Dickens, unlike Smith however, influenced the novels he published and was himself influenced by his fellow authors. In many ways *All the Year Round* enjoyed the atmosphere of what we might call a writing workshop. It is wonderful to think of the ferment of ideas about fiction that were current there at this period. Dickens and Collins were reading Lytton's story and passing expert judgement, Wills—the 'commonplace' mind—was acting as guinea pig for the ordinary reader. Dickens and Wills were reading Collins's *No Name* in proof and offering their suggestions. (Collins had tried the 'outline' on Dickens in July.) Forster was reading Lytton's work and was a confidant for the germs of narrative for *Our Mutual Friend* which was beginning to stir in Dickens's mind. And Lytton was reading *Great Expectations* in proof and making his proposals for alteration. These are merely the few interactions we can trace because there is some recorded evidence. It is certain that there was much more verbal give and take which we shall never know about.

In spite of the journal's character as a writing community Dickens with Wills's help superintended and kept business affairs in order by the exercise of tact, diplomacy, economic good sense and personal authority. One is led to wonder what would have happened if other novelists had taken over the means of novel production in this way; *All the Year Round* shows it could be done. And in a less utopian way Dickens's journal performed a general service to the profession of novel-writing: 'the eminent author', declared the *Publishers' Circular* in 1861, 'may now descend from the six shilling Quarterly even to the penny weekly without the slightest fear of losing caste.'[71] It was the appearance of a story by Lytton in a twopenny periodical conducted by Dickens that inspired this sense of an important liberation.

9

Marketing 'Middlemarch'

To her contemporaries and even to herself there was something mysterious in the fact that George Eliot should have been such a successful novelist in terms of sales. Many, like Trollope, contemplated her popularity with frank bewilderment: 'I doubt whether any young person can read with pleasure either *Felix Holt*, *Middlemarch* or *Daniel Deronda*. I know that they are very difficult to many that are not young.'[1] John Blackwood, who had his money tied up in the novelist, shared the surprise but for him it was accompanied by relief. To appreciate *Adam Bede*, he told the novelist, 'I required to give my mind to it, and I trembled for that large section of hard readers who have no mind to give, but now I think the general applause is enlisting even noodles.'[2] It may be that Eliot's novels appealed to the self-improving reader who read without fully understanding, but was sustained by a strong sense of duty. Doubtless the firm evangelical cast of her morality made her fiction acceptable to strait-laced readers who might not otherwise have approved of novels. Blackwood was typical in praising Dorothea Brooke as 'better than any sermon.'[3] There was in this way a kind of social seal of approval on George Eliot. Blackwood sent free copies of her novels to all the top aristocratic Tories; Prince Albert on his own behalf sent a copy of *Adam Bede* to Baron Stockmar. Would he have done the same with *The Ordeal of Richard Feverel*? Probably not; certainly not, one imagines, with *East Lynne*.

Yet, paradoxically, there must have been those who sought out her novels for just the opposite reason, for the titillation which her unusually frank dealing with sex offered in an age of unofficial, but effective, censorship. George Eliot was not one of those who set out to reconcile those two irreconcilable things—'art and young girls'[4] and many must have found in her work the illicit pleasures of adult fiction.

Whatever the reason George Eliot was a prodigiously successful author, a 'cult' in her time.[5] As such she was a very valuable literary property to John Blackwood, who brought out all but one of her novels. So successful was she, in fact, that she could only be judged by her own remarkable standards. Although Blackwood sold just under 5,000 of the three-volume *Felix Holt* in 1866 the venture was judged to be something of a failure. Such a sale, the good reviews and the £5,000 which went with them would have had any other novelist jumping with joy. Nonetheless for those concerned with producing her novels it might be suspected that George Eliot was slipping in public favour. This, as it happened, was the usual pattern with novelists who had enjoyed massive popularity for ten years. Charles Reade, for instance, had been level-pegging with George Eliot at the beginning of the sixties. (It was a set-piece of criticism of the period to contest the superiority of *The Cloister and the Hearth* or *Romola.*) But by the end of the decade Reade was suffering badly from over exposure and bemoaning his low earnings:

Yesterday I treated with Mr. Frederic Chapman for 'A Terrible Temptation'. He gives me £600 for a 3 volume edition of 1500 copies. Should this be exhausted, fresh arrangements to be made. This is a pitiable decline on former sales. He gave me £1500 for limited copyright of 'Griffith Gaunt'. Bradbury and Evans gave me £2000 for ditto of 'Foul Play'.[6]

Wilkie Collins offers an even more striking parallel case. *The Woman in White* and *Adam Bede* were runaway bestsellers at the same period around 1860. Arising from his success Collins had an offer of £5,000 from Smith for his next serial novel. ('No living novelist (except Dickens) has had such an offer as this for *one* book,' he proudly noted.)[7] The next year Smith offered George Eliot £10,000 for *her* next novel. In 1868 Collins was reduced to £600 and aftersales profits from his publisher Tinsley (who was significantly less reputable than Smith, Elder and Sampson Low who had previously handled his work). The two novelists were clearly no longer in the same division. Mrs Henry Wood, who had made her name with *East Lynne* in 1861 wrote glumly in 1869: 'I do not get much more than half what

I once had for a three volume work. It used to average one thousand guineas for the guinea and a half edition. Now it is six hundred.'[8] For her next work it was, in fact, to sink to £500.

Felix Holt marked a comparable decline in George Eliot's career. But in her case it was hardly 'pitiable'—a low point certainly, but a low point which was still well above most novelists' highest. And with her there were unique problems; it was not that she did not still sell but that it was difficult to predict exactly *how* her work would sell. The real trouble with *Felix Holt*, for example, came not with the three-volume issue but with the cheaper 12s. two-volume reprint. Over the years Blackwood had developed a definite sales strategy with George Eliot's novels: massive printing of the three-decker followed, after only a few months, by a similarly massive two-volume reprinting, which, in turn would be followed by a judicious 6s. issue at the end of the publisher's term of copyright. The figures for *Adam Bede* illustrate the avalanche of sales Blackwood achieved with this sequence:

	3 vols. 31s. 6d.	*2 vols. 12s.*	*1 vol. 6s.*
Jan. 1859	2000		
May	750		
May	500	3000	
June		3000	
Sept.		2000	
Nov.		2000	
June 1860		1000	
June 1861		500	
Oct.			3000
Feb. 1864			1000
Aug. 1866			500[9]

The 'Bedesman', as Blackwood called it, sold indefatigably. So too did *The Mill on the Floss*. The best part of 6,500 three-and 2,000 two-volume copies were sold off within a year; the 1,500 6s. single volumes which were printed two years after the novel's first publication sold out completely. *Felix Holt* did not conform to this pattern, however, and it was worrying. Blackwood printed 5,000 in June 1866 of which only 385 were left on hand at the end of the year. This was doubtless gratifying. But the 12s. edition which was brought out in December 1866 fared unexpectedly badly. 2,000 were printed of which only 613 were sold in the year; 1274 were still on hand in 1876. No 6s. version was embarked upon. The novel, in short, was a failure, and uniquely for George Eliot, made a loss entry in the publication ledger. Blackwood was annoyed with himself for letting it happen: 'I never was so far out in calculating what a sale would be.'[10] he told the novelist. He might well have blamed two of his *bêtes noires*, Mudie and the 'yellow books which seem to haunt the rising generation worse than any plague of Egypt' (i.e. W. H. Smith's cheap yellow backs).[11] But he must also have wondered whether George Eliot herself were not in eclipse with the mass of readers.

II

It was in the shadow of *Felix Holt's* perplexing failure that George Eliot began work on her 'English novel'—*Middlemarch.* First ideas for this work began to take form in 1867; thereafter it became an increasingly ambitious project involving the fusion of two separately conceived elements, one centred around Dorothea Brooke, the other around Lydgate.[12] But by 5 April 1871, the genetic problem was solved and Lewes could write to the American publishers Osgood, Ticknor and Company, offering them the work as a proposition to 'turn over in your minds at leisure...Mrs. Lewes sees her way to finishing her new novel by this autumn. It is a story of English provincial life—time 1830—and will be in three volumes.' But unfortunately George Eliot, who had some 240 pages written, was already beginning to exceed even the ample proportions of the three-decker and it was evident that something more capacious would be needed. Blackwood had been making polite enquiries as to what Mrs Lewes had in mind for some months. On 7 May Lewes wrote to him with a definite proposal, which is interesting enough to quote in its entirety:

My dear Blackwood

Here we are quietly settled for the summer and I hope you will be able to run down and see us (station Haslemere) some day and get out of the vortex of London.

Meanwhile here is something for you to turn over in your mind, and come prepared to discuss. Mrs. Lewes finds that she will require

4 volumes for her story, not 3. I winced at the idea at first, but the story must not be spoiled for want of space, and as you have more than once spoken of the desirability of inventing some mode of circumventing the Libraries and making the public *buy* instead of borrowing I have devised the following scheme, suggested by the plan Victor Hugo followed with his long *Misérables*—namely to publish it in *half-volume parts* either at intervals of one, or as I think better, two months. The eight parts at 5/– could yield the 2£ for the four volumes, and at two month intervals would not be dearer than Maga. Each part would have a certain unity and completeness in itself with separate title. Thus the work is called *Middlemarch*. Part 1 will be *Miss Brooke*.

If in a stiff paper cover—attractive but not bookstallish—(I have one in my eye) this part ought to seduce purchasers, especially if Mudie were scant in supplies. It would be enough to furnish the town with talk for some time, and each part thus keep up and swell the general interest. *Tristram Shandy* you may remember was published at irregular intervals; and great was the desire for the continuation. Considering how slowly the public mind is brought into motion this spreading of the publication over 16 months would be a decided advantage to the sale—especially as each part would contain as much as one ought to read at a time.

Ponder this; or suggest a better plan![13]

It is a provocative letter, if only from the number of roles that its writer adopts. Lewes is at once the friend, the literary agent, the apologist, the market analyst, the husband and the high-pressure salesman. At this period, of course, many contracts stipulated that 'in the event of the author being a married lady this agreement should be countersigned by her husband'. Chapman and Hall were obliged for form's sake to do business through William Gaskell, the Unitarian minister, rather than his novelist wife. But Lewes was doing much more than mere formal arranging. What he was attempting was a diplomatic compromise between alternatives one of which was unacceptable to the publisher (the four-volume novel) and the other of which was unacceptable to the author (serialisation). And his freedom of movement was limited by the memory of *Felix Holt's* sales.

Blackwood, despite his friendliness with the Leweses was not to be won over that easily. In 1862 Eliot had broken the established relationship with the Edinburgh house and sold Smith *Romola*, her historical novel of the Italian middle ages. Blackwood had not protested for two reasons. First because he did not believe in 'fancy'—or as he called them 'wild'[14]—prices like those offered by Smith (who was prepared to go to a five-figure payment for the novel). Secondly, he was probably convinced that George Eliot's *métier* was the novel of regional, midland life with which she had made her name. The publisher was noticably cooler when she 'returned to her first friend'[15] with *Felix Holt* which Smith (who in his turn did not like politically strong fiction) had turned down. 'I read the first two MS volumes before concluding anything,' wrote Blackwood to W. Lucas Collins, stressing the independence of his decision.[16] This is not to say that there was any estrangement or that the firm did not welcome George Eliot's work. (Langford, Blackwood's manager, 'became positively radiant' when he heard the news of *Middlemarch*.)[17] But Blackwood was no longer the simply acceptive patron he had been in the early sixties when he would, out of the goodness of his heart, make *ex gratia* payments. And Lewes, as we see, did not confide in Blackwood that he was simultaneously making arrangements with an American firm, which might well have the work first.[18]

Blackwood had other factors to weigh up. The sixties closed on a period of considerable confusion for the producer of novels. The old order was giving way, but to what was not entirely clear. Should the progressive publisher invest in a few great authors or disperse his interest over a wider field? Blackwood was, one may guess, not sure of how to go forward into the 1870s. In 1869 he turned down novels by Trollope and Mrs Oliphant on the grounds that he was fully extended. At the same time, however, he was enquiring of George Eliot 'Are you writing anything?'[19]

Lewes had one strong card. Blackwood was at this time furious with the libraries, and especially Mudie, for the 'enormous discounts' which they wanted to exact from him. Almost every one of his business letters through 1871 contains some reference to the detested Mudie. Langford, Blackwood's business manager, actually saw it as the time when the final pitched battle must be fought:

Mudie's position cannot be helped, must be faced and either we must yield henceforth more and more to him or take our ground and defy him. The only other course is to publish our novels openly at a lower price.[20]

In this fighting mood they would be more inclined to listen to Lewes's proposals for a new way to sell fiction. That *Middlemarch* would help the firm 'get out of the clutches of Mudie'[21] was a view put forward more than once in the Blackwood-Langford correspondence.

Something else in Lewes's favour was that Blackwood had no reason to love the four-volume form any more than he did. As Bentley stiltedly pointed out to G. P. R. James when his *Louis XIV* threatened to overflow three volumes: 'work in four volumes is not within the class of publications termed popular.'[22] Reade had found this out with his *The Cloister and the Hearth* which had more success of esteem than of sales. And Blackwood had had some personal experience of the curse that lay on the four-volume production with Lytton's *My Novel* (1853) and *What Will he Do with It?* (1858). The second of these, which had cost Blackwood £3,000, was offered as a reduced remainder by Mudie only a few months after it came out. As for *My Novel*, this work had turned out to be so long that Lytton, with unusual levity, suggested they might retitle it *The Boa Constrictor*. Langford was unamused and wrote in anguish from London on hearing that the new work would be in four volumes although it had been announced in the *Publishers' Circular* as three:

I am greatly alarmed at the prospects of My Novel there is so general an objection to its being in four vols—I *know* that it will materially affect the subscription and when Kate Stewart [Mrs Oliphant's concurrent work] was being subscribed about the library people all strongly objected to the 4 vols…Mr. Miles told me today that he should only take half what he would if it had been in 3 vols.[23]

As it happened *My Novel* sold well enough in four volumes, but there were clearly extraordinary risks involved in the over-size form.

In fact Lewes's letter must have induced a certain sense of *déjà vu* in Blackwood. Twenty years before something oddly similar had occurred in connection with this same work, *My Novel.* In 1849 Lytton, then a new Blackwood's author, had declared himself

more and more inclined to think that for great *sales*—the usual 3 volume form is wearing out and think something great might be done by a popular book in a new shape—avoiding what has been done before in mere form whether by Dickens etc. or the orthodox Circulating Library editions—Tristram Shandy and Clarissa Harlowe came out volume by volume—Don Quixote was published in parts.[24]

Encouraged by Blackwood Lytton went on to propose an exotic form for his forthcoming *My Novel.* It should be published in the magazine and finally in volumes, as was orthodox, but in between an intermediate issue should be made in '*livraisons*', on the French pattern. Forster, Chapman and Hall's literary adviser, had suggested to him that the reissue should be in twelve 1s. volumes, which would bind up into four or six volumes eventually. Blackwood on the other hand suggested 5s. numbers, which would comprise four of the magazine instalments. At first Lytton was cool towards this proposal, preferring 2s. or 2s. 6d. *livraisons* of two numbers. But after some months he came more and more to the publisher's way of thinking: in June 1850, when he sent the first four numbers for inspection he was on the brink of accepting Blackwood's scheme:

I own I entertain great doubts of the efficacy of a serial at 2s. containing the two numbers, already just read by so many thousands in the Magazine—I almost doubt whether your first idea of 5s. parts be not better. But this must be well weighed and deliberately considered after you have read the specimens sent. In your present idea the 4 numbers comprise 2 parts at 2s. each. There will be 12 parts in all—It may therefore be a doubt (returning to the old idea) whether the present specimens should form rather one part at 4s. being 6 parts in all instead of 12. But you will think over this...[25]

In the event the publisher's nerve was not up to the experiment and the 5s. venture was quietly shelved. *My Novel* was run through *Blackwood's Magazine* and then issued in four volumes.

In the case of George Eliot's novel, however, it appeared the publisher did not want four volumes. On the other hand George

Eliot did not want to go in for the magazine serial which was the obvious vehicle for the over-size narrative. She had very strong ideas about the artistic propriety of the arbitrary divisioning which serialisation enforced. This is shown by her dealings with Smith over *Romola* ten years before. Smith had bid for the novel after hearing the author read the beginning of it at her home. It seems to have been a finely organised piece of salesmanship on Lewes's part. Smith afterwards reported that till then, 'I had not known how deeply a woman's voice could charm.'[26] The next day, with the author's voice still ringing in his ears, apparently, he wrote to Lewes offering £10,000 for *Romola*, stipulating only that the length should be sufficient for sixteen numbers of the *Cornhill*. But when the work was 'almost completed' George Eliot insisted that the work must be reduced to twelve, over-size, parts. Smith remonstrated, pointing out that these large portions would unbalance the layout of his magazine, and that he would be out of pocket since he would have to start paying another novelist four months earlier. Lewes apparently took Smith's part but George Eliot was adamant; she would not transgress 'the canons of her art'. In May 1862 she signed an agreement for twelve instalments, at £583 6s. 8d. each. Smith thus gave up four parts, George Eliot £3,000.[27]

In fact George Eliot miscalculated; the work over-ran to fourteen numbers after all. But this was no concession to Smith and his editor. The novelist was simply not prepared to force her work into any shape that did not suit. And often, of course, these things only made themselves evident during, or after, the writing. Not for her the Procrustean rigours of the monthly serial or the exactly measured magazine instalment.

One convenience of the form Lewes suggested for *Middlemarch* was that it would not require George Eliot to fit within a definite frame—ten or so pages either way would not matter. Nor would she have to break down the presently existing 'Miss Brooke' narrative so as to intermix it with other material. A third benefit, though Lewes is too tactful to mention it directly, is that she would not be bound to regular or constricted output. *Les Misérables* was a notoriously digressive book. The *Publishers' Circular* for 16 November 1868 had a long, jocular piece about

M. Hugo's habit of taking up to ten volumes for his stories and particularly the voluminousness of this one novel:

> Its inordinate length reminds one of the *mot* of the newspaper editor, who, having received from a contributor a leading article on Turkish finances six columns and a half long, was advised to hang it up as country housewives hang a flitch of bacon, and carve leading articles out of it when required.

Nor, if one thought about it, was the allusion to *Tristram Shandy* entirely reassuring. That novel came out very irregularly. It was also unfinished and was a work in which, as its author jocularly calculated, digression had outweighed progression by a factor of 364 to 1. For a novelist who already feared that she had 'too much matter, too many momenti' it was not an altogether happy comparison.

Finally, despite his appeal to venerable literary models, it is likely that Lewes's eyes were fixed on the dollars. In late 1857 Charles Reade had his two-volume *White Lies* issued by Ticknor and Fields in four 'half volumes' each selling at 25 cents and coming out monthly. The reason for this eccentric form was practical. In order to get a return from American sales it was necessary to send early sheets to one's contracted transatlantic publisher so that he, working at breakneck speed, could get out an authorised edition. Releasing the copy in half-volume units had the advantage that it kept the unprinted material together while reducing the danger period—which was the time between the author parting with the manuscript in England and the accredited American publisher putting out the printed article before the pirates could steal it.

Lewes was heavily involved in the American market and this, too, resulted in complicated negotiations. Although it first appeared that *Middlemarch* would come out in *Every Saturday*, it was eventually Harper's who got the novel for their insatiable *Weekly*, with two-volume production to follow, at £120 for early sheets. Lewes, therefore, was proposing a form of serialisation which would reconcile the opposing demands of three parties. It would suit his American paymasters, who wanted secure early sheets; Blackwood, who was reluctant to take a four-volume work which might not catch on; and George Eliot, who would not write in short instalments for anybody—however much they paid her.

III

Although he does not mention it outright, Lewes is clearly proposing an experiment in serialisation. Such experiments were fairly common at this period when it was felt that the traditional forms like the three-volume novel and the monthly thirty-two-page serial had had their day. At Smith's suggestion, for example, Trollope brought out his *Last Chronicle of Barset* in thirty-two weekly 6d. parts from December 1866 onwards. (At Lewes's suggestion Smith had actually toyed with this idea for *Romola,* the bitty form would have suited the novel even less than the *Cornhill* did.) This was in line with an increasing and more imaginative use of magazine serialisation, and some novelists were beginning to look at newspapers as a vehicle for their fiction. Trade journals like the *Publishers' Circular* solemnly discussed the possibility of a new generation of writers in numbers to rival their 'great originator' Dickens.[28] In general, however, the tendency was to shorter, more rapidly recurrent and cheaper instalments. To judge by the fiction they preferred, the reading public's attention span seemed to have lessened somewhat over the years. On this score alone there was some risk in Lewes's proposal.

As Jerome Beaty demonstrates in his *Middlemarch from Notebook to Novel*, George Eliot had begun by looking for something to suit the disparate narrative blocks with which she started. Had there been a future for a four-volume *Middlemarch* there is no doubt she would have brought it out in that form. But Blackwood, like Lewes, now 'winced' at the idea of four-volume issue. In 1870 people would no longer, it seemed, pay two guineas for a novel unless the sum were spread out. And as his comments about Mudie make clear, Lewes appreciated that after *Felix Holt* the libraries could no longer be relied on for massive orders.

What was involved here in an acute form was the perennial struggle which had gone on through the century between fiction for buying and fiction for lending. What Lewes put forward was a hybrid of the two which would cream both markets without being completely dependent on either. *Middlemarch* should have the stiff covers and narrative wholeness associated with the library volume; at the same time it should have the reduced price and deferred payment associated with the serial. It would thus be both bought and hired. The scheme certainly had a certain novelty though, paradoxically, it would also appeal to the more traditional kind of reader who felt that standards should be kept up in a world where fiction was increasingly becoming the property of the newspapermen. William Tinsley was one such old-fashioned reader and comments in his *Recollections*:

> A book rich in talent or genius, has as much or more right to good dress as a rich man. Where is the intellectual man or woman who is not proud to possess the glorious octavos of Thackeray, Dickens, Lever and even some of Frank Smedley's volumes, which are little monuments of book building, as are some of Anthony Trollope's original editions? And even though the original editions of George Eliot's (Miss Evans's) books are mostly in crown octavo, they are beautifully printed, in good readable types, and on good paper. There is no huddling the type and matter together, and making the pages a conglomeration of almost invisible lines hard to decipher. It must be well remembered that George Eliot published her two last great fictions in eight volumes each, or at least in eight five shilling parts, made into four volumes, at two pounds each book; and, as all the reading world knows, the first editions of *Daniel Deronda* and *Middlemarch* are lovely specimens of English printed books.[29]

This question of the 'dignity' of *Middlemarch* weighed heavily with George Eliot and Lewes. The novel must not be 'thin'—each 'book' must be indeed a book. It was only later that Lewes admitted the possibility of an advertiser, which with paper covers was the hall-mark of the monthly number. And even then a prime value of advertisements in Lewes's eye was that they would make each volume appear thicker.

IV

John Blackwood, who normally acted as his own publisher's reader, decided to trust his judgement. As it would happen the first part of *Middlemarch* was full of the provincial matter and character which 'intensely delighted' him; 'quite wonderful' was his private opinion on 19 July.[30] It is also likely that he was disposed to accept the idea promptly since he could legitimately claim that he had put forward the notion of 5s., bimonthly 'books' himself, to Lytton twenty years earlier. (One wonders if Lewes knew of this, and of Lytton's comparison with *Tristram Shandy* and the French *livraisons*; he must surely have picked it up from Blackwood in one of their conversations.) Moreover, Blackwood had suggested after *Felix Holt* that next time 'we must experiment in a new form.'[31] The multi-volume form was consequently approved and Blackwood continued to be delighted by the portions of the story which he saw. Emboldened by the publisher's warmth Lewes wrote a sharper, more precise business letter on 21 August:

> Since the plan is novel and may not realize all that one hopes from its novelty the choice is open to you to speculate or not as you think fit. Assuming that the work will consist of 4 volumes to sell at 40/– if you propose to take the risk we should be willing to part with the *English* right only, for 4 years (which would bring it into your other term of copyrights) for the sum of £6,000—payable in the course of 1872–*3* in any instalments you may think fit.
>
> Or if we take the risk we should require a royalty of 2/– per copy sold, on each 5/– part, in the original form, and an equivalent royalty on copies in cheaper editions. Half yearly accounts.
>
> We ought to sell 10,000 at this cheap rate, because soon the Libraries will find it more profitable than ordinary novels since they will have 8 vols. to distribute in lieu of 4. But no one can tell.[32]

The argument about the Libraries was dubious since they would, as with other serials, wait for the reprinted volume form before buying in bulk (though W. H. Smith might be expected, as he did in fact, to order substantially). But it is evident that the balance of power was with Lewes; it is he who dictates terms for Blackwood to accept. The implied reference to American arrangements puts a coercive pressure on the publisher, suggesting that Lewes had already some agreement made in that quarter. The first alternative he offers would attract Blackwood if he were really confident; it would mean he could extract all the revenue from the market with first and cheap impressions.

But because of the novelty of the form it might be difficult to know how much to print and mistakes could be costly. Six thousand pounds was a heavy sum. There was the memory of *Felix Holt*. Who was to say that the public had not turned against George Eliot as they did against Reade, or the older Trollope? Finally, there was Lytton. Was not the idea his—could one honourably appropriate the serialisation which he, in a sense, had pioneered but had not yet taken advantage of?

The firm, not least Blackwood himself, was inclined to tread very warily on the 'Middlemarch experiment'.[33] Langford wrote from London on 1 September 1871 confirming his chief's cautiousness:

I quite agree with you that Lewes's terms are out of the question. It would never do to pay absolutely any very large sum when we are about to try an experiment. I would much prefer to stretch to the utmost with a royalty, as our object must be first to secure ourselves against loss...the experiment must not be tried altogether at the publisher's expense. That the sale would reach 10,000 is a mere assumption, based on no facts.[34]

Meanwhile Blackwood had written to Lewes demanding clarification of the American arrangement and an assurance that no part of the work would be published before it came out in England. He also had a counter-proposition for Lewes:

My idea of terms is to give you a smaller lordship than you propose but at the same time to guarantee you a particular sum whatever the result might be. I would be disposed to risk the £6000 but our experience of Felix Holt is that we had given too much in that case.[35]

But Lewes was immovable and apparently he would give no firm commitment on the American affair. Langford was furious and exploded in a letter to Blackwood:

As a matter of feeling and dignity I would have nothing to do with any book by an English writer that appears first abroad. This is another instance of the excessive greed that characterizes the proceedings at the Priory. It puts me in mind of the two partners in David Copperfield one of whom does the sentiment and the other the severity. Whatever arrangements authors make with America the English publisher should have precedence. I have no patience with such modes of proceedings.[36]

And with a final fling at Lewes's philosophical affiliations he observed: '*Comptism* [sic] ought to be spelt *Count*-ism.'

Having turned all this over in his mind Blackwood announced his opinion to his nephew William, together with his misgivings:

I enclose Lewes' letter. I think we had best just go in for the Lordship which will not be a bad thing.

Unless they have got a big sum I do not think they are wise as to their Yankee arrangement. It has a confounded trading look.[37]

The worry of the affair was sufficient to prevent him playing golf the next day (an activity which meant not much less than publishing to him) but he submitted and wrote to Lewes on 6 September accepting the second of Lewes's propositions, the 40 per cent royalty. This would mean some degree of loss- as well as profit-sharing (nonetheless he declared himself sanguine of a great coup).

Was his caution justified? We may find an answer in the printing figures for the novel in its various forms:

Date	*Printed*	*Accumulating Profit*	*Form*
Nov. 71–Dec. 73	5650		5s. numbers
Dec. 73	366 (bound up from above)	6602	4 vols. at 42s.
Feb.–Nov. 73	2724		4 vols. at 21s.
	525	386	,,
May 74–Apr. 76	18406	2084	7s. 6d. edn
Nov. 76	2100	518	,,
Oct. 77	2100	339	,,
Sept. 78	2100	541	,,
Mar. 80	2100	319	,,
Feb. 81	3150	542	,,

The *Middlemarch* experiment had paid off. What is interesting is that Blackwood, following Langford rather than Lewes, may have grossly underestimated the market of 'actual buyers'. The serialisation imprint was modest compared to what Dickens or Thackeray notched up (e.g. 28,000 for the monthly issue of *Our Mutual Friend*, 13,000 for *The Virginians*).[38] *Middlemarch* in parts sold completely out. There was only a minimal number left over to sew up into the four-volume, two-guinea sets that had been conceived as a safety net. What might have happened if Blackwood had tried for the 10,000 Lewes proposed? For it was clear that the serial had managed to catch the buying, as opposed to the borrowing, readership. The Edinburgh branch of the firm reported that they were 'selling copies over the counter in George Street to people who never think of buying an ordinary novel'.[39]

One voice, however, was raised up against *Middlemarch*'s success, that of Lytton. In October the novelist despatched an angry note to Edinburgh:

> I observe in the paper an announcement that you are bringing out a new novel by George Eliot in single volumes. If this be true, it occasions me, naturally, much chagrin—for you will probably remember that I was very desirous of bringing out 'My Novel' and 'What will he do with it' in that form—but, after consideration *you* were against it. Still I always cherished the idea—and had intended so to bring out the next novel published in my own name.
>
> Of course, therefore, it is annoying to see the design I had conceived to be my own, forestalled and appropriated by another novelist. The chance of success in such an experiment is in favour of the author who first starts it—those who may follow the example are looked upon as imitators—And of course it would not become me to imitate any other writer.[40]

It makes a curious little epilogue to the *Middlemarch* experiment and although demonstrably the initiative for the novel's serialisation came from Lewes one cannot help wondering whether the idea had an obscure and distant origin in Lytton's discussions with Blackwood in 1850.

V

Bearing in mind what we have seen of the preparatory dealings it would be a mistake to think that what we have is merely the record of a great novel instinctively finding its proper form. Rather it is something arrived at by an adjustment of reciprocal interests and by some carpentering with standard forms of outlet for the novel. Nonetheless the arrangement seems to have suited George Eliot well enough. When she returned to serious work again, late in the year, she set herself to master all the problems of fission and fusion which the bimonthly serial set. Jerome Beaty has traced how the original joins were made between the 'Miss Brooke' and 'Middlemarch' elements. To begin with there is a palpable disjunction evident, even to the reader of the printed page. Dorothea and Lydgate, the two centres of the early narrative, inhabit separate worlds, and the story alternates awkwardly between them. But gradually George Eliot interweaves the plot more and more until in the seventh book the strands are inextricable. Dorothea is involved in Lydgate's affairs, Lydgate is involved with Bulstrode's and, through Raffles, Bulstrode is involved with Ladislaw's. In the last books we can detect George Eliot using short chapters to accelerate the narrative pace (in the manner of Reade or Collins) and chapter alternations between groups of characters (in the manner of Dickens). Most surprising, perhaps, is the way in which she uses the tricks of the serialists that one expects she would have despised most—the working up of mystery and the suspense ending to a number. The seventh book ends with resolution to 'clear' Lydgate and the reader is left a month before he finds out how this will be done. In fact since George Eliot introduces sensational crime, mystery, a guilty love plot and suspense in the last stages of her novel, and since it was decided to speed up issue from two months to one, it is likely that she, as much as Lewes or Blackwood, became rather concerned with keeping the public on the end of her line.

Despite the increasing narrative activity in *Middlemarch* George Eliot did not sacrifice the original intention of books, each of which was to have 'a certain unity and completeness in itself'. Even after *Middlemarch* was collected into volume-form she determined to let the serial divisions stand so that the novel is invariably printed in eight subtitled 'books'. To keep the physical divisions of the serial in this way was extremely unusual, if not unique. Dickens, Thackeray, Trollope and others would always dissolve then regroup the parts of their serials into new wholes when they reprinted in volumes. It would be a very perceptive reader who could, without calculation, work out the original sections of *Pendennis* or *Copperfield* from a standard edition. But clearly George Eliot wanted to retain the complex interaction of small and large unities in the novel.

What had begun as a practical way of getting round problems of narrative lumpiness became, finally, the way in which George Eliot 'thought' about her work and its organisation.

According to Henry James, *Middlemarch* is 'a treasure-house of detail, but it is an indifferent whole'.[41] Critics will probably take sides on that issue forever. But one may be sure that whatever integrity *Middlemarch* does have is directly attributable to the marketing decisions that permitted it to appear in what was, by the commercial standards of the age, an exotic form.

10

Hardy
Breaking into Fiction

One of the discomforts of nineteenth-century authorship was to be pestered by letters from would-be writers wanting to know the secret of success. Thackeray had a short answer for such tyros:

> Dear Sir,
> I can give you little help or advice in the matter. You must know yourself in what literary subjects you are most interested—knock at publishers' doors, be refused, be accepted as all of us have done. I was a known and tolerably successful author when I tried 3 or 4 publishers with Vanity Fair…I was staying with Mr. Blackwood when the first of the Adam Bede papers arrived from an unknown hand—you may have to try once, twice thrice before you succeed.[1]

The advice could well have gone to the young Hardy who, in the sixties, was doing the rounds of the publishers. The earliest letters in Smith, Elder's and Macmillans' files from the young author are awkward accompanying notes to an unsolicited sample of fiction, hopefully submitted 'for your consideration'.

The author's uneasiness was understandable. To have a manuscript to submit for approval was in itself an admission of a kind of failure. The established author would sell his novel before composition, sometimes before he even had an idea of what it was to be about. Usually, once the agreement was signed, he by-passed the publisher's reader and often the publisher himself, sending copy direct to the printer. Many reputable authors, like Charles Reade, refused outright to permit judgement on their work by possible literary inferiors: 'I will never,' vowed Reade, 'under any circumstances submit a MS. of mine to the chance of any other writer comprehending it and seeing its merit.'[2]

This was very well for Reade but the unfledged novelist had little choice in the matter. His work's future was entirely dependent on this one 'chance'. If he had ability and were wise the best thing he could do would be to regard the process of 'knocking at publishers' doors' as an opportunity to pick up some useful tips, if nothing else. To his credit, this seems to have been the young Hardy's attitude.

Unless he had a sponsor or a contact the first hurdle which the starting author had to tackle was the publisher's reader. The growth of the power of the 'reader' in this period is an interesting phenomenon. It marks, among other things, the elevation of unbiassed critical intelligence as the guide to making the publisher's list. It may be seen as the reviewer's judgement advanced to a position before, rather than after, commercial investment in a work. But the publisher's reader did more than read. His alternate, grander title—'literary adviser'—often does better justice to his status in the firm. It was his task to balance the artistic idealism and economic ambition of the house; not merely to pass judgement on a manuscript but to predict whether or not it would sell. His specialised skills on these matters might give him dictatorial power. John Forster and George Meredith with Chapman and Hall, for example, had an authority that went far beyond mere opinion on manuscripts. When Mrs Wood brought her *East Lynne* to 193 Piccadilly, she did so with a warm introduction from Harrison Ainsworth an old friend of the house. Meredith's verdict, 'opinion decidedly against it', was queried by Ainsworth who as an editor with twenty years' experience might presume to know the value of a manuscript. Chapman asked Meredith to look again and reconsider. Meredith repeated his prohibition against the firm's taking it; the book was 'foul'.[3] So, in the face of the author's hopes, an influential friend's recommendation and the proprietor's inclination, the reader had his way. *East Lynne* went to Bentley's where it made a fortune.

Bentley seems to have used his readers in a somewhat lower capacity than his rivals.[4] Forster and Meredith were salaried. They had a place in the business and a strong voice on policy decisions. (It was Forster who worked out the form of profit-spreading together with lump-sum agreement which reconciled

Dickens to his publishers in the early 1840s.) So too with Smith Williams at Smith, Elder and Morley at Macmillan's and Langford at Blackwood's. From Bentley, however, Geraldine Jewsbury had a usual piece rate of a guinea a novel. Her influence, and that of her fellow readers for the firm, extended only as far as a favourable or dismissive opinion had weight with the head of the business. (She it was, incidentally, who recommended Bentley to take *East Lynne*.)

Since he was best known as a publisher of library three-deckers Bentley probably needed someone like Miss Jewsbury to keep his house from being engulfed in a wash of mediocre fiction. Certainly the general standard of the huge number of aspirant manuscripts does not seem to have been high; Miss Jewsbury would greet an egregiously bad work with the comment 'greater rubbish than usual'. The late sixties and seventies, the period when Hardy was trying to break into fiction, was still the heyday of the novel. 'I wrote novels', recalled Shaw, 'because everybody did so then.'[5] The glamour exerted by the literary profession on weak minds encouraged hordes of would-be Dickenses and George Eliots. Innumerable Victorian women hoped to emulate Charlotte Brontë and write themselves out of the restrictions which the age imposed on their sex.

Despite the inevitably rubbishy standard of most of it, the publishers did not attempt to staunch this stream. The more manuscripts a house had, the better chance of getting a winner. Henry Holt, the American publisher, expresses the trade mentality on this point wittily:

> I have lately awakened with a bang to the realization that all the time I have spent over American fiction during over forty years, has brought us just two books that paid a decent profit. I feel about it, however, a good deal as the Cuban must feel about continuing to pay for lottery numbers—that the time when they will win a prize must be nearer at hand than it was when he began.[6]

Nonetheless, although they rarely returned a novel unlooked at, many publisher's readers must have been, to put it mildly, cursory. *Wuthering Heights* went through six publishers in eighteen months. Charlotte Brontë's *The Professor* 'had the honour of being rejected nine times by the "Tr–de" '.[7] As for

Branwell, he became so desperate he superscribed *Condemn Not Unheard* on his submissions.[8] It is possible that the 'Tr–de' may have been put off by the Brontës' frugal habit of using old wrapping paper, with the previous publishers' addresses still visible on it.[9] But even so it is surprising that they were not picked out before they had peddled their manuscripts through so many unsympathetic English publishers.

One can view the sufferings of the Brontës with relative complacency. Posterity has atoned for these early humiliations. But for the majority of the pathetically expectant novelists who knocked at the publishers' doors there was never to be fame, during their lifetime or after it. And for many there was never even to be the satisfaction of seeing their work in print. The archives of publishing houses contain no more disturbing and emotionally fraught material than the files of correspondence with hopeful Victorian authors. The letters run from the gauche to the hectoring. Some wheedle, others cajole; a few misguided souls attempt to bully the publisher into taking their manuscripts. Frequently one comes across the kind of genuinely harrowing supplication that Thackeray describes so movingly in his essay 'Thorns in the Cushion'. Take the following extract from a letter to Richard Bentley:

> I am now employed upon a story, which promises to be good—'Dorothy Chance or the Fortunes of the Foundling.' When completed would you like to see it?—If you could help me to dispose of it you do not know what an act of kindness it would be—The dark clouds of adversity have gathered so thickly over me, that I can see no bright lining to their stormy edges. My dear husband is well nigh heart-broken, and the infirmities of age are upon him...to add to our many sorrows my dear daughter Agnes has within a few weeks lost her husband and been left with six small children...we have no income.[10]

Not surprisingly the publisher was often glad to interpose the impersonal 'reader' as a barrier between himself and such suffering.

II

Macmillan's, with whom we shall be mainly concerned in this chapter, were a conscientious house who seem to have thoroughly scrutinised any work that was submitted to them. Their readers' comments were recorded in exercise books, the first of which, covering the period 1868–71, contains reports on each of Hardy's first three novels.

Some interesting statistics may be derived from this book. During 1868–70 Macmillan's published, out of a combined list of 450 titles, only 30 novels and children's tales (in which they had a small speciality). Of these 30, a mere 6 were originally unsolicited manuscripts which passed through the reader's hands. (The other 24 were from authors of reputation, with some kind of *entrée*, or from Macmillan's regular stable of writers.) These 6 novels were sifted out of 143 manuscripts on which reports were made. In spite of being in a ratio of 1:15 in Macmillan's published list, fiction preponderates over verse and non-fiction prose in the reader's book thus: 30 (verse), 103 (non-fiction), 143 (novels). It is a daunting imbalance.

One can deduce from the descriptions of them that the bulk of these novels were unrelievedly awful, below even that minimal threshold for nineteenth-century fiction which Shaw wryly observed: 'a novel cannot be too bad to be worth publishing, providing it is a novel at all, not an ineptitude.'[11] Many of these 143 would seem to fall into the 'ineptitude' class. Most were by women: women, 80; men, 39; sex unidentified, 24. Given that many in the 'unidentified' section must also have been women, and that some of the men's names must have been transvestite *noms de plume* it may be assumed that female pretenders outnumbered male by more than 2:1. This did not reflect the situation as regards the printed novel. In the 1871 Mudie's clearance sale there are 441 works of fiction listed of which 212 are by men, 229 by women.[12] This would suggest that published novelists of the period were almost equally divided as to sex.

It is likely that the vast majority of manuscript novels considered by Macmillan's in this period were from writers who had never published before and, presumably, never achieved print thereafter. The kinds of fiction they wrote were predictably formulaic, and one can categorise the novels from the stale reek of the titles, without having to read the works themselves. Typically numerous are three-volume love stories, built round a conventional heroine (*Muriel*, *Nina's Disappointments*, *Gabrielle and her Guardian*, *Madelane*, *Honora's Governess*); problem and sensation novels (*Wife or Sister?*, *Adventures of Prior Claims*, *The Price he Paid for it*, *Will She Fail?*); historical romances (*The Quest of the Sangraal*, *Ralf Skirlaugh*, *The Normans or Kith and Kin*, *Guido the Adventurer*); Trollopian chronicles (*Mrs Vernon and her Daughters*, *Brookfield Rectory*, *Miles Wentworth's Heir*, *The Tremaines of Trevingdon*, *Aunt Barbara's Heir*); simple romances of high life, what in earlier times were called 'silver fork' tales (*La Contesse Estelle*, *Wooed and Won*, *Donna Catherina's Legacy*, *Incognito*, *Regent Rosalind*, *Hedging an Heiress*).[13]

The profile of the average novel submitted emerges: effeminate, romantic, untalented and extremely prolific. A similar situation is found in Geraldine Jewsbury's reports for the same period. A lively, intellectually able woman she liked to send her comments to Bentley in the form of chatty letters. Her key comments on fiction for the year in which Hardy was making his first attempts will give a closer-up picture of the state of unpublished fiction:

8 Feb. 1868	*Change* Clever—certainly clever—but...I do not think the Book wd. be a success, it is so hard and cold.
11 Feb.	*Lance Urquart's Lover* it wd. be perhaps worth yr. while to take if the lady were not likely to require a large sum for the MS.
17 Feb.	*Two Sons of One Mother* respectable but *dull* and slow.
29 Feb.	*Nelly Brooke decline it altogether*. It is dreadfully dull.
3 March	*Married in Haste* it is *very weak—the style* is *flat* and commonplace.
10 March	*Thro' Flood and Flame* the story is poor—the *scenes* are *good. You may take it if* he does not ask too much.
23 March	*George Grey* It is great rubbish and I recommend you to have nothing whatever to do with it.
27 March	*Between Life and Death* if published wd. make everybody *laugh*.
28 March	*The Dream Painter* the story itself is not likely to be successful, it is too foolish...The style...is poor and commonplace.
28 March	*On the Brink* it is not altogether a bad novel—but it is not a good one...I shd. say decline it.

13 April	*Colston refuse* it altogether...the style is dry and commonplace—the story is stupid.
(?) April	*The Wilverdens of Summerdown* moderately interesting ...if you don't have to pay much for it you might accept it.
4 May	*The Birthright* the style...dull and the story an exaggerated piece of sensational *nonsense.*
8 May	*Lord Nemmo* utter and entire *rubbish.*
19 May	*After Three Years* I was much interested...but if it is to succeed you must insist on careful revision.
19 May	*Compton Friars* an extremly poor washy story.
28 May	*Guy Loval Carrington* very dry and very dull.
3 June	*Parvenant* it is very *nearly* good—but not quite.
3 June	*The Two Rubies* a dull unwieldy story, ill put together.
5 June	*On a Summer Evening* utter nonsense and rubbish.
18 June	*The Countess Conningston utter rubbish.*
18 June	*Garibaldi's Novel* DO NOT TAKE IT!
30 June	Unnamed MS. *I do not like the work...great dullness.*
4 Aug.	*Who Will She Marry?* It is not bad but it is very dull.
7 Aug.	*The Guards* you must please *refuse* it altogether and give no encouragement to the author.
19 Aug.	*Silversprings reject it* without hesitation...dull.
21 Sept.	*Lois Eto* quite *unworthy* of your notice.
10 Oct.	*The Tenants of the White House* all but *unreadable.*
20 Nov.	*Why did she leave him? imbecile.*
20 Nov.	*Natural Protectors* a foolish and *very vulgar* novel.
20 Nov.	*Passion Flowers worse* than rubbish.[14]

It is not quite what Geraldine Jewsbury called it, a 'universal No',[15] but one may safely assume that the aperture Bentley offered to unsolicited manuscripts was a very narrow one. As far as I can discover, four of the above works were eventually published: *Nelly Brooke* and *Through Flood and Flame* by Bentley, *Colston* by Newby and *The Two Rubies* by Tinsley.

III

Hardy submitted all three of his first novels to Macmillan's, for the tribunal by publisher's reader. They accepted none of them but they perceived in the young writer an outstanding talent—even if they were unprepared to put their money behind it. Arguably Hardy derived from his experiences with Macmillan's what amounted to an education in writing fiction. He gained a practical acquaintance with the mores, fashions and taboos which regulated the selection of novels for publication, for purchase by the circulating libraries and reading by the general public.

The story begins in July 1868 when Hardy submitted *The Poor Man and the Lady* to Macmillan's:

In writing the novel I wish to lay before you—*The Poor Man and the Lady* (sent by today's post)—the following considerations had place.

That the upper classes of society have been induced to read, before any, books in which *they themselves* are painted by a comparative outsider.

That, in works of such a kind, unmitigated utterances of strong feeling against the class to which these readers belong may lead them to throw down a volume in disgust; whilst the very same feelings inserted edgewise so to say—half concealed beneath ambiguous expressions, or at any rate written as if they were not the chief aims of the book (even though they may be)—become the most attractive remarks of all.

That, nowadays, discussions on the questions of manners, rising in the world, etc. (the main incidents of the novel), have grown to be particularly absorbing.

That as a rule no fiction will considerably interest readers poor or rich unless the passion of love forms a prominent feature in the thread of the story.

That novelty of *position* and *view*, in relation to a known subject, is more taking among the readers of light literature than even absolute novelty of subject.

Hence the book took its shape, rightly or wrongly.[16]

The first lesson Hardy had to learn was that he in fact had something to learn. Moreover it was a situation in which the publishing house had all the power. This first letter is grossly misjudged in tone—aggressive, brusque, *de haut en bas* practically. John Morley reported on the fierce young man's manuscript. Later famous as the editor of the *Fortnightly* and author of Gladstone's *Life*, Morley was a scholar of cultural omnicompetence who could as easily assess a work of philosophy, sociology or medicine as a novel. His comments on *Poor Man* were conscientious, detailed and ultimately shortsighted.

(Although Hardy later destroyed the manuscript of *Poor Man*, enough trace of it survives for its outline to be reconstructed. The bones of the novel were what was to become Hardy's favourite plot—the love of a lower born man for a lady—but what makes this different from its successors was that it seems to have incorporated a lot of radical satire on the London rich. The work was thus more political than much of what we recognise in the later author.) Morley wrote:

A very curious and original performance: the opening pictures of the Christmas Eve in the tranter's house are really of good quality; much of the writing is strong and fresh. But there crops up in parts a certain rawness of absurdity that is very displeasing, and makes it read like some clever lad's dream: the thing hangs too loosely together. There is real feeling in the writing, though now and then it is commonplace in form as all feeling turning on the insolence and folly of the rich in face of the poor is apt to sound: (e.g. p. 338). If the man is young, there is stuff and promise in him: but he must study form and composition, in such writers as Balzac and Thackeray, who would I think come as natural masters to him.[17]

Alexander Macmillan chose to answer Hardy himself, at great length, mixing endorsement of his reader's criticism with an avuncular sermon on the dangers of cynicism in fiction:

I have read through the novel you were so good as to send me, with care and with much interest and admiration, but feeling at the same time that it has what seem to me fatal drawbacks to its success, and what, I think, judging the writer from the book itself, you would feel even more strongly—its truthfulness and justice.

Your description of country life among working men is admirable, and, though I can only judge of it from the corresponding life in Scotland, which I knew well when young, palpably truthful. Your pictures of character among Londoners, and especially the upper classes, are sharp, clear, incisive, and in many respects true, but they are wholly dark—not a ray of light visible to relieve the darkness, and therefore exaggerated and untrue in their result...You see I am writing to you as to a writer who seems to me of, at least potentially, considerable mark, of power and purpose. If this is your first book I think you ought to go on. May I ask if it is, and—you are not a lady, so perhaps you will forgive the question—are you young?[18]

Hardy, then, 'must study form and composition' and labour

to write less 'darkly'. The actual question of publication Macmillan left open. On tenterhooks Hardy waited until he could stand it no longer, and wrote again. But now his tone was humble, wheedling almost. He concluded his letter of inquiry with a postscript accepting the 'young apprentice' or 'clever lad' role into which Macmillan and Morley would cast him. (He was 28.)

Would you mind suggesting the sort of story you think I could do best, or any literary work I should do well to go on upon?[19]

It is likely that Macmillan's could not make up their mind on the book. They therefore declined it, but gave Hardy an introduction to Chapman and Hall who had a tradition of publishing dangerously anti-social novels (or perhaps Morley had a word with Meredith—they were both contributors to Chapman and Hall's *Fortnightly*). But with this second house Hardy had a similarly inconclusive experience. They accepted his novel, with the proviso that the author should put £20 of his own money into the production. But then they had second thoughts. Hardy was called for interview with the house's legendary reader, George Meredith, who seems to have enjoyed delivering 'vocal criticism'[20] to nervous young authors. The encounter is recalled in Hardy's *Life*:

Meredith had the manuscript in his hand, and began lecturing Hardy upon it in a sonorous voice. No record was kept by the latter of their conversation, but the gist of it he remembered very well. It was that the firm were willing to publish the novel as agreed, but that he, the speaker, strongly advised its author not to 'nail his colours to the mast' so definitely in a first book, if he wished to do anything practical in literature; for if he printed so pronounced a thing he would be attacked on all sides by the conventional reviewers, and his future injured...the tendency of the writing being socialistic, not to say revolutionary...the upshot of this interview was that Hardy took away the MS. with him to decide on a course.

Meredith had added that Hardy could rewrite the story, softening it down considerably; or what would be much better, put it away altogether for the present, and attempt a novel with a purely artistic purpose, giving it a more complicated 'plot' than was attempted with *The Poor Man and the Lady*.[21]

It is likely that Meredith was thinking of the reception of his own early novel, *The Ordeal of Richard Feverel*, ten years before. This work had been considered scandalously frank by early readers and critics, doing his reputation much harm. Mudie, with his 'petticoated mind', had cramped the novel's circulation by taking 300 then holding back on issuing it. *The Ordeal* was 'denounced over the country by clergymen, at book clubs, and it fell dead'.[22] In his later works the elder novelist took refuge in plots of baffling complexity and a style of riddling impenetrability. In a way he seems to have been urging the same kind of protective obliquity on the young, and probably bewildered, Hardy. (In 1895, when he too had fallen foul of the British Public, Hardy said he had never heard 'so much good criticism packed into so little space'.)[23]

From Macmillan's Hardy had had a schoolboy's lesson in 'composition'; Meredith gave him a 'lecture'. He had been offered some conflicting encouragement. He understood he was to write fiction with intricate plot like Wilkie Collins (*The Moonstone* was the hit of 1868) and to write of 'rural scenes and humble life' like George Eliot (*Silas Marner* was a recent best-seller). He had been instructed to avoid the shocking and try for a 'light chatty tone which gave no offence'. In other words he was to write like Collins, George Eliot, Thackeray and Meredith himself. A literary Proteus would have had difficulty in adapting to all these roles.

Hardy's first novel had at least two more rebuffs and he finally gave it up as a lost cause. In his next work he decided to follow Meredith's advice first. *The Poor Man and the Lady* was 'A Story with no Plot'; his next novel, *Desperate Remedies*, is all plot. Its narrative is a serial of accidents, coincidences and improbabilities. In defiance of chapters it is sectioned, presented as a calendar of 'events' (a device borrowed from Wilkie Collins). The final act of the plot, the alliance of a heroic trio against the villainous, murderous husband has more than an echo of *The Woman in White* about it. The bigamous husband's killing his supposed-dead first wife in a park has a distinct resemblance to *Lady Audley's Secret*. ('Dead, yet not dead' was one of the stand-bys of the sensation plot and in Miss Braddon's novel the villainess pushes her supposed-dead first husband down a garden well.) This is not to say that the novel is entirely stale. *Desperate*

Remedies is Hardy's only investigation of the really criminal mind and is, as such, interesting enough. But by 1870 the sensation novel, in whose conventions the criminal Manston is contained, was worn out and clichéd.

In March 1870 Hardy submitted the work to Macmillan's. But again the piece was too strong for them to take on. The structural 'looseness' had been rectified and the young writer had studied composition and form to some effect, apparently. But Morley shuddered away from the central, sexual event and advised his employer to shun it as something unclean:

Shews decided talent for invention and construction, the plot being complex and absolutely impossible, yet is worked out with elaborate seriousness and consistency. The dialogue is good, and there is a general firmness and closeness of texture about the style.

But the story is ruined by the disgusting and absurd outrage which is the key to its mystery. The violation of a young lady at an evening party, and the subsequent birth of a child, is too abominable to be tolerated as a central incident from which the action of the story is to move. After reflection, I don't see how this could be modified in any way...

Don't touch this—but beg the writer to discipline himself to keep away from such incidents as violation—and let us see his next story.[24]

The schoolmaster's tone has hardened: the writer was to be kept in order not by 'study' and 'lectures' but now by 'discipline'. Alexander Macmillan returned the manuscript in April 1870 as 'far too sensational' for them to use.

So far Hardy had had the benefit of probably the best critics of unpublished fiction in England—Morley, Macmillan, George Smith,[25] Chapman and Meredith. But he was not in print and might well have felt himself thoroughly confused. Publishers all recognised his talent but they were not prepared to put any money on it—he was too dangerous. ('Revolutionary' is a revealing term, so too is 'disgusting'.) He might have been forgiven some irritation. Here he was with 'a story quite foreign to my own instincts, and which...owed its existence to Meredith'.[26] Yet it would appear that neither Meredith's firm, nor Macmillan's, who originally directed him there, were prepared to take it.

Hardy finally found a house willing to accept the risk in a lower rank than that at which he had been aiming, Tinsley Brothers. A day after receiving the rejected manuscript from Macmillan's, Hardy sent it on its way to this less reputable publisher. Tinsleys' reader had misgivings like 'the woman who is Mrs. Manston's *substitute* [being] put forward quite so prominently as his *mistress*',[27] yet he found the book 'clever' and they were willing to bring it out when revised. It is likely that Tinsley was hoping that if it did not run riot, the novel's 'almost ultra sensational matter' might be a selling point. Hardy would profit from what, in the light of later literary history, might be called the 'Lady Chatterley' factor. It was a reasonable gamble from the publisher's viewpoint. *Lorna Doone* had recently been turned down by the editor of the *Cornhill Magazine* as morally 'objectionable' and was later to become one of the century's best sellers. Even if it did not become a hit, *Desperate Remedies* might catch on with the average circulating library reader for whom Tinsley catered.

IV

Hardy's involvement with William Tinsley is an interesting episode and has been subject to certain misrepresentations (most emanating from Hardy himself). The terms of agreement for *Desperate Remedies* were simple enough. Hardy had a half-profits contract and an edition of 500 three-volume copies was planned for. This was a usual arrangement for a first novel by an untried author. What was slightly unusual was that Hardy advanced £75 in ready money to the publisher as 'guarantee'. This would be repaid the novelist out of net profits—if there were any. In fact Hardy never recovered his money. Tinsley calculated that the 372 copies sold yielded a half share of only £60 after expenses, leaving the novelist £15 out of pocket on his first published work.

Hardy gives a wryly comic account of his dealings with Tinsley in the *Life*, presenting the publisher as a seedy cockney with an unsure control of the English language and an eye to the main chance. Other contemporary accounts picture Tinsley as less dishonest than naive: 'a dear, kind soul, quite witless and quite "h"less'.[28] Taking their cue from such hints as these some critics have been very severe on Hardy's first publisher. Guinevere Griest, for example, in *Mudie's Circulating Library* is extremely suspicious of the publisher's honesty in his transactions with the young novelist:

It is difficult to understand how Tinsley could have legitimately charged Hardy £15 for the publication of his first novel, *Desperate Remedies*...If Trollope's estimate of £200 is used for production and advertising costs (and Tinsleys', lower in reputation than Chapman and Hall, may well have spent less), and if 370 copies were sold at 14s. 6d., gross receipts would have exceeded expenses by about £68 5s. Thus Hardy would have received his £75 back, plus £34 2s. 6d., or a total of £109 2s. 6d., instead of the £60 he actually got. It is possible, of course, that Tinsley could not sell the novel for as much as 14s. 6d.; but even at 10s. 6d. a copy, the book would have come within £6 of covering a cost of £200. Just how the sum of £60 was determined is not clear.[29]

The implication that Tinsley was underhanded and exploited an inexperienced writer is unfair, at least in this instance. He had taken *Desperate Remedies* after better-off publishers had turned it down. Moreover he took its successor, *Under the Greenwood Tree*, after having made, as he maintained, a loss on the first work. In his version of the relationship Tinsley feels justified in putting himself forward as Hardy's benefactor:

I read a good many manuscripts almost every year during the time I was a publisher. One I read and took an especial interest in was Thomas Hardy's first novel, called 'Desperate Remedies.' In fact, I read the work twice, and even though I never thoroughly made up my mind that it was the sort of work to be a great success, I certainly thought it contained some capital characters and character drawing. But Mr. Hardy had dragged into the midst of excellent humorous writing almost ultra-sensational matter; in fact, incidents unworthy of his pen and the main portion of the work. Still, I quite thought that there was enough of the bright side of human nature in it to sell at least one fair edition. However, there was not, but for a first venture I do not think Mr. Hardy had much to complain about.[30]

As for his book-keeping and accounts with the young author not being 'clear', they seem, on the contrary, to have been crystalline. Tinsley was not a good correspondent, holding the cheerful view that 'letters answer themselves';[31] but he informed

Hardy how sales were going in October and January and in February 1872 he sent the following statement:[32]

DESPERATE REMEDIES

	£	s.	d.		£	s.
1871				By Author	75	
To paper				280 sold	209	
27 rms. at 22/–	29	14		50 sold to		
,, ¾		15		Mudie at 6/–	15	
Composing and				20 sold to		
printing 500				Smith at 7/6	7	10
27½ sheets at 2.15	75	12	6	22 sold to		
½		16	6	Smith at 6/–	6	12
Corrections	12	10		22 Press, author		
Binding 444	26	12	9	5 Public Libs.		
Advertising	48	4	9	45 on hand (bound)		
Balance	119	5	2	56 on hand (quire)		
	313	10	8	500	313	10

[The balance of £119 5s. 2d. yields £59 12s. 7d. each to publisher and author, some £15 short of Hardy's £75 advance.]

It is not hard to see where normal calculations might go wrong. In fact Tinsley had managed to keep production and advertising costs under the £200 Trollope allows by some £12. He had sold 280 at the trade price (though with the added discount of 25 for the price of 24, a usual bonus for pre-publication subscription). But where the discrepancy comes in is with library sales. Mudie had got his copies at a paltry 6s. and Smith's most of their 42 at the same minimal price.

There can be little doubt that the account is an honest one. If Tinsley had wanted to cheat Hardy he would have inflated his moderate production costs rather than falsifying verifiable library receipts. What this episode shows, in fact, is the power of the libraries to bully smaller publishers into taking ludicrously low prices for their books. Six shillings represents something considerably less than cost. Tinsley was releasing a third part of all the copies he sold for less than it cost him to produce them; on the face of things it would appear a recipe for commercial suicide.

A number of reasons, other than self-destructive philanthropy towards Mudie, may be put forward to explain this apparent anomaly. The first, and probably least important, is that Tinsley personally had an exaggerated notion of the value of library sales and was prepared to knock down his prices to a near give-away level. It is true that in his *Recollections* he professes an excessive respect for the three-decker and declares roundly: 'Fiction is, and always was, meant more for lending rather than for buying.'[33] It was probably for this reason that the reader he employed to look at *Desperate Remedies* was William Faux—the chief of W. H. Smith's lending department.[34] But there is more to this transaction than the demonstration of a publisher's crotchet. It would seem that the less substantial houses—like Tinsley's, Newby, Hurst and Blackett, Saunders and Otley—had particular reasons for wanting to get on Mudie's and Smith's lists and were prepared to pay heavily for the privilege. It is hard to investigate how such firms did business since unlike the major concerns their papers have rarely been considered worth keeping. The evidence suggests, however, that the cachet of a place in the big Libraries' catalogues and newspaper advertisements warranted making books over as virtual presentation copies.

This was an accepted fact of the publishing world of the 1870s. In 1879, for example, Mudie wrote imperiously to Bentley:

> dear Mr. Bentley
>
> Can you let me have 50 No Surrender at 9/–...If so I will keep it in my advertisement...

Or again in January 1873:

> I wish to do what I can for 'Burgoyne' and if you will let me have 520 as 480 in the terms proposed I will place it near the top of my list (with 'Dickens' and 'Slickman') and give it a leading position in a few special advertisements.[35]

If he could take this tone with a major publisher one may well imagine how he dealt with such as Tinsley.

We may reconstruct what happened. *Desperate Remedies* was published in March 1871. Mudie and W. H. Smith took a few at a reasonable price (15s.?). The novel caused no stir and in June Hardy observed it being remaindered by Smith at 2s. 6d. the three volumes. Tinsley had managed to clear 280. In early October interest in the book revived with a very warm review of it in the *Saturday Review* (probably by Hardy's friend H. M.

Moule). Rising to this bait Smith and Mudie offered to take a job lot of almost 100 copies between them, but at very reduced price. The publisher who had nothing to lose let them go to make money for the libraries while they lost money for him and his author.

Presumably the return on the publisher's investment came with the follow-up orders, if the novel was popular, and cheap reprints for which the library copies had laid the way. For Hardy there was no reprint and no popularity. He had only the dubious joy of having attained print at last. He could console himself with the conventional trade wisdom that 'first novels are never paid for'—except sometimes by their authors, he might have added.

In the meanwhile he had followed the other of the publishers' suggestions and written a story of rural life, what was later to be known as *Under the Greenwood Tree.* (It incorporated some bits of *Poor Man* that Morley had approved of.) Writing as the 'author of *Desperate Remedies*' Hardy submitted the manuscript, as usual, to Macmillan's for first refusal. It was, he ingratiatingly pointed out, 'entirely a story of rural life, and the attempt has been made to draw the characters humorously without caricature...I thought it just as well not to dabble in plot again.'[36] Nor in 'violation', presumably.

Macmillan's, as usual, were in two minds. They hummed and hawed over whether they would take it: they felt that the Christmas season was too busy for them. There was something of a misunderstanding and Hardy, irritated or bewildered, felt he had been rejected yet again. Then, by a stroke of luck, Tinsley stepped back into the picture:

Quite soon after, while reading in the Strand a poster of the Italian Opera, a heavy hand was laid on his shoulder, and turning he saw Tinsley himself, who asked when Hardy was going to let him have another novel.

Hardy, with thoughts of the balance-sheet, drily told him never.

'Wot, now!' said Tinsley. 'Haven't you anything written?' Hardy remarked that he had written a short story some time before but didn't know what had become of the MS., and did not care. He also had outlined one for three volumes; but had abandoned it. He was now doing better things, and attending to his profession of architect.

'Damned if that isn't what I thought you wos!' exlaimed Mr. Tinsley. 'Well, now, can't you get that story, and show it to me?'

Hardy would not promise, reminding the publisher that the account he had rendered for the other book was not likely to tempt him to publish a second.

' 'Pon my soul, Mr. Hardy,' said Tinsley, 'you wouldn't have got another man in London to print it! Oh, be hanged if you would! 'twas a blood-curdling story! Now please try to find that new manuscript and let me see it.'[37]

Tinsley's blood did not curdle on reading the second manuscript, and he offered £30 for the copyright, which Hardy accepted. The publisher found no more luck with *Under the Greenwood Tree* than with *Desperate Remedies*, however:

in that book [wrote Tinsley] I felt sure I had got hold of the best little prose idyll I had ever read…I almost raved about the book, and I gave it away wholesale to pressmen and anyone I knew interested in good fiction. But, strange to say, it would not sell. Finding it hung on hand in the original two-volume form, I printed it in a very pretty illustrated one-volume form. That edition was a failure. Then I published it in a two-shilling form, with paper covers and that edition had a very poor sale indeed; and yet it was one of the best press-noticed books I ever published.[38]

In spite of its hanging in the bookshops *Under the Greenwood Tree*, as Tinsley records, won golden opinions in the reviews. Moreover Macmillan, as if to amend for the bungling over Hardy's latest novel, had been broadcasting the young author's name around the trade. On 19 June 1873, the American publisher Holt wrote:

I'm reading 'A Pair of Blue Eyes' by our friend Hardy. Judging from the portion I've been through I should advise you to make any sacrifice within reason to get hold of that fellow. I don't forget that you put me on to his track.[39]

Macmillan had clearly been instrumental in getting Hardy an American publisher while he was still having trouble getting one in England. Holt was more than enthusiastic about their protégé and assumed (mistakenly) that Macmillan's shared his unqualified enthusiasm. In July, sending the novelist a copy of the American publication of *Under the Greenwood Tree* via

Macmillan's office he noted: 'I suppose that you will not consider any little commissions that bring him to your doors of more trouble than they are worth.'[40] But in fact Macmillan's did not get Hardy, even after taking so much trouble in promoting his career. Nor did Tinsley hold him after publishing his first three novels, *Desperate Remedies*, *Under the Greenwood Tree* and *A Pair of Blue Eyes* at an overall loss. After Hardy had made his name, at his first publisher's expense, Leslie Stephen wrote to him on behalf of the *Cornhill*, requesting a serial. It was Smith's usual tactic, using his money to buy property that was coming up in the world.

So now the publishers were knocking on Hardy's door. Henceforth if there were objections the novelist would change not his manuscript but his house.[41] It is hard not to feel rather sorry for Macmillan's and Tinsley. The one firm had invested time, the other money in the developing author. Neither was to reap the reward, at least not directly. (Macmillan's, however, got Hardy later in his career and Tinsley had a valuable copyright to sell when he went bankrupt in 1878.)

The course of these three novels through the publishing houses gives one some insight into the educative force which the publishers, through their selection and rejection processes, exercised on young talents. Conditioning might, perhaps, be the better term. Clearly the authorities Hardy came into contact with were interested in two things, to decontaminate his fiction of its 'dangerous' qualities, and to fashion him after the model of proven and established authors—Wilkie Collins, Thackeray, George Eliot and Balzac.

It is a nice question whether the influence was baleful or benign. Hardy was at this time, as he said with a striking phrase, 'feeling his way to a method'.[42] Do those tremendous, sensational scenes and the creaking plot machineries in the later novels owe something to the hour with Meredith? Is the somewhat *appliqué* nature of much of Hardy's rural scene painting the outcome of the early preferences of Alexander Macmillan? And does the crashing attempt at a tone of light badinage which so often jars in Hardy's fiction arise, in part at least, from the advice at an impressionable age to write like Thackeray?

These are largely unanswerable questions. What one can say is that Hardy gained from his early contact with the trade a sure awareness of the rules and fashions which dominated English fiction; he came to know his enemy. Hardy in later life seems to have regarded his experiences with Tinsley, at least, in this light: 'Tinsley...was a shrewd chap when dealing with young authors. However, I always think that on a first novel a writer must not expect to make money.'[43]

Notes

Abbreviations

PML; Pierpont Morgan Library
Bodley: Trollope Papers, Oxford (Pressmark MS. Don. C 9–10*)
Forster: Dickens business accounts, Victoria and Albert Museum, Dyce Forster Collection (Pressmark F. D. 18. 1–3)
BM: British Museum manuscript departments (Add. Mss. throughout)
Huntington: Henry E. Huntington Library, California
Berg: Berg collection, New York Public Library
Smith, Elder: Smith, Elder Papers
Blackwood: Blackwood's Papers, National Library of Scotland
Urbana: Bentley Papers, University of Illinois

I have not attempted a bibliography, thinking that the first half of the book is too general and the second too specific for any such compilation to be useful. Comprehensive bibliographies may be found in Richard D. Altick, *The English Common Reader* (Chicago, 1957) and in F. A. Mumby, *Publishing and Bookselling* (London, 1954, new edition with supplementary material by I. Norrie, 1973).

Introduction

1 See A. Waugh, *A Hundred Years of Publishing* (London, 1930), pp. 84–5.
2 Bacon was taken to be Richard Bentley, Bungay his erstwhile partner, Henry Colburn.
3 BM 46641: letters of Richard Bentley to Herman Melville, 4 March 1852, 5 May 1852. See also R. A. Gettmann, *A Victorian Publisher* (Cambridge, 1960), p. 158. For Melville's dollar earnings see E. Exman, *The House of Harper* (New York, 1967), p. 39.
4 See Mrs M. O. Oliphant, *Annals of a Publishing House*, iii, *John Blackwood*, by Mrs G. Porter (Edinburgh and London, 1898), 39.
5 A. L. Walker, *The Autobiography and Letters of Mrs M. O. W. Oliphant* (London, 1899), p. 5.
6 Mrs M. O. Oliphant, *Annals of a Publishing House*, ii (Edinburgh and London, 1897), 426.
7 *The Letters of Mrs Gaskell*, ed. J. A. V. Chapple and A. Pollard (Manchester, 1966), p. 772.
8 See C. Morgan, *The House of Macmillan* (London, 1943).
9 F. A. Mumby, *Publishing and Bookselling* (London, 1954), p. 248.
10 A. Trollope, *An Autobiography*, ed. F. Page (Oxford, 1950), p. 141.
11 R. G. G. Price, *A History of Punch* (London, 1957), pp. 353–5.

12 Waugh, p. 61. Dickens's meaning is slightly ambiguous: he might have meant the printer Clowes as well as Bradbury and Evans.
13 Urbana, Richard Bentley's Diary, 1861(?).
14 *Autobiography*, p. 110.
15 For a comprehensive examination of the publication of *Endymion* see Annabel Jones's chapter in *Essays in the History of Publishing*, ed. A. Briggs (London, 1974), pp. 141–86.
16 *My Miscellanies* (New York, 1874), p. 140.

Chapter 1: Novel Publishing 1830–1870

1 See L. Huxley, *The House of Smith, Elder* (London, 1923), p. 3.
2 T. Hughes, *Memoir of Daniel Macmillan* (London, 1882), p. 116.
3 Mrs M. O. Oliphant, *Annals of a Publishing House*, ii (Edinburgh and London, 1897), 163.
4 G. H. Putnam, *George Palmer Putnam* (London, 1912), p. 379.
5 F. A. Mumby, *The House of Routledge* (London, 1934), p. 3. The newly founded house of Richard Bentley took the novel and did well with it, bringing out two 31s. 6d. editions in 1831–2.
6 Mrs M. O. Oliphant, *Annals of a Publishing House*, i (Edinburgh and London, 1897), 518. The fate of Scott, Constable and Ballantyne was publicised in the most widely read of all nineteenth-century biographies, Lockhart's *Life of Scott*.
7 BM 46611, 9 Dec. 1831. *The Conspiracy*, by Dr Johnston, eventually came out in three volumes in April 1834. The winter of 1831 was a difficult period for Bentley in other respects as he was engaged in breaking his unlucky partnership with Colburn (see R. A. Gettmann, *A Victorian Publisher* (Cambridge, 1960), p. 20). It should also be pointed out that, though it was a slack period for the good literary work, the reform era was marked by a notable demand for cheap reading matter. The best account of the situation given by A. S. Collins, *The Profession of Letters* (London, 1928).
8 See Waugh, p. 98. Smith, Elder revived the dinner sale during their most expansive phase in November 1859 but dropped the dining part in 1864. Bentley's seem to have been the most assiduous in the upkeep of the tradition, possibly because so much of their trade was with the libraries.
9 See 'The Price of the Novel', *The Author* (1894), pp. 94–9.
10 See the initial editorial, 2 Jan. 1828. The novel's aura of luxury accounts, I suspect, for the vogue of 'silver fork' fiction in the 1830s—works with such titles as Smith, Elder's *The Bar Sinister* by the Honourable Lady ****. (1836).
11 Walter Besant hazards this estimate in his *The Pen and the Book* (London, 1899). It is probably on the low side.
12 The 6s. reprint was established with Bentley's 'Standard Novels' in 1831. Bentley and Colburn specialised in the 6s. reprint, almost unchallenged, throughout the 1830s. In the 1890s 6s. became the normal first-form price for fiction.
13 Urbana, Arthur Mudie to Bentley, 21 Dec. 1894.
14 G. L. Griest, *Mudie's Circulating Library* (Bloomington, Indiana, 1970), p. 95.
15 Urbana, Reade to Bentley, 21 March 1853(?).
16 This account, and the figures, are largely taken from the *American Literary*

Gazette and Publishers' Circular, 1 Jan. 1864, on the book trade in England, which is largely taken, in its turn, from Chambers' *Encyclopaedia* (London, 1860–8). All the figures given must be taken with a certain elasticity when applied to actual day-to-day trading. Bentley, for example, would often give higher allowances for cash settlement; country orders were sometimes supplied at a different rate from those in town.

17 BM 46595 (publication ledger).

18 With the various discounts this came to be the normal trade price for the three-decker.

19 See John Chapman's article, 'The Commerce of Literature', *Westminster Review*, April 1852.

20 Huntington, Lever to his wife, 22 April 1857.

21 A. Waugh, *A Hundred Years of Publishing* (London, 1930), p. 142.

22 Blackwood, Acc. 5644. Blackwood resolutely held out against giving Mudie special terms, hence most of the sales were at 22s. 6d.

23 BM 46641, Bentley to Ticknor, 5 April 1850. See C. E. Frazer Clark's article 'Hawthorne and the Pirates', *Proof*, 1971, pp. 90–116 for a discussion of the publication of Hawthorne's books in England.

24 A. Trollope, *The New Zealander*, ed. N. John Hall (London, 1973), p. 184. Trollope alludes specifically to American fiction reprinted for the railway reading trade.

25 Information taken from advertisements in the *Publishers' Circular* and from M. Sadleir, *XIX Century Fiction* (Cambridge, 1951), ii, 170.

26 See S. H. Nowell-Smith, *International Law and the Publisher* (Oxford, 1968), pp. 28–31 for the account of 'Murray's Colonial and Home Library' and its problems in paying authors while providing cheap literature.

27 By the end of the century the 6d. reprint was reached as the standard form; see R. D. Altick, *The English Common Reader* (Chicago, 1957), pp. 313–17.

28 BM 46642, G. Bentley to Miss Sinclair, 12 Sept. 1854.

29 BM 46613, 28 Oct. 1839.

30 These figures are derived from the accounts Dickens's publishers rendered the novelist, now in the Forster collection.

31 See Q. D. Leavis, *Fiction and the Reading Public* (London, 1932), pp. 151–7.

32 *The Letters of Anthony Trollope*, ed. B. A. Booth (Oxford, 1951), p. 269.

33 George Eliot eventually had £7,000 for the serialisation of *Romola* in the *Cornhill* (see Chapter 9).

34 J. C. Jeaffreson, *Novels and Novelists* (London, 1858), ii, 313.

35 Forster. Remission of the paper tax in the 1860s accounts for one reduction. All the others result from more efficient production. Bradbury and Evans's figures (for *Dombey*) must be used with caution since they itemised expenses more fully than Chapman and Hall and I have engrossed their specific accounts to tally with those of Dickens's later publisher.

36 Griest gives the authoritative account of the growth of Mudie's in her opening chapters.

37 Urbana, R. Bentley's diary, 1861.

38 See J. Shaylor, *The Fascination of Books* (London, 1912), pp. 28–9 and Griest, p. 42. Bentley, for example, sent his obligatory copy of *Oliver Twist* in 1838 to the British Museum in sheets.

39 See H. Maxwell, *Life and Times of the Rt. Hon. W. H. Smith* (London, 1893), i, ch. 2. Free enterprise at railway stations in the early 1840s sucked in a large number of French novels (whose copyrights were unprotected

and could be more cheaply produced). The dubious tone of these works helped Smith to his franchise.

40 E. Marston, *After Work* (London and New York, 1904), p. 43.
41 Urbana, Mudie to Bentley, 11 March 1876.
42 *Saturday Review*, 3 Nov. 1860, p. 550.
43 Meredith's phrase. See S. M. Ellis, *George Meredith* (London, 1919), p. 103.
44 Bodley.
45 See A. Trollope, *An Autobiography*, ed. F. Page (Oxford, 1950), pp. 103–4, and M. Sadleir, *Trollope: A Commentary* (London, 1927), p. 174.
46 *The Bookseller* (25 May 1859) reports, probably apocryphally, that publishers sent the proof sheets of novels to New Oxford Street for approval or correction.
47 His advertisements reveal that Bentley, before Mudie's dominance, was very keen to cut prices. His major, unsuccessful attempt, came in 1853, however (see Chapter 3).
48 BM 46641, Bentley to Mudie, 13 Sept. 1850.
49 BM 46642, Bentley to Mudie, 7 June 1858. Mudie in fact took more than he wanted. Bentley drove the bargain as part of a package deal allowing the library credit instead of cash payment.
50 *The Letters of George Eliot*, ed. G. S. Haight (Oxford, 1954–5), iii, 283. Longman's did Mudie severe damage by bringing out a cheap edition of *Endymion* prematurely; see *Essays in the History of Publishing*, ed. A. Briggs (London, 1974), p. 185.
51 Altick, *The English Common Reader*, p. 296.
52 See Griest, p. 38 for an indication of how much Mudie's stock increased over the next few years.
53 *Letters of George Eliot*, iii, 317. See also Griest, *Mudie's Circulating Library* pp. 112–19. For a devastating analysis of the authorial and publishing inflationary tricks see C. E. and E. S. Lauterbach, 'The nineteenth-century three-volume novel', *PBSA*, li, (1957), 263–302.
54 Huntington, Reade to J. T. Fields, 1855.
55 Forster.
56 PML, Lever to Spencer, 10 May 1847.
57 Urbana, Reade to Bentley, no date though a reference to *Peg Woffington* suggests 1852.
58 Huntington, Lever to his wife, 23 May 1856. Lever had this information from Chapman who told him that Routledge had already sold 45,000 of Lytton's novels but was still out of pocket to the tune of £10,000. See also Mumby, *The House of Routledge*, pp. 58–9.
59 Blackwood, 4102, Lytton to J. Blackwood, 15 Oct. 1853.
60 Figures quoted by Q. D. Leavis, *Fiction and the Reading Public*, p. 306. See also the *Saturday Review*, 31 Jan. 1857, for Smith's information on 'railroad reading'.
61 A. J. Church, 'Authors and Publishers', *Nineteenth Century* (May 1907), p. 865.
62 BM 46611, correspondence of September 1832 with the owners of Jane Austen's copyright. In October 1833 the outstanding copyright, of *Pride and Prejudice*, was bought for £21.
63 Taken from the advertisement in the *Athenaeum*, March 1847.
64 Forster.
65 PML, Lever to Spencer, 8 Oct. 1847.
66 Urbana, Reade to Bentley, 'Tuesday' 1856. Reade, as usual, was even more

courageous than any of his novel writing colleagues. The *London Journal* had a somewhat sensational reputation.

67 See F. D. Tredrey, *The House of Blackwood* (Edinburgh, 1954), p. 117.

68 Forster. There is some unconvincing evidence that magazine serialisation did hurt subsequent volume sale. Smith, Elder occasionally missed out three-volume republication of a serialised work (see Huxley, *The House of Smith, Elder*, p. 91). On the other hand Smith turned down *East Lynne*, of all novels, on the ground that prior magazine publication 'would leave no purchasers for the 31s. 6d. book' (Huxley, p. 123). Bentley's experience with the bestselling *East Lynne* belies this apprehension.

69 E. Downey, *Twenty Years Ago* (London, 1905), pp. 246–7.

70 Forster.

71 Blackwood, 4094, Langford to J. Blackwood, 29 Oct. 1851.

72 Quoted Altick, *The English Common Reader*, p. 305 with a discussion of the state of the trade after 1852. See also, J. L. Barnes, *Free Trade in Books* (Oxford, 1964).

Chapter 2: Mass Market and Big Business: Novel Publishing at Midcentury

1 According to H. Curwen in *A History of Booksellers* (London, 1873), 80,000 sets were sold.

2 Forster. See also A. Waugh, *A Hundred Years of Publishing* (London, 1930), p. 129.

3 PML, letters from Collins to his mother, and to Ward, 22 Aug. 1860 and 16 April 1861. See also K. Robinson, *Wilkie Collins* (London, 1951), p. 146.

4 This figure is pencilled into the publication ledger. Dickens's influenza prevented the first number of *Oliver Twist* from appearing in the first issue of the magazine. The sale seems to have settled down at 8–9,000 (see R. A. Gettmann, *A Victorian Publisher* (Cambridge, 1960), p. 143).

5 *The Bookseller* (26 April 1860) p. 213. Smith began by printing 50,000 all of which sold before the nominal publication date. He pushed the printing number up until by February 1860 he was selling the 'unprecedented' number of 100,000. Circulation fell drastically in the 1870s (see L. Huxley, *The House of Smith, Elder* (London, 1923), p. 120).

6 Huxley, *The House of Smith, Elder*, p. 100.

7 G. N. Ray, *Thackeray: the Age of Wisdom* (London and New York, 1958), p. 296.

8 Huxley, *The House of Smith, Elder*, p. 45. When Smith took over in the 1840s the firm, which had been embezzled by a dishonest partner, was financially insecure. Smith seems to have dedicated himself to the agency side first, building up the firm's commercial base. In the 1850s he increasingly took an interest in publishing.

9 *Hodson's Booksellers Publishers and Stationers Directory* (1855, repr. 1972 with introduction by G. Pollard.)

10 See, for example, *The Letters of Mrs Gaskell*, ed. J. A. V. Chapple and A. Pollard (Manchester, 1966), p. 250.

11 Bodley. See also M. Sadleir, *Trollope: A Bibliography* (London, 1928), Section 6. The full account of Newby's dealings with Trollope is given by Lance Tingay, 'The Publication of Trollope's first Novel', *T.L.S.*, 30 March 1956, 200.

12 *Letters of Mrs Gaskell*, pp. 428–9. All references to Newby were removed

from the printed text—presumably as a trade courtesy. In the MS. of the *Life* Mrs Gaskell, apparently, names the publisher.

13 PML, Collins to W. Tinsley, 11 July 1868.

14 The agreement for *The Moonstone*, dated 10 June 1868, is in the Huntington Library.

15 See W. Tinsley, *The Random Recollections of an Old Publisher* (London, 1900), i, 115.

16 A. J. Church, 'Authors and Publishers', *Nineteenth Century* (May, 1907), p. 856.

17 See W. Gerin, *Emily Brontë* (Oxford, 1971), ch. 15.

18 *The Brontës: Their Lives, Friendships and Correspondence*, ed. Wise and Symington (London, 1932), ii, 154.

19 Bodley. See also Sadleir, *Trollope: A Bibliography*, p. 262.

20 A. Trollope, *An Autobiography*, ed. F. Page, (Oxford 1950), p. 98. But see Sadleir *Trollope: A Bibliography*, p. 262 for a contradictory account of what happened to the surplus copies of the novel.

21 BM 46641, Bentley in correspondence with Miss Wilson (later Mrs Oliphant), 8 Nov. 1851.

22 Their name appears after the fourth number. At this point the advertiser becomes organised and the aspect of the serial generally improves. Chapman and Hall's other regular printer was Whiting who did the concurrent *Library of Fiction*.

23. E. Howe and H. Waite, *The London Society of Compositors* (London, 1948), p. 148.

24 *The Truth About Publishing* (London, 1947), p. 111–12.

25 Forster.

26 Mrs M. O. Oliphant, *Annals of a Publishing House*, i (Edinburgh and London, 1897), 70, quoting Lockhart.

27 Mrs M. O. Oliphant, *Annals of a Publishing House*, ii (Edinburgh and London, 1897), 256.

28 Urbana, from the memoir of Bentley's manager, Morgan.

29 Princeton, Morgan to Ainsworth, 13 Nov. 1840. See also R. D. Altick, *The English Common Reader* (Chicago, 1957), p. 277.

30 Urbana, 30 March 1833(?), Lytton to Bentley which mentions a book on the English—presumably *England and the English* for which Bentley drew up a joint contract with *Pompeii*.

31 BM 46611. 'The Countess' was the subject of a contract of 24 October 1832. For £400 Lytton permitted the publisher to print an edition of 1,750 copies, the book 'to be published anonymously'.

32 PML. Insertions to the agreement are bracketed.

33 PML, Lever to Spencer, Dec. 1838. In the early days Bentley did not always bother with contracts either. In 1831–2 he took *Sir Ralph Esher* from Leigh Hunt with no written agreement and paid the novelist every Saturday as the copy arrived.

34 In the 1850s Bentley was still negotiating the sale of the *Pompeii* stereotype plates: see BM 46642.

35 *Annals* ii, 57. Colburn is supposed to have made £20,000 a year from 1826 to 1829; see *The Profession of Letters 1780–1832*, p. 157.

36 *Annals* ii, 349.

37 On 1 Dec. 1861, for example, Lever signed an agreement with Chapman and Hall for *Barrington* which prohibited him from publishing any other new novel during the course of its serial issue; PML.

38 PML, Lever to Spencer, 20 Dec. 1838.
39 BM 46640, Bentley to James, March 1839.
40 M. Sadleir, *Bulwer: a Panorama* (London, 1933), p. 366.
41 Bk. 2, ch. 4. Bulwer was in Italy with Rosina from September 1833 to March 1834.
42 The bulk of the surviving MS. of *Pompeii* is at PML.
43 Samuel Bentley did volumes 1 and 2, Moyes volume 3 which has a noticeably different appearance. Correspondence dealing with this awkward division of labour is at Urbana, Lytton to Bentley, 24 Sept. 1834.
44 Urbana, Morgan to Bentley, 1834. See also Gettmann, *A Victorian Publisher*, p. 235.
45 Urbana, Lytton to Bentley, 27 September 1834. *Pompeii* actually appeared in its first three-decker form with an erratum list—a great rarity.
46 Lytton mentions it in dealings with Bentley in April 1839: '...[a] collected Edition of my work...After the plan and form of the Waverley Novels' (Urbana).
47 PML, 13 Aug. 1847.
48 W. Besant, *Essays and Historiettes* (London, 1903), p. 285.
49 Forster.
50 Lytton to Bentley, April 1839 specifies this as a novel 'on an English subject' for a mere £750 (Urbana).
51 BM 46641, Jan. 1854.
52 Urbana, Morgan to Bentley, 14 July 1846. In March 1848 a contract was arranged for two romances, one on the subject of Harold the other on 'a Greek subject' (elsewhere in the negotiations a 'Norman subject' is mentioned), see BM 46615.
53 PML, Lytton to Chapman, 19 Jan. 1848.
54 PML, Lytton to Chapman, 23 Feb. 1849.
55 PML, Lever to Spencer, 26 Jan. 1846.
56 R. D. Altick, *Studies in Bibliography*, vi (1954), 4.
57 J. F. Wilson, *A Few Personal Recollections by an Old Printer* (London, 1896), pp. 9–10.
58 See F. E. Comparato, *Books for the Million* (New York, 1971), p. 49.
59 Their London agent Cadell died in 1839. See *Annals*, ii, 242.
60 *The Fascination of Books* (London, 1912), p. 185.
61 Huntington, *All the Year Round* Letterbook, 28 April 1859.
62 Walter Besant, *The Pen and the Book* (London, 1899).
63 *Fiction and the Reading Public* (London, 1932), p. 151.
64 Huntington, Lever to his wife, 22 May 1856.
65 In 1858 Macmillan's opened a branch at Henrietta Street, Covent Garden. In 1863 they moved their publishing headquarters to London, leaving the retail selling side of the business at Cambridge.
66 BM 55376. See also Chapter 5.
67 *American Literary Gazette* (Jan. 1864) p. 174.
68 F. A. Mumby, *The House of Routledge* (London, 1934), p. 53; A. Trollope, *The New Zealander*, ed. N. John Hall (London, 1973), p. 183.
69 PML, correspondence early May 1849.
70 *The Bookseller* (24 Feb. 1859), p. 729.
71 Tinsley, *Recollections*, i, 52.
72 In 1864. See *Annals* ii, 462. Mudie's problems are mentioned in Blackwood's and Bentley's correspondence of the period. It seems the trade rallied round to support the Library. The episode, however, is rather hazy.

Mudie's stock figures suggest that he may have over-extended himself between 1858 and 1862. Much of the self-glorifying brashness disappears from the Library's announcements and advertisements after this period.

73 They did this for Ainsworth's *New Monthly* for which he paid them £100 a year (Urbana, Ainsworth to Bentley, 29 Sept. 1854). They also did something similar for *All the Year Round*, handling the magazine's out of town distribution.

74 *American Literary Gazette* (1 Jan. 1864).

75 Compare Melville's contracts with Harper's and with Bentley's for *Moby Dick* as given by H. Hayford, 'Contract', *Proof* (1971), 1–7. The 'American' system of royalty payment was held up as a model to backward English publishers by James Spedding, *Publishers and Authors* (London, 1867).

76 W. S. Tryon and W. Charvat, *The Cost Books of Ticknor and Fields* (New York, 1949) p. 311.

77 E. Exman, *The House of Harper* (New York, 1967), p. 36.

78 Ibid. p. 10.

79 *Autobiography*, p. 313. Charles Reade was unique among English novelists in getting as much from American as from English publishers; see *Publishers' Circular* (10 Dec, 1868), p. 754.

80 Exman, *The House of Harper*, p. 54.

Chapter 3: Craft Versus Trade: Novelists and Publishers

1 R. D. Altick, *Studies in Bibliography*, vi (1954), 18–19.

2 S. Unwin, *The Truth About Publishing* (London, 1947), p. 11.

3 R. A. Gettmann, *A Victorian Publisher* (Cambridge, 1960), pp. 24, 120.

4 BM 46642, Bentley to Crowe, 17 July 1854.

5 Mrs M. O. Oliphant, *Annals of a Publishing House*, i (Edinburgh and London, 1897), 26.

6 Mrs M. O. Oliphant, *Annals of a Publishing House*, ii (Edinburgh and London, 1897), 248.

7 A. Trollope, *An Autobiography*, ed. F. Page (Oxford, 1950), p. 210.

8 PML, Lever to a friend, 25 May 1841.

9 PML, Lever to Chapman and Hall, 7 May 1846.

10 See, for example, the appendices to Altick, *The English Common Reader*.

11 F. A. Mumby, *Publishing and Bookselling* (London, 1954), pp. 263–4.

12 E. Downey, *Twenty Years Ago* (London, 1905), p. 4.

13 Smith, Elder, contract dated 9 April 1859 (later superseded).

14 The appendices to the recent Pilgrim edition of Charles Dickens's letters (Oxford, 1965–) are illuminating in the way that they show the novelist's publishers habitually defining future novels in terms of those successful in the past.

15 *Publishers' Circular* (15 Dec. 1842), p. 355.

16 E.g. BM 46213 where Bentley had written into the contract of Henry Cockton's *Modern Rake's Progress* (8 Nov. 1839) that the work was to have the same format as 'the work recently published under the title of Nicholas Nickleby'.

17 Urbana, Mrs Wood to Bentley, July 1861. An advertisement in the *Publishers' Circular* (15 March 1860), declares that 12,000 copies of *Danesbury House* had been sold, at 1s. plain, 2s. fine binding, and that the first two editions had been exhausted in fifteen days.

18 See Chapter 10. Meredith read the work for Chapman and Hall. Cassell's did not list *East Lynne* when they advertised a new serial by Mrs Wood in 1862.
19 Urbana, Mrs Wood to Bentley, 10 March 1862.
20 Thackeray, 'The Dignity of Literature' (letter to the *Morning Chronicle*), 12 Jan. 1850.
21 Mrs M. O. Oliphant, *Annals of a Publishing House*, iii, *John Blackwood*, by Mrs G. Porter (Edinburgh and London, 1898), 392.
22 L. Stevenson, *Dr Quicksilver* (London, 1939), p. 225.
23 PML, 28 Sept. 1863. I take the text from G. G. Grubb, 'Some Unpublished Correspondence of Dickens and Chapman and Hall', *Boston University Studies in English* (1955), pp. 98–127.
24 Berg; contract is dated 21 November.
25 See the third chapter of Forster's *Life* of Dickens for one, perhaps biased account of this complicated passage in the novelist's career.
26 Urbana, Morgan to Bentley, 7 July 1837.
27 A. Waugh, *A Hundred Years of Publishing* (London, 1930), p. 26.
28 Huntington, Lever to his wife, 22, 29 Jan. 1859.
29 *The Letters and Private Papers of William Makepeace Thackeray*, ed. G. N. Ray (London and Cambridge, Mass., 1945–6) i, 351–2.
30 Smith, Elder, 16 June 1856.
31 R. G. G. Price, *A History of Punch* (London, 1957), p. 103.
32 *Autobiography*, p. 109.
33 *Annals*, ii, 425.
34 He had a fellowship at Magdalen that brought him £500 a year: see Compton Reade, *Charles Reade: a Memoir* (London, 1887), p. 151 and M. Elwin, *Charles Reade* (London, 1931), p. 54.
35 *The Brontës: Their Lives, Friendships and Correspondence*, ed. Wise and Symington (London, 1932), iii, 21.
36 *The Letters of Mrs Gaskell*, ed. J. A. V. Chapple and A. Pollard (Manchester, 1966), p. 74.
37 *The Brontës*, iii, 21.
38 *Letters of Mrs Gaskell*, p. 721.
39 Smith, Elder, Charlotte Brontë to Smith, 14 Sept. 1849.
40 So he asserts in a letter to Gleig in 1831, BM 46639.
41 She had £50 advance for the novel from the publisher, 'not to be recalled' —a clause that suggests no great hopes for the novel.
42 See Gettmann, *A Victorian Publisher*, p. 111.
43 Urbana, Mrs Wood to Bentley, Feb. 1862. See also Gettmann, p. 142.
44 PML, Lever to Spencer, 26 Feb. 1850.
45 PML, Reade to *Atlantic Monthly*, 10 Oct. 1858(?).
46 *Annals*, i, 223–4.
47 Urbana, Bentley to Reade, 11 June 1857.
48 Urbana, Reade to Bentley, 1857.
49 Details of the Bentley-Reade controversy are to be found in Bentley's *List of Principal Works* for 1852.
50 *The House of Smith, Elder*, pp. 38–9. Smith took his last two three-deckers from James in 1848. Newby published ten James three-deckers in the next four years.
51 Compton Reade, *Charles Reade: a Memoir*, pp. 9–10, Elwin, *Charles Reade*, p. 85.
52 Huntington, Reade to Fields, 12 Sept. 1855.

53 PML, Lever to Spencer, 25 March 1847.
54 BM 46641, Bentley to Harwood, 29 March 1851.
55 *Dr Quicksilver*, pp. 138–9. He first had a very brief alliance with Colburn, who brought out *Arthur O'Leary* in three volumes in 1844.
56 I have taken details from a letter of 10 Nov. 1846 to Hugh Baker (PML), who had agreed to help Lever.
57 See *Dr Quicksilver*, pp. 158–9. Irish publishers like Curry pioneered the cheap reprinting of popular novels in large numbers.
58 PML, Lever to Spencer, 15 Aug. 1845.
59 PML, Lever to Spencer, 8 Sept. 1845.
60 Ibid. Curry credited the novelist with only the thirteenth and fourteenth thousands on *Hinton*, and this partly explained the deficit.
61 PML, Lever to Baker, 10 Nov. 1846. Lever was being charged for the production of 20,000—i.e. 4,000 more than had been sold—and this was set against the profit on 16,000.
62 PML, Lever to Spencer, 25 March 1847. Curry claimed not to have kept separate accounts.
63 PML, Lever to Baker, 10 Dec. 1846.
64 PML, Lever to Spencer, 15 Aug. 1846.
65 PML, Lever to Baker, 10 Nov. 1846.
66 BM 46642, correspondence between Bentley and Reade, June 1857. The court case established the very ambiguous definition that an edition was not an impression set up from fresh type but whatever batch of copies a publisher chose to put out at any one time. This definition helped neither party.
67 PML, Lever to Baker, 10 Feb. 1847.
68 PML, Lever to Spencer, 20 Feb. 1847.
69 PML, Lever to Baker, 2 Jan. 1847.
70 PML, Lever to Spencer, 1 Nov. 1848.
71 In Feb. 1847; Lever notes the fact in his letters. Chapman contracted to bring out a cheap edition for Lytton in Oct. 1847.
72 All this time Lever was living expensively abroad.
73 The lawyer was Baker, in Feb. 1847.
74 PML, Lever to Spencer, 26 May 1847.
75 Urbana, Bentley's Diary, 1860. A new edition of Isaac D'Israeli's *Calamities and Quarrels of Authors* was brought out by Routledge in 1859.
76 Charles Reade, *The Eighth Commandment* (London, 1860), p. 5. For a discussion of the complex issue of copyright see S. H. Nowell-Smith, *International Law and the Publisher* (Oxford, 1968).
77 BM 46611, Agreement, Reynolds with Bentley and Colburn, 28 Nov. 1829, for the *Dramatic Tourist*, a novel in three volumes. Bentley was keen to get authors to sign their copyrights over to him entirely as he had a thriving reprint series, the 'Standard Novels'.
78 Frederick Evans, as representative of his firm who were unsatisfied creditors, was on the inspectorate. See Urbana, Bentley's Diary, 1860.
79 PML, Lever to Spencer, 5 Oct. 1847.
80 PML, Lever to a friend, 18 Aug. 1845.
81 E. Marston, *After Work* (London and New York, 1904) p. 64.
82 PML, the receipt is dated 11 Dec. 1848 and signed by her husband.
83 *Letters of Mrs Gaskell*, p. 56.
84 Ibid. p. 69.
85 PML. She received £500 on 24 Jan 1853.
86 PML, William Gaskell to Chapman, 17 April 1855.

87 PML, 8 May 1855. The next paragraph, not quoted here, concerns the volume of tales. This is the earliest payment by royalty I have seen.
88 *Letters of Mrs Gaskell*, p. 407. See also the brisk dealing with George Smith for *The Life of Charlotte Brontë* in Dec. 1856, *Letters*, p. 430.

Chapter 4: 'Henry Esmond': The Shaping Power of Contract

1 H. Vizetelly, *Glances back through Seventy Years* (London, 1893), i, 283–6.
2 This is evident from advertisements for future numbers in the monthly serialised version of the novel.
3 The contract is given as an appendix to G. N. Ray, *Thackeray: The Uses of Adversity* (London and New York, 1955), pp. 433–4. Throughout this chapter I am indebted to the account of Thackeray's dealings with Bradbury and Evans given by Peter L. Shillingsburg in *Victorian Studies Association Newsletter*, March 1973.
4 PML, agreement 28 May 1845 for *The Knight of Gwynne*.
5 L. Stevenson, *Dr Quicksilver* (London, 1939), p. 149.
6 See, for example, *Fraser's Magazine* (Jan. 1851), p. 86.
7 A. Trollope, *An Autobiography*, ed. F. Page (Oxford, 1950), pp. 138–9.
8 Mrs Gaskell, *The Life of Charlotte Brontë* (London, 1933), p. 298.
9 Anne Ritchie, *Chapters from Some Memoirs* (London, 1894), p. 130.
10 L. Huxley, *The House of Smith, Elder* (London, 1923), p. 61.
11 Ibid. p. 39.
12 See Chapter 3.
13 I take this information from Vineta Colby, *Yesterday's Women* (Princeton, 1974), p. 230.
14 Smith, Elder. See also *The Letters and Private Papers of William Makepeace Thackeray* (London and Cambridge, Mass., 1945–6), ii, 736.
15 See G. N. Ray, *The Buried Life* (London and Cambridge, Mass., 1952), pp. 78–96.
16 See Lewis Melville, *William Makepeace Thackeray* (London, 1910) ii, 268–70.
17 Smith, Elder, Thackeray to Smith, 8 Aug. 1852.
18 PML, Lever to Chapman, 26 June 1866.
19 W. Tinsley, *The Random Recollections of an Old Publisher* (London, 1900), i, 80–1.
20 Smith, Elder, Thackeray to Smith, 28 Aug. 1854.
21 B. R. Jerman, 'The Production of Disraeli's Trilogy', *PBSA*, lviii (1964), 239–51.
22 PML, Lever to Spencer, 17 June 1866.
23 Tinsley, *Recollections*, i, 54.
24 'Mr. Thackeray's long-promised Novel is, at last, announced to appear in the course of October,' the *Publishers' Circular* announced (prematurely) in its issue of 1 October 1852. The delay in delivery may have hurt the novel's sales somewhat.

Chapter 5: 'Westward Ho!': 'A Popularly Successful Book'

1 Berg. The notes appear to be jotted down on the spur of the moment.
2 BM 46642, Bentley to Crowe and Skene, 17 July 1854, 20 Apr. 1855.

3 Urbana, Collins to Bentley, 12 July 1854.
4 'Sir Walter Raleigh and his Times', *North British Review* (repr. Ticknor and Fields, Boston, 1859), p. 459.
5 BM 54911, Kingsley to Macmillan's, 22 July 1854.
6 The Chevalier Bunsen on *Hypatia*, quoted Amy Cruse, *The Victorians and their Books* (London, 1935), p. 275.
7 See S. H. Nowell-Smith, *Letters to Macmillan* (London, 1967), pp. 34–6.
8 See J. Foster, *A Bibliographical Catalogue of Macmillan and Company's Publishing from 1843 to 1889* (London, 1891).
9 BM 55376, D. Macmillan to Kingsley, 12 Dec. 1854. In the early nineteenth century William Lane's Minerva Press was famous for its tepid romances and Gothic tales.
10 C. Morgan, *The House of Macmillan* (London, 1943), p. 2.
11 S. H. Nowell-Smith, *The House of Cassell* (London, 1958), pp. 77–8.
12 C. L. Graves, *The Life and Letters of Alexander Macmillan* (London, 1910), p. 12.
13 See Nowell-Smith, *Letters to Macmillan*, p. 34 where Kingsley talks of 'your novel'.
14 BM 55376, D. Macmillan to Tetley, 2 March 1855.
15 T. Hughes, *Memoir of Daniel Macmillan* (London, 1882), p. 252.
16 BM 55376, A. Macmillan to Rev. and Mrs Crowfoot, 2 Nov. 1854.
17 BM 55376, D. Macmillan to Mrs Paine, 6 Nov. 1854.
18 BM 55376, D. Macmillan to Kingsley, 2 Feb. 1855.
19 BM 46642, Bentley to Mrs Costello, 17 April 1854. According to the *Publishers' Circular*, 15 Feb. 1854, 'one half of the publication issued appear to have some bearing upon the scene or question of the contemplated war.'
20 PML, Kingsley to an admirer, 26 Nov. 1855.
21 BM 55376, Macmillan's to Clay, 31 Oct. 1854.
22 Morgan, p. 43.
23 BM 55376, 20 Feb. 1855.
24 BM 55377, A. Macmillan to Kingsley, 2 March 1855.
25 BM 55377. A. Macmillan to Mrs Kingsley, 5 April 1855.
26 Ibid.
27 Foster, *Bibliographical Catalogue*, p. 31.
28 Nowell-Smith, *Letters to Macmillan*, pp. 34–5.
29 BM 54911.
30 BM 54911, 22 July 1854.
31 BM 54911, 12 Aug. 1854.
32 Urbana, Kingsley to Chapman and Hall, 6 March 1850.
33 18 June 1854; the archaic form, Thackeray said, had 'injured *Esmond's* sale'.
34 BM 46642, Bentley to R. Meikleham, 20 Dec. 1855.
35 BM 54911, Kingsley to Macmillan's, 29 Oct. 1854.
36 BM 54911, 2 Nov. 1854.
37 BM 54911, Kingsley to Macmillan's, 1 Feb. 1855. The *Publishers' Circular* of 1 March 1855 announced the novel as 'unavoidably delayed'.
38 Macmillan's tried to persuade Kingsley to postpone publication until Easter (BM 55376, Macmillan's to Lord Cardigan, 13 Feb. 1855).
39 BM 55377, A. Macmillan to Kingsley, 21 April 1855.
40 M. F. Thorp, *Charles Kingsley* (Princeton, 1937), p. 118.
41 *The Warden*, ch. 15.
42 BM 55376, D. Macmillan to Kingsley, 31 Oct. 1854.

43 BM 54911, 12 Aug. 1854.
44 BM 55376, Macmillan's to Trübner, 26 Sept. 1854.
45 Graves, p. 94.
46 Urbana, Kingsley to Parker on *Hypatia's* conclusion, 1852(?).
47 C. Woodham-Smith, *The Reason Why* (London, 1953).
48 BM 54911, letters of 22 July, 15, 29 Sept. 1854.
49 *Charles Kingsley* (London, 1891) i, 331.
50 BM 54911, Kingsley to Macmillan's, 11 Dec. 1854. Kingsley had bad influenza at this period.
51 BM 54911, 21 May 1855.
52 T. Hughes, 'Prefatory Memoir' (printed with *Alton Locke*, London, 1900), p. xxxiv.
53 Cruse, *The Victorians and their Books*, p. 275.

Chapter 6: Trollope: Making the First Rank

1 I take this figure from 'On the Forms of Publishing Fiction' (probably by William Tinsley), *Tinsley's Magazine* (May 1872), p. 412.
2 PML, contract of 2 Aug. 1859.
3 See M. Sadleir, 'Anthony Trollope and his Publishers', *The Library*, v (1924–5), 215–42.
4 A. Trollope, *An Autobiography*, ed. F. Page (Oxford, 1950), p. 98.
5 Bodley.
6 P. 126. But *The Bookseller* (23 April 1859) reports that it went into a second 31s. 6d. edition.
7 Bodley. Trollope evidently drew up the table for his autobiography.
8 *The Letters of Anthony Trollope*, ed. B. A. Booth (Oxford, 1951), p. 37. Longman's had already poured cold water on Trollope's proposed novel satirical of advertising (which later emerged as *Brown, Jones and Robinson*) and on *The New Zealander*, parts of which were included into *The Three Clerks*. For details see N. John Hall's edition of *The New Zealander* (London, 1973).
9 *Autobiography*, p. 110–11.
10 BM 46617, agreement of 15 Oct. 1857.
11 BM 46642.
12 BM 46637. Since Trollope shortened the text somewhat for Bentley, it is possible that he had some small extra emolument.
13 BM 46642.
14 *Autobiography*, p. 117.
15 PML.
16 PML.
17 PML.
18 PML, agreement of 10 Nov. 1858.
19 Smith, Elder, Thackeray to Smith, 1859(?).
20 A. Trollope, *Thackeray* (London, 1909), p. 52. Smith denies this in his account (given by Huxley) asserting that Thackeray was capable of providing the necessary front serial, but courteously gave Trollope first place. The evidence of the contracts is against Smith. In an agreement of 9 April 1859 Thackeray undertook to provide two serials for *Cornhill* of full length (sixteen numbers). In a subsequent contract of 20 August these serials were postponed 'to be published as separate serial works in monthly parts in

place of in a magazine'. Thackeray agreed, in their place, to provide a short story of six parts, the first part to be given to Smith by December 9.

21 *Autobiography*, p. 138.

22 Bodley, Smith to Trollope, 26 Oct. 1859.

23 *Letters of Trollope*, p. 29.

24 See the opening Trollope added to *Castle Richmond*.

25 *Thackeray*, p. 51.

26 L. Huxley, *The House of Smith, Elder* (London, 1923), p. 97.

27 See *Autobiography*, p. 121.

28 *Autobiography*, p. 143.

29 *Letters of Trollope*, p. 57 (13 April 1860, to Catherine Gould).

30 Urbana, Morgan to Bentley, 21 Sept. 1840.

31 BM 46612, 27 April 1836. The 'Unco' Good' was renamed *The Vicar of Wrexhill*.

32 *The House of Fiction*, ed. L. Edel (London, 1962), p. 89.

Chapter 7: Lever and Ainsworth: Missing the First Rank

1 See R. A. Gettmann, *A Victorian Publisher* (Cambridge, 1960), p. 86 for alternatives proposed by Ainsworth.

2 There were five editions of the novel by 1837. It was taken over by Macrone in 1835.

3 BM 46640, Bentley to Barham, 24 Sept. 1839. Ainsworth let Bentley down when he failed to write two novels for which he signed contracts in 1836—'Monaldeschi' (about the Queen of Sweden) and 'Caesar Borgia'.

4 George Smith's jaundiced opinion of Ainsworth, quoted in L. Huxley, *The House of Smith, Elder* (London, 1923), p. 39.

5 Urbana, Ainsworth to Bentley, 29 Aug. 1851.

6 It was, however, completed some years later. There is some mystery over the subsequent career of *Clitheroe*. Routledge completed the novel in 12 numbers, not the 20 originally intended by Chapman and Hall, who began publishing the work. It is asserted by M. Sadleir in *XIX Century Fiction* (Cambridge, 1951), i, 6, that the resumed serial was a success. There is no evidence I can find, beyond the assertion of Ainsworth's very sympathetic biographer S. M. Ellis, that the oddly disjointed novel made any impression on the reading public at either period of its publication. But Routledge who were reissuing Ainsworth in a collective in the mid-1850s probably bought the incomplete copyright from Chapman and asked the novelist to bring it up to full weight so they could slip it in with the other titles, which they did.

7 Forster.

8 In a letter of 4 July 1863 (Urbana) Ainsworth bitterly accuses Bentley of 'a flagrant violation of our agreement'. In February 1866 Bentley took over *Temple Bar*, a direct competitor to Ainsworth's magazine.

9 All the agreements are held in PML. I have, however, been unable to locate that for *Cardinal Pole* which Chapman and Hall brought out in 1863.

10 PML, Ainsworth to Chapman, 11 March 1862.

11 Urbana, Ainsworth to Bentley, 26 April 1866.

12 PML, Ainsworth to Chapman, 8 April 1865.

13 See A. Waugh, *A Hundred Years of Publishing* (London, 1930), p. 83 for

the publisher's problems in recovering Ainsworth's own stereotype plates from Bohn.

14 Smith, Elder, 12 Sept. 1847.

15 Urbana, Ainsworth to Bentley, 23 April 1865. Ainsworth was using the dispute over the periodical as a lever—unsuccessfully.

16 Mrs M. O. Oliphant, *Annals of a Publishing House*, iii, *John Blackwood*, by Mrs G. Porter (Edinburgh and London, 1898), 245.

17 S. M. Ellis, *W. Harrison Ainsworth* (London, 1911), ii, 251.

18 Huntington, Ainsworth to Tinsley, 13 Feb. 1873, 26 May 1875.

19 Urbana, Morgan's memoir of Bentley's.

20 Ibid.

21 BM 46613, agreement 10 Dec. 1838; £300 'check', £200 promissory note.

22 In a package with *Rookwood*, *Crichton* and *Guy Fawkes*, BM 46615.

23 BM 46613, agreement 2 Feb. 1839. Bentley offers £30 a month primarily 'for the use of his name'. Dickens had £20 initially.

24 Ellis, *W. Harrison Ainsworth*, ii, 264.

25 Bodley.

26 PML, agreement 22 Jan. 1845. The printing number was later raised to 6,000.

27 PML, Lever to Chapman, 25 Jan. 1845. Lever wanted a 'squarer book' than Dickens's and thought the cover might be less ornate.

28 PML, agreement of 28 May 1845, publication to start March 1846. In Feb. 1846 Chapman and Hall proposed an extension to the full issue of monthly numbers.

29 PML, Lever to Spencer, 26 Jan. 1846.

30 PML, Lever to Chapman and Hall, 14 Nov 1846; Lever gloomily reflects on *Dombey's* success, in the same letter.

31 PML, Lever to Chapman, Dec. 1845.

32 PML, Lever to Chapman, 14 Nov. 1846.

33 Lever to a friend, 4 Dec. 1845.

34 PML, Lever to Spencer, 27 Feb. 1850.

35 PML, Lever to Chapman, 9 Jan. 1847.

36 PML, Lever to Spencer, 9 Jan. 1847.

37 PML, Lever to Spencer, 31 May 1847.

38 PML, Lever to Chapman, 14 Aug. 1848.

39 L. Stevenson, *Dr Quicksilver* (London, 1939), p. 166.

40 Huntington, Lever to his wife, 24 June 1859.

41 *Annals*, iii, 226.

42 *Annals*, iii, 234.

Chapter 8: Dickens as Publisher

1 A. Waugh, *A Hundred Years of Publishing* (London, 1930), p. 44.

2 *The Letters of Charles Dickens*, ed. W. Dexter (London, 1939), iii, 65.

3 Waugh, p. 61. The obvious thing for Dickens to have done was to publish his works on commission. But he had had a bad experience doing this with *A Christmas Carol* which seems to have predisposed him against the practice for life (see Waugh, p. 66).

4 E. Johnson, *Charles Dickens* (New York, 1952), ii, 943.

5 *Letters of Dickens*, iii, 220.

6 *Letters of Dickens*, iii, 194. 'Bradbury and Evans' had appeared at the foot

of the last page of *Household Words*. The absence of this together with the changed name was the only obvious difference between the journals.

7 *All the Year Round* began in April 1859 and overlapped a few weeks with *Household Words*.

8 Information taken from the *All the Year Round* Letterbook (Huntington).

9 Huntington Letter book, 19 May 1859.

10 R. C. Lehmann, *Charles Dickens as Editor* (London, 1912).

11 *Letters of Dickens*, iii, 193–4, and Huntington Letterbook 7 Aug. 1860.

12 *Letters of Dickens*, iii, 303.

13 Bodley, 'M.D.F.' to Trollope, 5 Aug. 1861.

14 See, e.g., Dickens's letter to George Eliot, *Letters of Dickens*, iii, 111.

15 *Letters of Dickens*, iii, 311. *All the Year Round*'s staff, like that of *Household Words*, went in for some group composition at Christmas. See Deborah A. Thomas's articles on 'Contributors to the Christmas Numbers of *Household Words* and *All the Year Round*, 1850–1867', *The Dickensian*, Sept. 1973 and Jan. 1974.

16 PML, agreement, 31 Jan. 1862.

17 See M. Elwin, *Charles Reade* (London, 1931), p. 133. For a discussion of Dickens as employer and the terms he gave see G. Grubb, 'The Editorial Policies of Charles Dickens', *PMLA*, 58 (1943), 1110–24 and W. Buckler, 'Dickens the Paymaster', *PMLA*, 66 (1951), 1177–80.

18 Huntington Letterbook, 12 March 1860.

19 *Letters of Dickens*, iii, 110.

20 *Letters of Dickens*, iii, 145.

21 PML, Collins to Ward, 1860(?).

22 PML, Dickens to F. Trollope, 1866(?).

23 *Letters of Dickens*, iii, 184.

24 Huntington Letterbook, 27 April 1859.

25 *Letters of Dickens*, iii, 118.

26 *The House of Cassell*, p. 121.

27 *Letters of Dickens*, iii, 194. The publisher was usually Sampson Low because their American agency made for easy transatlantic relationships; see E. Marston, *After Work* (London and New York, 1904), p. 57.

28 Compton Reade, *Charles Reade: a Memoir* (London, 1887), ii, 139.

29 Thackeray resigned *Cornhill* in March 1862. Smith had trouble replacing him.

30 *Letters of Dickens*, iii, 184.

31 PML, 17 Aug. 1860.

32 PML, 26 June 1860.

33 Huntington.

34 *Letters of Dickens*, iii, 151.

35 PML, 27 Feb. 1860.

36 From Dickens's postscript to *Very Hard Cash* in *All the Year Round*, Dec. 1864.

37 *Letters of Dickens*, iii, 165.

38 Letterbook 11 July 1860.

39 Letterbook, 13 Aug. 1860.

40 *Letters of Dickens*, iii, 183.

41 Ibid.

42 A. Trollope, *An Autobiography*, ed. F. Page (Oxford, 1950), p. 42.

43 *Letters of Dickens*, iii, 182.

44 *Letters of Dickens*, iii, 184.

45 *Letters of Dickens*, iii, 187.
46 *Letters of Dickens*, iii, 184.
47 PML, Lever to Spencer, 17 June 1866, about Chapman.
48 PML, 20 Oct. 1860.
49 PML, Collins to Ward, 18 Aug. 1859.
50 *Letters of Dickens*, iii, 145.
51 *Letters of Dickens*, iii, 124.
52 *Letters of Dickens*, iii, 282.
53 *Letters of Dickens*, iii, 169. Tact was needed. Lytton expressed the private opinion that *The Woman in White* was 'great trash'. See Robinson, *Wilkie Collins*, p. 149.
54 Blackwood, J. Blackwood to Lytton, 10 Jan. 1861. Blackwood also lost the cheap reprint which went to Sampson Low.
55 *Letters of Dickens*, iii, 207.
56 *Letters of Dickens*, iii, 219.
57 *Letters of Dickens*, iii, 214.
58 *Letters of Dickens*, iii, 221.
59 *Letters of Dickens*, iii, 241.
60 *Letters of Dickens*, iii, 268.
61 *Letters of Dickens*, iii, 269.
62 Ibid.
63 See *The Life of Edward Bulwer*, by his grandson the Earl of Lytton, ii (London, 1913), 345–7. For a close analysis of Dickens's interaction with Lytton see R. L. Wolff, *Strange Stories* (Boston, 1971), part iii, chapters 5 and 6.
64 *Letters of Dickens*, iii, 270.
65 See the dedication to *Zanoni*, 1845.
66 PML, June 1861. *Strange Story* ran in *All the Year Round* from 10 Aug. 1861 to 8 March 1862.
67 *Letters of Dickens*, iii, 225.
68 *Letters of Dickens*, iii, 236.
69 *Letters of Dickens*, iii, 234.
70 *Letters of Dickens*, iii, 218, 229.
71 *Publishers' Circular* (31 Dec. 1861), p. 694.

Chapter 9: Marketing 'Middlemarch'

1 A. Trollope, *An Autobiography*, ed. F. Page (Oxford, 1950), p. 246.
2 Mrs M. O. Oliphant, *Annals of a Publishing House*, iii, *John Blackwood*, by Mrs G. Porter (Edinburgh and London, 1898), 48–9.
3 *Annals*, iii, 380.
4 The phrase is George Moore's in *Literature at Nurse* (London, 1885), his blast against Mudie and the circulating library system. See also G. L. Griest, *Mudie's Circulating Library* (Bloomington, Indiana, 1970), p. 138.
5 *Annals*, iii, 53.
6 Compton Reade, *Charles Reade: a Memoir* (London, 1887), ii, 236. S. H. Nowell-Smith in *The House of Cassell* (London, 1958), p. 94, suggests that the outspokenness of *A Terrible Temptation* hurt the prospects of a large library sale for the novel.
7 PML, Aug. 1861.
8 Urbana, Mrs Wood to Bentley, 16 Aug. 1869.

9 Blackwood, Acc. 5644, Publication Ledgers. There is always a large element of printer's tolerance to be allowed for in Blackwood's figures. In the cost column for *Felix Holt*, for example, 5,000 three-volume copies are charged for. Yet Blackwoods had 5,252 copies credited in the receipts column.
10 Blackwood, Acc. 5643, J. Blackwood to George Eliot, 29 Dec. 1868.
11 Blackwood, Acc. 5643, J. Blackwood to Mrs Oliphant, 25 Apr. 1871.
12 The composition of *Middlemarch* is discussed authoritatively by J. Beaty, *Middlemarch from Notebook to Novel* (Urbana, 1960).
13 *The Letters of George Eliot*, ed. G. S. Haight (London, 1956), v, 145–6.
14 *Annals*, iii, 80.
15 *Annals*, iii, 158.
16 Ibid.
17 Blackwood, 4270, J. Blackwood to W. Blackwood, 13 May 1871.
18 E. Exman, *The House of Harper* (New York, 1967), p. 62, seems to suggest that Lewes was actually playing one American publisher against another.
19 Blackwood, Acc. 5643, John Blackwood to George Eliot, 4 Dec. 1868.
20 Blackwood, 4277, Langford to J. Blackwood, 28 Oct. 1871.
21 Blackwood, 4277, Langford to J. Blackwood, 20 Oct. 1871.
22 BM 46640. One might also cite Trollope's jest that as proof of his personal industry he had sent to the Great Exhibition four four-volume novels (all failures), *The Letters of Anthony Trollope*, ed. B. A. Booth (Oxford, 1951), p. 17.
23 Blackwood, 4099, Langford to J. Blackwood, 23 Dec. 1852. In fact Blackwood cleared almost all the 2,000 copies of the first edition.
24 Blackwood, 4086, Lytton to J. Blackwood, 12 Nov. 1849.
25 Blackwood, 4089, Lytton to J. Blackwood, 27 June, 1850.
26 L. Huxley, *The House of Smith, Elder*, (London, 1923), p. 101.
27 Smith, Elder, agreement 21 May 1862. I have followed Smith's account, as given in Huxley (pp. 101–2) which is probably faulty in certain details. In his biography of George Eliot (Oxford, 1968) G. S. Haight reports that when publication of *Romola* began in July only three numbers were finished. The agreement for twelve parts was signed in May. But although Smith's memory played him false on this matter it is unlikely that he made up the fact that there was an argument about the number of installments and that he wanted more than George Eliot was prepared to provide. Smith does not mention that term of copyright was also an important factor in negotiations. (See *Letters of George Eliot*, iv, 17–20, 34–5.)
28 *Publishers' Circular* (1 Nov. 1866), p. 650. Some other experiments in serialisation may be mentioned parenthetically. In 1859 Sampson Low issued Harriet Beecher Stowe's *The Minister's Wooing* in 16-page parts, 2d. plain, 6d. illustrated. In the same year Dickens's *Tale of Two Cities* was issued in eight monthly parts simultaneously with its serialisation in *All the Year Round*. After the 1870s serialisation through syndicated agencies in newspapers was not unusual; both Trollope and Collins dabbled in this (although Ainsworth pioneered the practice thirty years before). See Graham Pollard's 'Novels in Newspapers', *R.E.S.* xviii (1942), 72–85.
29 W. Tinsley, *The Random Recollections of an Old Publisher* (London, 1900), i, 54–5. The editions of Thackeray, Dickens etc. to which Tinsley refers are those large octavos made by binding up the part issues.
30 Blackwood, 4270, J. Blackwood to W. Blackwood, 19 July 1871.
31 Haight, *George Eliot*, p. 433.
32 *Letters of George Eliot*, v, 179–80.

33 Phrase used by Langford, Blackwood, 4277, 20 Oct. 1871.
34 Blackwood, 4277, Langford to J. Blackwood, 1 Sept. 1871.
35 Blackwood, Acc. 5643, J. Blackwood to Lewes, 30 Aug. 1871.
36 Blackwood, 4277, Langford to J. Blackwood, 6 Sept. 1871.
37 Blackwood, 4270, J. Blackwood to W. Blackwood, 4 Sept. 1871.
38 The figure 5,650 given for the serialised *Middlemarch* represents the smallest number printed on any single installment The actual printings per part were: I, 6,700; II, 5,913; III, 5,675; IV, 5,760; V, 5,650; VI, 5,650; VII, 5,650; VIII, 5,900.
39 Blackwood, 4277, Langford to J. Blackwood, 2 Dec. 1871.
40 Blackwood, 4278, Lytton to J. Blackwood, 29 Oct. 1871.
41 *The House of Fiction*, ed. L. Edel (London, 1962), p. 259.

Chapter 10: Hardy: Breaking into Fiction

1 Smith, Elder, nd, but a reference to *Cornhill Magazine* puts it after 1860.
2 PML, Reade to *Atlantic Monthly*, 10 Oct. 1858(?).
3 S. M. Ellis, *George Meredith* (London, 1919), p. 238.
4 See R. A. Gettmann, *A Victorian Publisher* (Cambridge, 1960), ch. 7.
5 S. H. Nowell-Smith, *Letters to Macmillan* (London, 1967), p. 191.
6 D. Sheehan, *This was Publishing* (Bloomington, Indiana, 1952), p. 32.
7 Smith, Elder, Charlotte Brontë to Smith, 5 Feb. 1851.
8 Mrs M. O. Oliphant, *Annals of a Publishing House*, ii (Edinburgh and London, 1897), 180.
9 L. Huxley, *The House of Smith, Elder* (London, 1923), p. 37.
10 BM 46653, S. Moodie to Bentley, 1865. Mrs Moodie, née Strickland, is best known for her work *Roughing it in the Bush*. There is no mention of *Dorothy Chance* in the British Museum Catalogue of Printed Books.
11 Preface, *Plays Unpleasant* (Harmondsworth, 1961), p. 8.
12 H. Curwen, *A History of Booksellers* (London, 1873), p. 429.
13 BM 55931.
14 BM 46658.
15 BM 46653, Jewsbury to Bentley, 26 May 1860.
16 Nowell-Smith, *Letters to Macmillan*, p. 130.
17 C. Morgan, *The House of Macmillan* (London, 1943), pp. 87–8. For the conjectured narrative see C. J. Weber, ed., *An Indiscretion in the Life of an Heiress* (Baltimore, 1935), pp. 5–12.
18 Morgan, *The House of Macmillan*, pp. 88–91.
19 BM 54923, 10 Sept. 1868.
20 See Ellis, *George Meredith*, p. 241. The interview took place in March 1869.
21 F. E. Hardy, *The Life of Thomas Hardy*, (London 1962), pp. 61–2.
22 Ellis, *George Meredith*, p. 103.
23 A. Waugh, *A Hundred Years of Publishing* (London, 1930), p. 149.
24 Morgan, *The House of Macmillan*, pp. 93–4.
25 On 15 April 1869 Hardy sent *Poor Man* to Smith. It was rejected. Oddly enough there is no evidence that Hardy actually submitted *Desperate Remedies* to Chapman and Hall, but it is hard to believe that he did not at least sound out the novel's prospects with the firm that had inspired it.
26 Ellis, *George Meredith*, p. 244.
27 R. L. Purdy, *Thomas Hardy: A Bibliographical Study* (London, 1954), p. 5.
28 G. Moore, quoted by E. Downey, *Twenty Years Ago* (London, 1905), p. 9.

29 G. L. Griest, *Mudie's Circulating Library* (Bloomington, Indiana, 1970), p. 60.
30 W. Tinsley, *The Random Recollections of an Old Publisher* (London, 1900), i, 126–7.
31 Downey, *Twenty Years Ago*, p. 26.
32 Purdy, *Hardy: A Bibliographical Study*, p. 5 reproduces this account.
33 Tinsley, *Recollections*, i, 55. Tinsley was also a notorious underseller. In November 1862 Bentley allowed him to attend his trade sale only on condition that he gave a guarantee that he would not undersell the trade (BM 46642, 5 Nov. 1862).
34 Downey, *Twenty Years Ago*, p. 22.
35 Urbana, 1 Aug. 1879, 25 Jan. 1873.
36 BM 54923, 7 Aug. 1871.
37 Hardy, *Life*, p. 88.
38 Tinsley, *Recollections*, i, 127.
39 BM 54891.
40 BM 54891, 24 July 1873.
41 In the mid 1890s, for example, Hardy left Sampson Low and Marston because he felt they were 'too old fashioned and too conservative' to take *Tess*. He took up instead with the newly established and go-ahead firm of Osgood (see E. Marston, *After Work* (London and New York, 1904), p. 266).
42 Preface, *Desperate Remedies*.
43 Vere H. Collins quotes this as a conversational remark by Hardy, long after his novel-writing career had finished in *Talks with Thomas Hardy, 1920–22* (London, 1928), p. 55.

Index